THE PARADIGM

The Definitive Guide
to Life and Happiness

The Paradigm

The Definitive Guide to Life and Happiness

Forrest Wong

PUBLISHED BY FORREST WONG

Cover Designer: Sydney Barnes
Publisher: Forrest Wong
Printer: CreateSpace at www.createspace.com
Library and Archives Canada Cataloguing in Publication
Wong, Forrest
The Paradigm: The Definitive Guide to Life and Happiness
Includes bibliographical references.
ISBN-13: 978-1544172637
ISBN-10: 154417263X

ASK YOURSELF TWO QUESTIONS:

1. Is the decision I'm about to make going to positively affect the future of humanity?

2. Will I regret not having made this decision when I am on my deathbed?

EVERYTHING ELSE WILL FOLLOW.

For all of my fellow human beings

TABLE OF CONTENTS

TABLE OF FIGURES

CHAPTER 5: HEALTH AND FITNESS

CHAPTER 6: PERSONAL HABITS

CHAPTER 7: GENUINE RELATIONSHIPS

CHAPTER 8: SOCIAL CONTRIBUTION

CHAPTER 9: YOUR LIFE PURSUIT

CHAPTER 10: CONTINUOUS GROWTH

QUICK REFERENCE GUIDE AND BOOK RECAP

APPENDIX 1

APPENDIX 2

FOREWORD

Every now and then, you come across someone who makes you better. Not just through their knack of inspiring with their words, or from their relentless pursuit of learning, or from their determination to excel in their work through practice. Make no mistake, when you meet and befriend someone who possesses any one of those traits, it can certainly motivate you to work harder and to strive toward becoming a better version of yourself. However, in my years of knowing Forrest, I've seen someone who not only possesses these attributes but exceeds them in one crucial way: his ability to listen.

I tout this seemingly unrelated trait of Forrest's because I believe it's an important quality when writing a book like this. I'm at ease when I reflect on my thoughts with him because of the way he asks questions and gently offers his opinions. When we sit down and mull over our lives and our decisions, there is an air of thoughtfulness as a result of his style. This means that when he speaks and gives advice, his thoughts are informed, contextualized, and calculated.

I always have and always will appreciate what Forrest has to say about life. Beyond being driven to succeed, his obsession with learning, and his ability to conjure up a spicy meme, he's always given me advice that, whether I use it or not, has a lot of weight because of its source. Because Forrest listens, I believe he is worth listening to.

NOEL FELICIANO
March 2018

PREFACE

The purpose of this book, in no uncertain terms, is to help the reader to achieve happiness and success in life. It aims to help the reader with the utmost practicality and specificity. Many self-help books in past decades have been written on the topic of achieving happiness, yet, in the eyes of this author, they have largely fallen short of their declared goal.

The above forms part of my motivation for writing the book you now hold in your hands. The other part of my motivation finds its origins in my own childhood. We all come into the world not knowing anything. Slowly, over time, we accumulate knowledge and learn how best to harness our talent and energy in productive ways for society. However, by the time many people "figure out" life, they are well into adulthood. We waste time and miss opportunities. That has certainly been my experience. If only there were a way to help people navigate that process more quickly and prudently, to get more out of life earlier…

I am reminded of a Steve Jobs quote from a speech he made in 1997, when he was just returning to Apple Computer Inc.:

> "Every good product that I've ever seen in this industry, and pretty much anywhere, is because a group of people cared deeply about making something wonderful that they and their friends wanted… They wanted to use it themselves. That's how the Apple I came about, that's how the Apple II came about, that's how the Macintosh came about.

That's how almost everything I know that's good has come about... If Woz and I could have went [sic] out and plunked down two thousand bucks and bought an Apple II, why would we have built one?"[1]

My book is born out of the same motivation that Steve Wozniak and Steve Jobs had during their youth. I wish there had been a book like this on the shelf of my local bookstore when I was younger. I sincerely hope this book helps you achieve your goals and gain greater satisfaction out of your endeavours in life.

Most of the existing self-help books on the market are vague at best. You will find little vagueness here. The Paradigm is penetrating, concise, and non-superfluous. It weeds through the theatrical and cuts to the heart of its subject matter.

Many people take a rather cynical view of the self-help genre of books in general. Fantasy and fiction are in vogue these days. They're great books; it's so easy to get lost in them. That's never been my goal, though. I'm more interested in helping people get lost in the biggest adventure of them all: their own lives.

Finally, I propose a movement—a movement for all of society to adopt The Paradigm as a way of life—to better not only our individual lives, but also society at large. Upon finishing this book, you can consider yourself to be a part of this movement.

INTRODUCTION

I would like to pose a question to the reader. What is the objective of the human condition? It may be tempting to say that the answer depends on the person asked. Such a reply seems eminently reasonable. However, within that reasonableness lurks a troubling problem. The problem is that the question remains slyly unanswered. It is merely an easy way to avoid answering a very fundamental and penetrating question regarding our existence and purpose on earth. However, the real answer is very simple. The objective of the human condition is to maximize happiness.

People's specific goals in life vary from person to person. From all walks of life, you will meet individuals who desire everything from raising a family, to becoming a world leader, to making breakthrough scientific discoveries in how we understand the universe. Regardless of the goal, all of these human aspirations fall within the province of *happiness*. From this self-evident fact, we can therefore derive a logical conclusion: all human desires fall under the banner of happiness.

THE PARADIGM OF HAPPINESS

It is very likely that you have read about Abraham Maslow's great work in this field. He too constructed a model of what he considered the fundamental building blocks of happiness itself. In general, this author has no qualms with Dr. Maslow's work. It is difficult to find anything inherently flawed with his reasoning. However, his one shortcoming is that he did not pursue his own work to its own logical conclusions. Abraham Maslow's hierarchy of needs can be found in psychology textbooks around the world, and is typically presented in the depiction that follows.[1]

FIGURE 1. A DEPICTION OF ABRAHAM MASLOW'S
HIERARCHY OF NEEDS

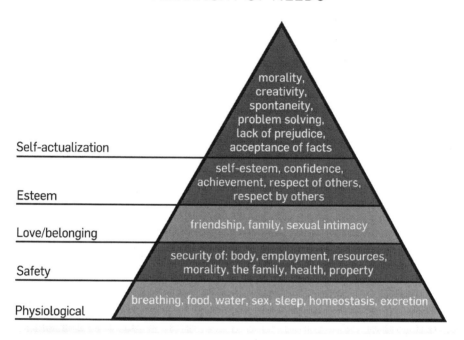

The inherent issue with Maslow's diagram is its lack of specificity and guidance. We are shown, in general terms, what will make us happy. We are not shown, however, exactly *how* we should go about achieving these goals in the modern world. Naturally, a model that strives for greater specificity must necessarily sacrifice at least some degree of universality. Perhaps, through this reasoning, we can give Maslow the benefit of the doubt as to why his model was fairly general. Even so, that realization does not address the issue of its relative vagueness. In response to this predicament, the author of this book created *The Paradigm of Happiness*—or more informally, referred to as simply The Paradigm. This model, as depicted, applies to practically all citizens living within industrialized nations.

The Paradigm, as you see in Figure 2, is stratified into three levels. The individual elements of each level work in concert to form the foundation for the level above it. While it is not strictly necessary to master one level before moving on to the next, doing

FIGURE 2. THE PARADIGM OF HAPPINESS

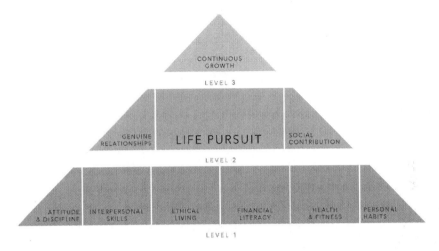

THE PARADIGM OF HAPPINESS

so is like providing a strong concrete foundation for a building. This strong foundation gives a building stability, whereas a building built on mud is not likely to last as long.

THE SIX COMPONENTS OF LEVEL 1

Level 1 concerns foundational life skills, the very bedrock that survival and efficient living are built upon. These six components—Attitude and Discipline, Interpersonal Skills, Ethical Living, Financial Literacy, Health and Fitness, and Personal Habits—can be considered life skills which need to be nurtured in order to fully support the upper levels of The Paradigm.

ATTITUDE AND DISCIPLINE

Everything in life starts within your own mind. Your perception is your reality. In life, your attitude determines your altitude. Your attitude towards life can be seen as the basis for which the rest of your life can either prosper or wither. Actively engaging your mind with the law of attraction and the power of positive mental reinforcement can open up possibilities for which the sky is the limit. However, by the same reasoning, a position of pessimism and a downtrodden demeanour can only produce the opposite.

A conscious and self-directed focus on the negative becomes like a prison cell that is too short to stand up in and too cramped to lie down in. Within this section of the book, I will offer a mental framework and a set of positive reinforcement techniques that will allow the reader to consciously shape their perspective on life. This mental framework is one of the most important elements within the first level of The Paradigm.

RELATIONSHIP SKILLS

Social skills are somewhat hard to define. They aren't always measurable. There are no hard and fast rules. This makes offering advice on the topic an exceedingly difficult matter. Nonetheless, useful social *principles* will be put forth in this chapter with the goal of increasing the reader's communication skills, confidence, and strength in their everyday relationships.

ETHICAL LIVING

The importance of ethics in one's life must not be understated. Ethical behaviour provides a foundation for succeeding in your endeavours from a place of integrity. Behaving ethically can be seen as forgoing immediate gain in favour of long-term and enduring gain. While adopting a high standard of ethical conduct is desirable in and of itself, the truth is that it is usually self-serving and beneficial to your own ends in the long run. In other words, you don't give up anything by being ethical!

Even a cursory observation will reveal that unless you are willing to act altruistically within society and help others, it is unlikely that you will receive help when you need it most. So, in reality, by helping others you are really helping yourself! This concept of altruistic selfishness is explained beautifully in Richard Dawkins' book *The Selfish Gene*.[2] Beyond this tit-for-tat concept lies something much more important: the creation and maintenance of meaningful and lasting relationships.

You will never form such relationships if the other party does not see you as worthy of trust. You will live a brutish and lonely life. I will unapologetically reiterate that behaving ethically is both the right thing *and* the self-serving thing to do! You will develop both self and peer respect. You have no reason not to behave ethically! In this book, I will strive to develop this point further and to postulate a framework for ethical decision making.

FINANCIAL LITERACY

Although money was not initially part of our evolutionary history, money is now our most basic tool in modern industrialized nations. Using and harnessing the power of money is not an inherent or natural skill. Successful money management is, at least for most of us, an acquired skill that must be learned.

Perhaps money cannot buy happiness, but it nonetheless provides one of its foundational pillars. For how can a person pursue their dreams—whether they be in arts, academia, athletics, or whatever they have a passion for—without money to meet their basic needs? How else does an individual eat three square meals a day or put a roof over their head? Money to the modern *Homo sapien* is what the stone axe was to the ancient *Homo ergaster*: a fundamental tool for survival. In this chapter, I will seek to instill a utilitarian attitude within the reader towards money and help the reader to develop a comprehensive savings and investment program.

HEALTH AND FITNESS

That an individual's health must be maintained as a foundation for happiness goes without saying. What is less certain is how we should go about pursuing good health. In this book, I have subcategorized the topic of health into three sections: nutrition, exercise, and mental health. This segregation allows us to tackle the vast topic of health in a more structured fashion. I will show that maintaining good health through these three facets is not as difficult, time consuming, or riddled with sacrifice as one may think, and that the benefits will pay for themselves. In this chapter, you will find diet and exercise plans that will help you along your way.

PERSONAL HABITS

The thread running through all the preceding elements of this level in The Paradigm can be tied together neatly through this section. The concept of "personal habits" includes things such as organization and time management, and are of utmost importance in increasing personal efficiency, reducing stress, and making the achievement of life goals that much easier. In this chapter, I will lay out an organizational plan to help you keep on top of your commitments at both work and in your personal life. Nobody plans to fail, but many fail to plan.

THE THREE COMPONENTS OF LEVEL 2

Building upon the foundational skills the reader will develop in Level 1, we proceed upwards in our happiness model. The elements within Level 1 were of a supporting role. The following three elements within Level 2 allow us to tap life's core sources of happiness: genuine relationships, social contributions, and succeeding in the pursuit of our life's purpose.

GENUINE RELATIONSHIPS WITH FRIENDS AND LOVED ONES

Take it from the experience of this author, who was rather slow in learning this lesson: happiness is not found in expensive gadgets, luxury cars, or fine clothing. It is often said that possessions are meant to be used and people are meant to be loved, but the reason why the world is in chaos is because possessions are being loved and people are being used. Happiness is found in experiences and deep connections with your friends and family, not through materialism or pretension. It is important to nurture, cultivate, and appreciate the friends and family you have around you while you can, as they will not be there forever. Fostering stronger and stronger relationships with friends and family is what will bring true happiness.

SOCIAL CONTRIBUTION

Give and you shall receive. Giving back to society and helping others is undoubtedly one of the greatest joys in the world. You will scarcely find happiness in any other endeavour. It can be said unequivocally that every reader of this book owes their good fortune to society in one manner or another. Enjoying the fruits of society and standing on the shoulders of the giants that came before us is a privilege. The most gratifying thing you can do with your time is to give something back. This might include intellectual contributions to certain fields, donating significant portions of personal wealth to philanthropic causes, or simply contributing your time to community initiatives.

ACHIEVING PERSONAL SUCCESS IN YOUR LIFE'S PURSUIT

This is the most important of the three cornerstone components discussed in Level 2. This is your raison d'être, your reason for existing. Achievement in your life's ultimate passion is where lasting happiness comes from. You and your life's calling can, in effect, be considered one and the same. This is your very identity. From this starting point, you can leave a legacy in ideas, culture, the arts, academics, or athletics that the mere genes of your progeny cannot hope to match. It will, and might, be your only lasting impression on this world. Your time is limited. It is of utmost importance that you realize that if you haven't found what your life's passion is, then your immediate task is to find it.

There is a temptation to equate success in one's life's work with being able to beat all others. While competition is certainly healthy, the real goal is to surpass personal bests and to become better than who you were yesterday. Comparing yourself to the Joneses—always looking at what the other people have—can only lead to despair. Your life's passion and your work will give your life meaning in a way that nothing else possibly can. It is better to conquer yourself than to win a thousand battles with others.

THE SINGLE COMPONENT OF LEVEL 3

CONTINUOUS GROWTH

The final level of The Paradigm of Happiness is that of continuous growth and improvement. This means that one must never settle for what they have accomplished in life. The beauty of achievement is that it is an endless journey. You will reach plateaus, but you must not stay there. Satisfaction in life comes from constantly pushing yourself to new limits. Humans have a need to build and create things; stagnation leads to a hollow existence.

ORIGINS OF THE PARADIGM OF HAPPINESS

As stated earlier, the fundamentals of The Paradigm of Happiness are built upon the work of Abraham Maslow and the examples set by many successful individuals. In writing this book, I sought out and researched the lives of the happiest and most satisfied people in history as a basis for building my model. I examined the qualities and the personal building blocks for the storied lives of Albert Einstein, Warren Buffett, Sam Walton, and many others. I distilled the common factors between all of these successful individuals until I had developed a comprehensive list. It is this list of qualities that became the component levels of The Paradigm. By juxtaposing my component list of qualities with Maslow's hierarchy of needs, I was able to determine which components were prerequisite factors for the fulfillment of other qualities.

The Paradigm is meant to be, above all, a guide. It is a framework by which people can solve life's problems and think about life's purpose. It is a way to consider how to move forward, be more productive, happier, and more accomplished. It is a book to help people navigate through life's ups and downs more intelligently, so as to avoid unnecessary and painful mistakes. Beyond helping people on the individual level, I hope this book has a far enough reaching influence to become a boost to society as a whole, as an influencing factor for a whole new generation of people in search of guidance.

One of the biggest reasons why people go through large portions of their lives (and for some, their whole lives) without much direction is because there is no manual or handbook for life itself. People are not given a guiding hand for how to proceed in life, for what they should seek from life, or how to overcome its most common pitfalls. What path should people take in life? What is the goal? How do they even decide this?

School, for all the general emphasis placed on its importance, does a remarkably poor job of preparing children for the real world upon graduation and entering adulthood. We are taught how to use a band saw in woodworking class or what year the Dutch East India Company was founded; however, beyond receiving some vague advice about finding a job, we are hardly ever taught about genuinely pressing matters such as how to invest personal savings, or how to truly contribute to society. This book intends to fill that educational gap and give people a guiding hand for how to live and make the most of life. I leave it to the reader to exercise his or her own critical judgment as to the success of my efforts.

THE STRUCTURE OF THIS BOOK

The content of this book has been logically organized in a manner reflecting that of The Paradigm of Happiness itself. There are four sections of the book, including the introduction you are currently reading. The second section covers all of the elements within Level 1 of The Paradigm, with each element occupying a chapter to itself, for a total of six chapters. The third section covers Level 2 of The Paradigm, with each of its three elements having their own chapters devoted to them as well. The final section of the book is devoted to the top of The Pardigm: the element of Continuous Growth. I hope you find this book helpful to you on your journey through life.

THE PARADIGM OF HAPPINESS
LEVEL 1

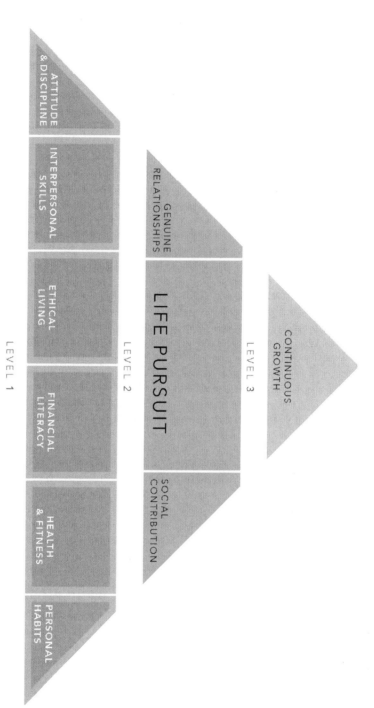

ATTITUDE & DISCIPLINE

INTERPERSONAL SKILLS

ETHICAL LIVING

FINANCIAL LITERACY

HEALTH & FITNESS

PERSONAL HABITS

LEVEL 1

GENUINE RELATIONSHIPS

LIFE PURSUIT

SOCIAL CONTRIBUTION

LEVEL 2

CONTINUOUS GROWTH

LEVEL 3

CHAPTER 1
ATTITUDE AND DISCIPLINE

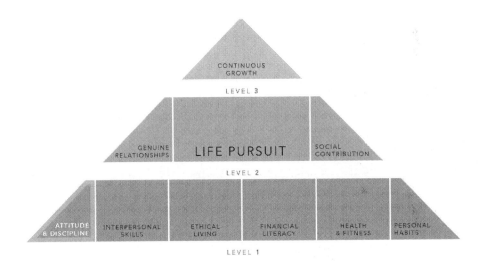

THE PARADIGM OF HAPPINESS

We begin our examination of the first element of the first level of The Paradigm with a simple premise: all positive changes and all happiness in life begin in your mind. The mind is the starting point for everything. From this premise, we develop a simple formula from which to build:

1. Make a conscious decision to focus on constructive thoughts.
2. Translate constructive thoughts into constructive action.
3. Let constructive action lead to positive outcomes in your life.

LET'S LOOK AT EACH STEP IN THE FORMULA

1. MAKE A CONSCIOUS DECISION TO FOCUS ON CONSTRUCTIVE THOUGHTS.

The first thing you must realize is that as a human being, you have control over the things that transpire within your mind. You have control over your thoughts. You can choose to think constructive thoughts, or you can choose to think destructive thoughts. That you can choose is an extremely powerful realization. To be happy you must first *choose* to be happy. To solve your problems, you must *choose* to focus on solving your problems. Gain awareness of the fact that you have responsibility for what happens in your life and how you deal with your problems. This sense of personal accountability is often referred to as an *internal locus of control* in psychological theory.[1]

The opposite attitude is called an *external locus of control*. Those with an external locus of control feel they have little to no responsibility for what happens in their lives. They see their day-to-day events, their schedule, and even their career paths, as being moulded and shaped by the forces surrounding them. This passivity is in contrast to the way we should be approaching our endeavours.[2] It is highly unlikely that a person will find life satisfying with an external locus of control. In industrialized, democratic societies, we are where we are in life because of the choices that we have made, for better or for worse. Attributing our circumstances to the actions of others is an abdication of our responsibility as human beings. Focus on developing an internal locus of control, and *choose your thoughts*.

2. TRANSLATE CONSTRUCTIVE THOUGHTS INTO CONSTRUCTIVE ACTION.

After making the conscious decision to engage in constructive and positive thoughts, we turn to the question of the content of those thoughts. Obviously, the ultimate choice is given to the reader in deciding what to think about. However, there is one particular type of thought *pattern* that has proven to be highly effective in the author's observation: goal-oriented thinking. Whatever you want to achieve in life, hold on to the thought of it tenaciously. The human mind will always tend to gravitate towards making its most common and powerful thoughts into realities. Keep your goal within your mind's eye and never let go of it. Begin with the end in mind.[3]

If you prefer, visualization is an extremely robust tool and can be effectively applied here as well. Imagine yourself as the person you want to become—a person who has achieved their goals. See yourself as accomplishing your dreams. Always keep this image in your mind. Make this image concrete. Think about what the details will be in addition to the general picture. If you dream of being a successful musician, for instance, imagine feeling the row of callouses that have developed on your fingers from years of playing. If you dream of being a successful entrepreneur, imagine the feeling of looking out at a crowd of young high school students listening to you giving a speech about success.

You may find it challenging to turn these positive thoughts into a habit at first. If this is the case, consider first approaching this task through the process of exclusion rather than inclusion. At first, it will not be terribly important what specific positive thoughts or thought patterns you decide to pursue. Start by simply refusing to dwell on the negative. From here, you can begin to move on to positive thoughts, whatever "positive" might mean to you personally.

It should be noted that my encouragement in focusing on positive as opposed to negative thoughts does not mean that you must always have positive *feelings*. The emotional balance of the human animal naturally swings between elation and despair. This swinging back and forth is entirely natural, and to be expected. The key is to accept those feelings and to work with them. You cannot change your feelings quickly. You can, however, learn to control your *thoughts*, which are inherently distinct from your feelings. More succinctly, it is vital that readers should focus on positive *thinking* even if their present *emotions* are dark.

As you harness your mental energies towards positive thinking, this leads to positive action, which is the theme of this second step of the formula. Your mind's renewed focus on constructive attitudes and activities you will give you both the energy and drive to pursue life goals and a resistance to lethargy. The mind persistently tries to fulfill and make real the image that it has formed for itself. From this canon, we develop the basis of the next principle in our formula.

3. LET CONSTRUCTIVE ACTION LEAD TO POSITIVE OUTCOMES IN YOUR LIFE.

While simple positive thinking can't miraculously change your emotions overnight, the resultant positive *actions* will produce life outcomes that can and will change your feelings for the better. Positive emotions follow your positive actions, not the other way around.[4,5] As stated earlier, the mind will always try to fulfill and make real the things with which it is occupied. As more and more positive actions and outcomes materialize through your attitudes, our formula will reinforce itself through a positive feedback loop. Positive outcomes from this stage will further catalyze your positive thoughts. This leads to greater action and then greater outcomes and so on indefinitely. All things excellent are as difficult as they are rare. Clearly, accomplishing anything worthwhile in life requires a deep commitment and sound work ethic. However, your passion will help your attitude, and you will see your work as being a gratifying hardship.

MOTIVATION AND INSPIRATION

After developing a constructive mind set, we now turn to the task of catalyzing that mindset with motivation and inspiration—the rocket fuel for your mind.

An extremely powerful tool for motivation and inspiration is emulating a role model. Ask yourself who you look up to. Who do you admire? Who is a hero to you? Who do you aspire to be like? I admire Warren Buffet. For years, the great Warren Buffett, philanthropist and successful businessman, has informally extolled the virtues of a very powerful formula for self-improvement. He would advise students to look around at the people they admire. Upon finding these role models, he would then instruct them to write a list of the qualities of those individuals that made them so successful and admirable. In making these lists, the students would find that none of those qualities were unachievable. They were all entirely qualities of character such as discipline and integrity. None of these fundamental qualities were ordained.[6]

Buffett would also advise students to write down a list of the qualities that they disliked in people. In a similar vein, none of those qualities were unchangeable either. They were all character traits such as unreliability or dishonesty that are based on behavioural choices. In the end, Buffet's logical conclusion was simple and irrefutable. If you aspire to be like the people you admire, then simply start behaving like them![7] Guided by this principle, you will soon find that nothing is impossible.

Buffett then summed up this philosophy with a remark that will be quoted for years to come: "Tell me who your heroes are, and I'll tell you how you'll turn out [to be.]"[8] From this statement, we can come to a further conclusion as well. You can decide who you do and who you don't want to be!

Beyond role models, consider your personal values. What do you feel deeply about? What values are you striving towards in life? What aspects of society do you hope to change for the better? Perhaps you draw strength from your religious values. If you carry a powerfully entrenched ideology within your psyche, draw upon that to nourish your motivation.

Find motivation. Part of this author's own morning ritual is to find and view a new motivational video every morning just after waking. Human motivation tends to dissipate quite quickly. Viewing a new motivational video on a daily basis from, say, YouTube, replenishes this reserve of personal inspiration. It is a simple act every morning that only takes a few minutes, but supercharges an individual to get things accomplished for the day. For maximum effectiveness, search for motivational videos made about people that you admire.

DEVELOPING CONFIDENCE

Confidence is a component of the attitudes that we have discussed thus far. Confidence is a quality that all people strive for in just about every field and every endeavour. There are two key aspects to note about confidence for those who have trouble conjuring it. They are not mystical and do not require divine insight. The first aspect is a strong desire. An aspiration to overcome nervousness and to become confident at whatever task you wish to engage in first requires an absolutely strong desire to do so.

The second key aspect to developing confidence is simple repetition. If you want to become more confident at public speaking, then the key is to practice more public speaking—perhaps building up to larger and larger audiences. If you wish to become more confident in a particular sport, then the key is to practice that sport. If you want to become more confident talking to those whom you may wish to date, the only way is to do it more often. Repetition! Repetition! Repetition!

These two key aspects of confidence tie in synergistically with the ideas of motivation and positive thinking discussed above. Remember that emotions follow actions, not the other way around. Repetition is the simple embodiment of that idea. Your desire will allow you to overcome your initial anxiety and to start pursuing a task. Act confidently. Repeat the task frequently, and eventually your feelings will follow your actions. You will find that with each repetition your nervousness and anxiety will subside.

Confidence is like a muscle. Your muscles don't become stronger just by thinking about wanting them to be stronger; they become stronger only when you subject them to forces that are greater than what they are used to. Little by little, you will find yourself enjoying whatever task you have set for yourself. This process mirrors The Paradigm's model for positive thinking, as these enjoyable experiences reinforce confidence until uneasiness disappears entirely.

THE PERSONAL BALANCE SHEET

There may be times when it seems like there is nothing in life that is going right for you and there is nothing but despondency. If your mood or personal situation is in an extreme funk, then it may be helpful to practice the following exercise for improving your perspective. Take a pen and a sheet of paper, and on the left side of the page simply start to list all of the positive things in your life that you are grateful for. List everything you can think of that you have going for you.

This list can be seen as a way to take stock of what resources you have for pursuing your personal goals. It is very empowering to see all of the positive elements in your life written down on paper, as then they will seem more concrete in your mind. Such things might include good health, family, friends, a retirement nest egg, or even the simple fact that you live in a society filled with opportunity. Take stock of what you have. You just might find that you are richer than you originally believed.

On the other side of the page, write down all of the negative things in your life such as unemployment, loneliness, or depression. Take stock of them as well. (Note that if you are experiencing a mental health issue, you should see a healthcare professional.) I will not presume to tell you that your problems are not real. However, what I will tell you is that every problem in this list is something that you must make an active effort to solve. You cannot allow these problems to linger, for if you do they will only grow worse over time. Ignoring them will not make them go away. The tools you are learning in this book will make it easier to remedy them.

What you have just created is a Personal Balance Sheet. This is very much analogous to a financial balance sheet, with which accountants will be familiar. Much like business leaders scrutinizing their company's statements, your goal will be to study your Personal Balance Sheet and determine how you can best use the resources on the left side to overcome the difficulties on the right side. Your ability to solve the problems present in your life has been much improved now that both your resources and your problems have been laid out in black and white.

After analyzing your immediate situation, your next task is to resolve to use the positive mental attitudes learned earlier in this chapter. Use them and make a conscious effort to increase the number of positive factors on the left side, while preventing negative factors from accumulating on the right side. Make this your goal. Has loneliness developed as a problem on the negative side of your Personal Balance Sheet? Seek earnestly to solve that problem. Go out and make new friends at school, at work, or wherever you decide is best. Upon doing so you can add your new friendship to the positive side of the Personal Balance Sheet and consider your life tangibly improved. The Personal Balance Sheet is a methodical and effective approach to solving life's problems. An example of a completed Personal Balance Sheet follows.

FIGURE 1.1 AN EXAMPLE OF A PERSONAL BALANCE SHEET

—————————— **MY PERSONAL BALANCE SHEET** ——————————

ASSETS
- Strong family relationships with my mother, father, and siblings.
- $3,340 in emergency savings.
- Personal vehicle with no loan.
- Applied skills in website development, graphic design, and photography.
- Computer, DSLR camera, and lighting equipment.
- Connections with Michelle and Tina, both good friends from high school.

CHALLENGES
- I have $22,230 in student loan debts.
- I am having a hard time finding a long-term partner.
- I am 27 lbs. (12kg.) above my ideal body weight.
- My current job is not in the career field that I want.
- I want to make more friends.
- I have social anxiety and shyness.

PASSION IS POWERFUL

One of the critical considerations for developing motivation and a positive mental attitude is your passion in life. This was alluded to earlier in this chapter in our discussion of goals. What is your calling? What do you love to do? You will recognize that this element of The Paradigm is placed explicitly in the second level. Even so, it is still worth mentioning here. I will reiterate that if you have not yet found your passion in life, then your immediate priority is to find it. Nothing will give you more drive than finding what you love. This point will be developed further in Chapter 9.

YOUR CORE PRINCIPLE

I saved the best for last. The one thing you'll need above all else when it comes to developing discipline, inspiration, and a positive attitude in life is *discovering your Core Principle*.

Every person's day-to-day actions are determined by their Core Principle. Some people actively develop it, some stumble upon it, while others operate on one that is instinctual.

As an example, there are many devout Christians who live their lives by the word of God. Many members of the church consider God to be the most important part of their lives. In turn, serving God becomes their Core Principle. All of their actions, their motivations, and the various philosophies to which they subscribe stem from their Core Principle. All of their actions and their life plans implicitly follow their concept of serving God. All the other theories, philosophies, and models of behaviour they adopt in life are simply extensions of this Core Principle. John D. Rockefeller, the great oil industrialist and founder of Standard Oil, adopted serving God as his Core Principle, and the drive from this principle is what gave him the strength of character to create his empire. Indeed, a Baptist preacher once told him to make as much money as possible, so that he could give away as much money as possible.[9,10]

I developed my Core Principle from experiences relating to my family life; more specifically, from my relationship with my mother and father. My mother and father, David and Hermia Wong, grew up extremely poor in China, during the Cold War years. Their story is very much a classic one. Shortly after arriving in Canada in the 1970s to study geology at the University of Regina, my father's own father passed away. Being the oldest of his siblings, he took it upon himself to drop out of university and begin an apprenticeship as a mechanic to support the family. It was the fastest way for him to start making reasonable money at the time, even if it meant sacrificing his dream of becoming a geologist.

By the same token, my mother grew up in a family that didn't have much in the way of wealth. Her mother never had the chance to attend school and couldn't read or write, so finding any work at all was difficult at best. My mother started working to help support the family when she was a teenager.

I grew up in the 1990s, and my mother and father—by working long hours and practicing the most prudent behaviour—did everything they could to make life better for me than it was for them. Their commitment meant never spending money on things that were not necessities, not drinking, not smoking, and carrying themselves with utmost integrity, to set a positive example.

Moreover, there were other smaller facets of their behaviour that became apparent as I grew up. My father, when taking on any task, would always accomplish it with great attention to detail and would never leave a job halfway done. My parents also both knew the value of education, especially since they had been robbed of the opportunity to finish school themselves.

My parents paid for my university tuition without ever having asked for a single penny of that money back. During my early years in university, I struggled to find my footing and was unsure about what career path I wanted to take. Despite my molasses-like progress, my parents never gave up on me, and they continued to support me and provide me with an education, even in the face of mounting costs and their advancing age. It was then that I realized I was squandering an incredible privilege that stemmed from my parents' incredible sacrifices. I was taking for granted their support and encouragement, and their integrity to "finish the job" of educating me. I felt that I had let them down.

My Core Principle is to *never* let my mother and father down ever again.

Whenever I am considering doing something or not doing something, I think about whether or not they would be proud of me for making that decision. I think about whether that action, or inaction, is in keeping with the hard work and sacrifices they made for me and for our family. My Core Principle guides my actions daily, and all the other ideologies and philosophies I have adopted in life are simply extensions to this Core Principle.

Those who lack positive attitude and discipline in life are those who have not developed a Core Principle.

If you have not discovered your Core Principle, your task is to find it as quickly as you can. It is the driving force behind everything you do, and a prerequisite to your entire life and career. Read as many books as you can. Talk with those you consider to be experienced and wise. Expose yourself to as many different ideologies as possible. Always exploring the new and unfamiliar is how you discover your Core Principle as quickly as possible.

BRANCHING OUT

Think of your Core principle as the hub of a network from which different ideas and concepts extend from and interconnect. This is the start of a mind map. See the Core Principle in the centre. The extensions make up the supplementary principles that form your overall *Personal Constitution*, an idea that I learned from a friend. A Personal Constitution, much like the Canadian constitution, is a document that outlines how you will run your life based on the values and principles that you have decided are important to you.

The mind map exercise will help you determine what those values are. The following is an example of my mind map, with my Core Principle in the middle. Using this exercise, I was able to see what principles and values supported my Core Principle. Take the time to do this exercise yourself. Keep in mind that this doesn't have to be too formal; you are just exploring ideas. Write down whatever comes to mind in order to stimulate introspection.

FIGURE 1.2: A MIND MAP OF THE AUTHOR'S CORE PRINCIPLE AND RELATED VALUES

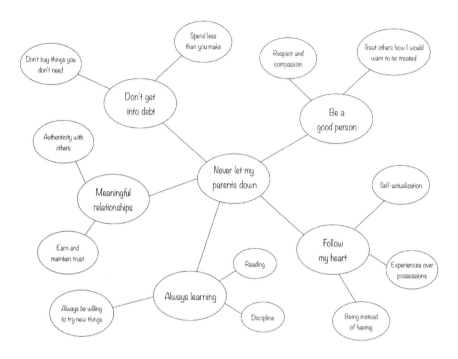

After using the mind map exercise above to determine what values were most important to me and my life, I took those ideas and formalized them into my Personal Constitution, which I've shared here for illustrative purposes.

PERSONAL CONSTITUTION

Preamble
I, Forrest Wong, pledge to uphold and defend my Core Principle through this Personal Constitution.

Statement of Purpose
I am devoted to achieving unity between my personal abilities, the needs of society, and the needs of my own self.

Article I. The Fundamentals
1. All of the actions in my life shall be in the service of self-actualization.
2. I will always follow my heart.
3. I will exercise discipline in all matters of life.
4. I will emphasize being over having.

Article II. Economic Principles
1. Economic decisions shall be governed by costs and benefits.
2. Money is my slave, not my master.
3. I will strive to maintain balance between working and learning.

Article III. Relationships
1. I will treat others with respect and compassion.
2. I will strive to cultivate deep and meaningful relationships with others.

Article IV. Personal Growth
1. I will always follow the three precepts of ethical decision making: The Global Test; The Golden Rule; and Phronesis (wisdom).
2. I will read, learn, and teach as much as possible, in all matters of knowledge.
3. I shall endeavour to develop both my physical and mental health to their maximum capacity.

Article V. Physical Environment
1. I will treat my home, wherever it may be, with respect and dignity.
2. I will strive to maintain cleanliness and order in all facets of my environment.
3. I will emphasize experiences over material possessions.

Take a minute every day to read your personal constitution and internalize it. This repetition will allow you to reprogram yourself to behave in ways that you have decided are ideal. Most of your behaviour in life is habitual. It won't happen overnight, but over the course of weeks and months, your habits will change for the better.

Additionally, you may find it helpful, as I have, to take individual components of your Personal Constitution and write them down in convenient places for reference. As an example, I have opted to write the three Economic Principles in my Personal Constitution onto a sticky note and place it my wallet. That way I am reminded of my rules for money every time I open my wallet. Similarly, I have placed a sticky note with the four tenets that make up The Fundamentals on my bathroom mirror. This way, I automatically see them every morning when I'm getting ready for the day. Think of other locations where placing reminders of the tenets you have pledged to yourself would be useful. An example would be putting the Physical Environment precepts on your bedroom wall if keeping that particular room tidy has been a challenge for you.

The encouragement to develop a Personal Constitution was given to me by a friend during my college years. This fellow (we'll call him Eddie) had a habit that I found curious at the time. Eddie would wake up every day at 5:45 a.m., regardless of his schedule. Even on weekends when there were no classes in session he would wake up at this time. I asked him, "Dude, why bother? It's the weekend."

I still remember his face turning somewhat stern before he responded. "It's all about the discipline, man. I can't afford to lose it. And what you don't use, you lose."

I was somewhat taken aback at Eddie's seriousness over what seemed to me to be a relatively trivial matter at the time. I didn't argue with him and simply nodded my head in agreement. Nonetheless, Eddie noticed a certain lack of enthusiasm on my part. He stalked over to his desk and pulled out what was obviously a well-worn sheet of paper from the top drawer. It was his Personal Constitution. He pointed to the first line of the first paragraph. "I promised myself that I would always '*carpe diem.*' It means 'seize the day'."

Carpe Diem was part of Eddie's Personal Constitution. More importantly, it was likely his Core Principle. It was only in the following weeks that I realized that if Eddie were not getting up at the same time every day, ready to go, he would not only be exercising a lack of discipline, he would be betraying himself. This realization struck me rather profoundly, and I got to work in producing my own Personal Constitution.

This constitution should not be cobbled together in 15 minutes off the top of your head. It should involve serious contemplation and introspection. Genuinely consider what is important in your life and what you value. Ensconce yourself in a place where you will not be distracted so that you can brainstorm. Feel free to use my own mind map and Personal Constitution, presented previously, as a framework for your own.

ACTION STEPS BEFORE READING THE NEXT CHAPTER

TO-DO: ATTITUDE AND DISCIPLINE

- Start determining what your Core Principle is by thinking about what drives your action in life and what values are most meaningful to you.
- Take stock of your life by writing down your assets and challenges on a personal balance sheet.
- Assemble your Personal Constitution.

FURTHER RECOMMENDED READINGS ON ATTITUDE AND DISCIPLINE

- *The Secret*, Rhonda Byrne
- *Meditations*, Marcus Aurelius
- *Think and Grow Rich*, Napoleon Hill
- *Awaken the Giant Within*, Anthony Robbins

CHAPTER 2
INTERPERSONAL SKILLS

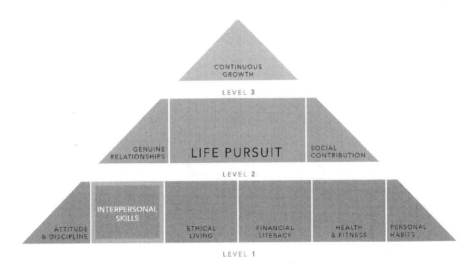

CONTINUOUS
GROWTH

LEVEL 3

GENUINE
RELATIONSHIPS

LIFE PURSUIT

SOCIAL
CONTRIBUTION

LEVEL 2

INTERPERSONAL
SKILLS

ATTITUDE
& DISCIPLINE

ETHICAL
LIVING

FINANCIAL
LITERACY

HEALTH
& FITNESS

PERSONAL
HABITS

LEVEL 1

THE PARADIGM OF HAPPINESS

Our relationships with the people in our lives make up the very fabric and texture of our day-to-day experiences. What are our lives without the people around us? This chapter is particularly important. Having strong relationships is absolutely paramount to achieving and maintaining a healthy state of mind for life. In this chapter, I'm going to tell you how to best develop and maintain strong relationships in four broad categories: platonic, familial, work, and romantic relationships. We shall begin our discussion with platonic relationships.

PLATONIC RELATIONSHIPS

Human beings are social animals. Our primitive forebears have lived in social groups since before even our ancestor, *Australopithecus afarensis*, developed the ability to walk on two legs—also known as bipedalism.[1] As our brains and bodies have developed and grown in complexity, so have our social systems. Generations later, our more recent ancestor, *Homo ergaster*, became the first of our ancient relatives to communicate with deep meaning through inferences of body language and telling glances of the eye.[2] Now, more than a million years after the age of *Homo ergaster*, the complexities and subtleties of our social lives have only increased.

Naturally, the biggest change in recent years to the modern social paradigm is the invention of mobile phones and the Internet. You would think that with the pervasive use of cell phones and social networking, our lives would have become more connected over the years. I think one can make a pretty good case for that. I, for one, find it much easier to keep up with friends I don't live close to, or to catch up with friends I haven't talked to in a while, thanks to Facebook. Cell phones, similarly, have given us a great leap forward in terms of personal communication, because they allow people to call a person, *wherever they are*, unlike landline phones that strictly allow you to contact a *place*. Beyond calling and texting, smart phones in particular are allowing us to be even more connected with each other with the advent of Internet connectivity. Now we can use Twitter, wherever we are, to update our friends about our lives. It seems great to be that connected to people, but I have some reservations.

Let's face it. Digital communication is extremely sterile. There just isn't the same feeling of interaction and connection with another person when you communicate with them digitally instead of physically. I'm sure you, the reader, have experienced this feeling as well. No matter how much we talk to our friends through Skype, Facebook, instant messaging, texting, or even a phone call, nothing compares to seeing and hanging out with our friends in person. That same energy just isn't there when we are connected through devices. More importantly, it's really not building our friendships either.

Aside from the convenience of contact, I would say that digital communication is most useful as a way of helping to *maintain* relationships, instead of building them. Have you ever had a friend move to a far away state or province and your only way of catching up with them on a regular basis was with the Internet? You know the feeling, then; no amount of Facebook personal messages stops you from missing that person. Only seeing them eases the experience of missing them. At the very least, though, this online contact can help to prevent the relationship from weakening over time. That's probably the extent of the usefulness of this impersonal medium, though. You would certainly be hard pressed to *make* new friends by meeting them online, although such a thing is not unheard of. (As always, exercise caution on the Internet, as befriending strangers can lead to disastrous consequences.)

Many of us—the younger generation in particular—have fooled ourselves into believing that by having a lot of Facebook friends, or a lot of Twitter followers, we are "networking." For the most part, that's not real networking. It's fake. The Internet has allowed us to believe that a tremendous amount of our empty networking constitutes real friendships.

Simply take this as a heed of caution. While these technologies have done great things for communication, never ever fool yourself into believing that strong relationships can be built and strengthened through electronic means alone. *Real* social contact is important for your mental health! While it is true that those who are introverted may prefer not to be in large and noisy gatherings, friendship still constitutes an important life component. Moreover, a strong network of friends will help, over time, to boost your career and personal prospects.

REAL FRIENDS

Everybody wants to have more friends. It's nice to have a lot of friends, and there's certainly nothing wrong with that. It's important to realize, however, that you need to be making friends for the right reasons. Are you looking to become friends with someone because you genuinely like who they are? Or do you want to become friends with someone so you can get to know that cute guy or girl they know? Maybe you want to be friends with them simply because they are popular, and you think they can boost your social status. Or worse, maybe you want to be friends with someone who's attractive just because you want to be seen with them. Such a line of reasoning is childish and self-defeating. Friendships based on these selfish and fake premises will not earn you true friends, particularly in the long run.

FIGURE 2.1: THE AUTHOR (RIGHT) AND HIS PARTNER IN CRIME CHANTELLE (LEFT)

Your thoughts and feelings, whether you want them to or not, do, over time, become reflective of your actions. As a result, relationships based on fake premises lead to fake relationships. Motivations matter greatly.

You want to have friendships and relationships because you like people for who they are. These are the people whom you are personally compatible with on a fundamental level. Why am I emphasizing this? Remember the whole point of this book.

It's my intention to try and help you live a happier life, and believe me, friendships built on honest and genuine interest in other people are key to having a fulfilling social life. Be true to people, be genuine, treat them as you would like to be treated, and you will both attract and keep the right people in your life. I am grateful for my true friends such as Chantelle, shown in Figure 2.1., who have stuck by me during trying times in my life.

One important thing to realize is that no matter who you are, I can practically guarantee you will have only a handful of true friends in your life. By "true friend", I mean the type of friend who knows you inside and out: the kind of friend in whom you can confide even the most embarrassing things; the kind of friend who begins to blur the line into family. In reply to the question of what a true friend is, Aristotle was once famously quoted as saying, "A single soul dwelling in two bodies."[3] These are the people who will bring real happiness into your life.

By saying that you will only have a few of these kinds of people in your life, I am in no way trying to imply that you are unlikable. I simply want to be sure you realize that having only a small number of true friends is not only the norm, but also that it's impossible to have many true friends. It's very much a question of friendship quality over quantity. It's not an exact science, but an empirical study suggests that the maximum number of true friends that most people can possibly maintain is about five. The number of close friends we can maintain is about fifteen. The number of what people would call "good friends" rises to about fifty. Beyond that, the maximum number of meaningful relationships the human brain can maintain tops out at around 150 people. This number (150) is often referred to as "Dunbar's number."[4]

In other words, don't fret or become depressed over not having very many true friends. That's just the way the human animal is built. When asked in surveys, an alarming number of people in the general population report that they don't have any true friends at all![5] Remember that the quoted number of five true friends was the practical *maximum*. Even if we only have one true friend, we are unbelievably lucky. One of the biggest reasons why the idea of having many close friends clashes with what's practical is the simple matter of time. Great friendships are formed and strengthened because of the oodles of time spent with those people. So, with only 24 hours in a day (and a good chunk of it spent sleeping and working), how many true friendships can we really have? There's an old saying that rings true: You can be friends with anyone, but you can't be friends with everyone.

In the end, building these few true relationships is what matters most. While you shouldn't shun the prospects of making friends with new people, the few true friends you have will be the relationships that bring you real happiness in the long run.

THE FIRST STEP TO MAKING FRIENDS

The first step in making friends is to *want* to make friends. This sounds absurdly obvious, but you would not believe the number of people you will meet in life that talk the talk, but aren't willing to walk the walk. They will make the claim that they want to go through with trying to accomplish something but their actions don't reflect the claim. The aspiration itself is not truly affirmed in their minds. You may know the type. These are the kind of people who say they want to hang out, but seem happy when plans are cancelled. In the end, you know what they say: *actions speak louder than words*. To make friends, you have to consciously want to achieve that goal. Remember to solidify the goal in your mind as we discussed in Chapter 1. Put a laser focus on that goal and do not let go of it. If talking to people—especially people you've just met—gives you a lot of anxiety, don't worry: that's perfectly normal—doubly so if it's someone you have a crush on or are attracted to.

Right now, sincerely say to yourself, "I want to make friends." Do this earnestly. Make this a real goal in your mind's eye.

Without consciously affirming goals and ambitions, they tend to become muted in our daily lives. We make half-hearted attempts at accomplishing them and give up too easily. You have to let yourself know that you want it. To give yourself motivation, remember that making real friends can make you happier. If you suffer from a lot of social anxiety, remind yourself of the satisfying feeling you will have after conquering your fear and striking up a simple conversation. Also remember that socializing becomes easier over time. It doesn't remain difficult forever. As you make friends, you will find yourself becoming more relaxed and easy going as time goes on. Your natural charisma and playfulness start to show themselves. Eventually, you will begin to realize that the vast majority of people around you have similar friendship aspirations. They would love to be friends with you—just as you would with them!

Most of all, though, remember that there is no rewind button in life. You only get to live life once, and you can only live it forward. Whether you are in high school, college, or in the workforce, remember that every time you pass up the opportunity to socialize and make friends, you are forgoing an opportunity that will never again make itself available. In life, you will either suffer the pain of discipline, or suffer the pain of regret. This might be the biggest motivator of all. The last thing you want is to look back on missed opportunities with regret.

ONCE MORE, WITH FEELING

So you've decided that you want to make and be friends with people. Notice how the decision, a real affirmation, was what we wanted first? The reason is because our thoughts, which are at least partially controllable, are what are really at the core of our behaviour. Both consciously and subconsciously, our affirmations become our actions—sometimes before we even realize it. Now that you've decided stronger friendships are what you'd like to pursue, let's build some precepts around that decision.

The first is confidence. Confidence is the key quality for social success. Beyond knowing that you want to make friends, you must have confidence in yourself. Being shy gets you nowhere. Yes, certainly, getting over shyness is easier said than done. However, remember that confidence, no matter who you are, will slowly but surely come to you as you interact with more and more people. Take it in baby steps if you experience a lot of social anxiety. Start trying to become more social with the people you are most comfortable with. Simply ask for the time or to borrow a pen— anything to start a conversation. Beyond that, strike up smaller conversations about music, or opinions on an item of clothing you wore that day. Over time, you will find that great conversation begins to happen and flow spontaneously. I mentioned before that the key to proficiency in any skill is repetition. Social skills are no exception. This is the one thing that will build confidence more than anything else.

Remember that your feelings over time become a self-fulfilling prophecy. What you feel is often subconsciously communicated to the people around you. Your feelings become transmuted into reactions, facial expressions, and body language. Getting this feeling of confidence, enthusiasm, and positivity is the most important part of being socially successful. If you begin to feel this way around people, you will naturally attract others to you and have the right kinds of conversations that seem to flow naturally and easily. Having interesting anecdotes in reserve for lulls in conversations might appear to be useful, but the real core of social success is the enjoyment and the positive feelings you get from those relationships. People will always forget what you've said. People will never forget how you've made them feel.

Besides repetition, one of the best techniques for building confidence in social situations is something called mental affirmation. Mental affirmations may seem kind of hokey on first consideration, but they really work. They are essentially positive statements, mentally spoken to yourself on a regular basis, that slowly begin to imprint themselves on your subconscious. Repeating statements such as, "I am confident and charismatic" or "every day in every way, it's getting better and better," begins to shift the way your mind perceives the world around you. Slowly but surely, these conscious, positive efforts change the way you feel. Many successful people such as John Lennon have been known to use this tool in their daily lives. These statements harden your resolve to become successful.[6]

Keep in mind that the statements don't always have to be mental. Sometimes, sticky notes to yourself, often on places like your bathroom mirror or at your desk, can help as well. Remember that the statements should be formed in the *present* tense. Any statement that is formed in the future tense will simply not have the kind of psychological impact needed to get your mental gears going. Nothing is stimulated when the success you aspire to is always postulated in the future instead of the present. Simply changing a statement such as "I will be confident" to "I *am* confident" stimulates the subconscious to work toward your goals. It doesn't happen immediately, but over time you really *can* change the way you feel.

Contrast these positive affirmations to the attitudes of most people: pessimism and cynicism. Whether they realize it or not, these people are polluting their own subconscious with negative statements such as "I can't do it", "I'll never be like him", or worst of all, "I'll do it tomorrow." Without making a conscious effort toward maintaining positive attitudes, these negative affirmations seem to become the human mind's default. It's incredibly important that you resist these negative thoughts as best you can.

Finally, what is perhaps the most powerful social realization is that *everyone* shares the same anxieties as you do. We all want to look good in the presence of others. We all fear what others may think of us. We all put up fronts to make ourselves look as good as possible. This is an incredible, worldwide facade that exists as part of the human condition. Knowing that we all perform this same act is truly an epiphany. Everyone—and I mean *everyone*—fears you as much as you fear them.

BIRDS OF A FEATHER

The best friendships are often formed over a similar interest, whether it be a sport, games, a club in school, or even a similar taste in music.[7] Eventually, out of this affinity for a similar interest, a bond for each other begins to form. It's all about getting to that point where the two of you can become super relaxed and comfortable with each other. One of the best ways to do this is through associating more and more with people who have the same hobbies as you. This alone can spur on the best conversations, debates, and fun times. Take advantage of the close interactions you have with people at work or in school; make an effort to find others with similar interests to you, and initiate conversations with them.

There are several instances where two people with similar interests who got to know one another spawned some of the greatest commercial ventures of all time. These would include Steve Jobs and Steve Wozniak, the cofounders of Apple; noted philanthropist Warren Buffett and Charlie Munger of Berkshire Hathaway (an investment company); and Tina Fey and Amy Poehler in the world of film. Birds of a feather really do flock together.

Even if you are an especially young reader of this book, I am confident there is something out there that sparks true curiosity and fascination in you. When I was in high school I was hardly the social butterfly, but despite my lack of social skills I bonded with a lot people over a common interest in technology (to this day, I am very much a technology enthusiast). So, while I wasn't the one who would normally ever be a significant part of a group conversation, I was certainly active amongst my fellow technology friends. This allowed me to build friendships I would normally be too shy to form. From this platform of commonality, you can build your confidence and begin to branch out. More recently, now in my twenties, pursuing an interest in theatre has given me the opportunity to meet many new friends and even my better half!

Beyond common interests, it's also great when you try to branch out by taking an interest in what other people have a passion for. What you will find is that good conversation is often sparked because people *love* to talk about their passions in life. People absolutely love to show off their knowledge, too. By expressing interest in what they are passionate about, you will have a topic that can provide oodles of conversational material. Also, since it's a field you don't already have intimate knowledge about, you are practically guaranteed to learn something along the way.

On the flip side of this topic, also remember that it really pays to be doing things in your life that are constructive and progressive. If all you ever do after school or work is sit at home and play video games, then it follows that that is probably the only thing you would ever really have to talk about. If you find yourself lacking anything interesting to contribute to conversations, it may be a sign that you're simply not doing enough with the time you have available to you. Get involved with the world around you. Join a club, play a sport, travel, write a book; any of these things will enrich your life and give you plenty to talk about.

THE FOUNDATION

"And the rain descended, and the floods came, and the winds blew, and beat upon that house; and it fell not: for it was founded upon a rock."
Matthew 7:25[8]

Think of your entire social life as a skyscraper. Each relationship you have adds a new floor to the building. Everyone wants to build their skyscrapers to impressive heights. Of course, the most important part of doing this is to have a strong foundation. So what exactly would this be in social terms? Is it your charisma? Your attractiveness? Your wit? No. A strong foundation for all your life relationships is: Who. You. Are. The qualities that give your own personal Empire State Building an unshakeable concrete foundation are those of good character: strong ethics, integrity, humbleness, honesty, loyalty, compassion, treating people the way you would like to be treated, giving credit where credit is due, and having an impeccable work ethic. These are the characteristics—practically born out of the classic Scout Law—that will make the foundation of great relationships for the rest of your life.

This section may sound trivial, and may even be just plain obvious, but I am absolutely pleading with you to take this seriously. If there is any part of this book that you should take to heart, it's this one. Remember: you reap what you sow—what comes around, goes around. Leading a life of cut-corners and dishonesty may bring you some short-term benefits—say, if you were to impress someone by claiming to have accomplished something you actually didn't—but ultimately you will incur nothing but long-term losses. What's more, even if you do manage to get away with immoral or unethical behaviour, you will know what you've done, and you won't like it when you look back on it in the future.

Behaving with honesty and integrity is the absolute cornerstone to building a happy life—social or otherwise. It's what your strong foundation is made of. Throughout life, you will find yourself in many situations in which telling a lie is simply easier than telling the truth. The truth may be embarrassing, hurtful, or difficult to say; but remember, you are above any of that. Only the strongest behave with unbreakable integrity. Lies, on the other hand, are for those who lack strength of character. And unfortunately, what tends to happen in life is that lies simply lead to more lies. Eventually, they won't do any service to you except to paint you into a corner. Sooner or later, you begin to lose both trust and friends.

You may recall the story of a former Wall Street money manager named Bernard Madoff, who was arrested in 2008. Madoff was a con artist in the investment world who ran a Ponzi scheme.[9] (A Ponzi scheme is essentially an illegal investment scheme where the returns to investors are bogus, and most victims end up losing all their money.) Madoff was never a real investor. He was a fraud. He earned great accolades, for a time, through his false investment fund. The money was easy and came fast. He never had to work hard or exercise any magical genius the way everyone thought he did to gain his unbelievable investment returns. The lies and deceit seemed to pay off.

What happened? In the end he got caught. The house of cards that he himself built came crashing down on him. In 2009, he was sentenced to 150 years in prison.[10] One hundred and fifty years. He will go down in history with shame and with the countless people he has hurt cursing his name.

It's an extreme example, but microcosmically, people get busted every day for building a rickety house of cards on a foundation of lies. Even on a small scale, don't give in to that temptation. Think about it this way: at one time, even Bernard Madoff was a decent and honest money manager. He simply fell victim to the slippery slope of his own temptations.

Moving beyond such dark topics, we must consider that there is a very real positive side here. The simple truth is that nobody has to be the next Bernard Madoff. You have a *choice* when it comes to who you are and what you want to become. If you see negative qualities of greed, dishonesty, jealousy, humourlessness, and laziness, you can get rid of them. These qualities are not ordained at birth. You do not have to have them. You can choose to become a better person!

Reflect on the people you look up to. Think of your heroes. What qualities do they have? What makes you admire them? I think that when you really get down to it, you will find that the core qualities of your heroes are not going to be their sheer abilities or feats. Rather it's their character, temperament, and tenacity that really make them who they are. You are not barred from having any of these great qualities. You can choose to emulate them. Choose to be like your heroes. And in the end, you can be the one that others will look up to.

FIGURE 2.2: PICTURED HERE IS BRUCE LEE – MARTIAL ARTIST, PHILOSOPHER, ACTOR, AND A PERSONAL HERO OF MINE

TREATING YOUR FRIENDS RIGHT

It may be tempting at times, perhaps even just for simple conversational fodder, to talk negatively about friends behind their backs. It happens so often that it has almost become a normal part of conversation. I would simply advise against this. You may think that saying something funny but offensive about a friend in a conversation might endear you to others, but it won't. More than likely, the person about whom you are speaking ill will hear of what you have said. An additional point of concern is the impression you are giving the person you are telling your stories to. That person can see how disloyal you are acting, and therefore will be less likely to trust you in the future. It's your friendships that will pay the price. On the other hand, doing the opposite and demonstrating loyalty to your friends will beget loyalty to you. What comes around goes around. Treat your friends well. This important concept is discussed further in Chapter 3, which deals with ethical living, and Chapter 8, which explores the concept of social contribution.

FAMILIAL RELATIONSHIPS

Familial relationships are likely going to be the most important and impactful relationships we have in our whole lives. The one thing I must stress above all else is that it is important to spend time with family. Your family—both immediate and distant relatives—are going to be the closest people to you in your entire life. Friends may come and go, but your family is for life. You can always make new friends, but you will never have another father or another mother. Those people are absolutely irreplaceable in your life. You may dislike them at times, but no one can deny that your brother is your family, your sister is your family, your daughter is your family, and so on.

People don't last forever. Spend time with your friends and family while you still have the opportunity to do so. Furthermore, try not to put your friends above your family. This may seem difficult at times as your family relationships may grow tedious, but it is more than worth the effort. I find it highly likely that you will regret not doing so.

Beyond spending insufficient time with family, it is always possible that a problem may appear of an opposite sort. When living with family, often times a relationship of casual exploitation forms over the years. What this usually means is taking family for granted: expecting them to clean up after you, never showing them appreciation, perhaps even expecting money from them. This could even be phrased as taking advantage of family. This tends to happen when living in close contact with anyone for an extended time. Remember to appreciate family and everything they do for you. Never take them for granted. From this you can expect the same respect in return.

FIGURE 2.3: FAMILY TIME IS PRICELESS

WORK RELATIONSHIPS

While proper behaviour within the workplace often falls along the same lines as other relationship protocols, there are nonetheless important potential problems to avoid. It can be said that, in general, the reader's behaviour simply needs to be more guarded and professional within the work context. This is particularly true in the corporate setting. With that rule firmly in mind, success will not necessarily follow, but at the very least it is usually enough to keep you out of trouble. To be especially successful as an employee in the work place (meaning increases in compensation and promotion), you must go a step further and realize what it is that your employer recognizes as desirable in an employee. That one thing is helping to generate profit. The more that you contribute to your firm's profitability, the more likely you are to advance within your career.

This advancement can be realized by first taking initiative. Those who demonstrate leadership through their behaviour shall be seen as leaders and potential members of upper management. These types of people are ripe for promotion. Pursuing leadership means being willing to apply yourself so that all your assigned work is completed with meticulous attention to detail. Being a leader also means being able to cooperate with others. Your coworkers must *like* you, for the most part.

Within reason, take charge of helping the company solve problems even if they are not specifically assigned to you or your department. Show that you take responsibility for a problem just by having seen it. This shows management that you are a cut above, and are more than just another employee.

Another particularly effective strategy for proving your mettle to upper management is to offer suggestions on improving your company's operating efficiency and effectiveness. Have you figured out a way to speed up the flow of customer orders? Tell them. Did you think of a better way to organize the inventory? Tell them. Have you discovered a machine that can do raw materials processing twice as fast as the current one? Tell them. These insights can help you a great deal in advancing your career.

Familiarize yourself with your employer's standards for employee conduct, performance appraisal, and the vision of the company. In doing so, you can align your actions with the goals of the organization. This alignment will make your actions much more conducive to effective collaboration with your coworkers, and, by extension, foster a more positive experience for you at work. Always be sure that your behaviour—particularly in relation to sales, hiring, and firing—is in keeping with acceptable conduct.

SOME ACTIONS THAT CAN LAND YOU IN TROUBLE

As mentioned previously, work relationships need to be more formal and guarded than casual friendships. In particular, be very careful of interoffice romances. These can land you in hot water. Rules regarding such policies can differ from workplace to workplace and country to country, but if you do get involved romantically with a coworker there is one rule in particular you must observe: Keep it out of the workplace. All of your romantic communications with this person should be reserved for when you have left work. When you are on the job, it should not be apparent to anyone that you and your significant other are involved.

Additionally, be careful of the simple act of even asking a coworker out. If management finds out, it can, alone, be grounds for being reprimanded, or even terminated, depending on how you go about doing it, and what the working relationship is. Generally, professional boundaries are crossed if there is a difference in power, or if there is any element of coercion or harassment. Furthermore, even if you go about it politely and free of conflicts of interest, it is always possible that you could simply be rejected. This may make your working relationship with this person awkward, going forward. Be very careful. Asking out a coworker is not like asking out a high school crush.

With the increasing ubiquity of complex technology, another point of warning in the workplace is in regards to surveillance. Be aware that anything you do within the workplace can be subject to monitoring by your employer. This includes your physical actions via security cameras. This is particularly true in large retail environments where management is often concerned with employee theft. Digital monitoring of computer activity is also common.

If you are an office worker, you may think it is relatively innocent to use your office PC to check your Facebook notifications as a quick five-minute break when your boss isn't looking, but it is likely that your employer knows exactly what web pages you are visiting. Furthermore, there are also forms of monitoring software that allow an administrator to see exactly what is on your screen at any given moment. Since employers own the computer equipment and telephones, etc., they have a right to set a policy regarding the use of such equipment. Be careful about what you do at work! Always assume that your boss is watching! There is no easy way to explain yourself out of being caught red-handed doing something you shouldn't be doing at work. The best way to solve such problems is to avoid them entirely.

PRESENTATIONS AND PUBLIC SPEAKING

Depending on the type of job you have, there may be many times throughout a given year that you will have to deliver presentations. This book isn't about public speaking, per se; nonetheless, public speaking is an important facet of your work relationships. The key is practice. Practice, practice, practice. Practice your presentations and speeches ahead of time, whether alone or in front of an informal audience. Either way, find time to *practice*. Plan your presentations methodically and give them a logical flow. This usually means stating a set of facts or a vexing problem and then making a proposal on how to proceed or solve the problem. Own the content.

Some other important considerations include:

Visual Aids   If you are going to use visual aids during your presentation, make them as simple as possible, and don't make them a direct copy of the words that you are speaking.

Simplicity means having as few words, graphs, and pictures on your slides as possible to communicate your message clearly. For an excellent example of this, watch the presentations of the late Steve Jobs when he was at the helm of Apple Inc. During his product introductions, Jobs would often have as little as a single word on an entire slide.

This strategy is effective because the human attention span is quite limited. A dizzying array of numbers and facts on a PowerPoint slide might seem impressive, but it will result in information overload to the vast majority of your audience members. Keep it simple.

Finally, avoiding repetitive content in your slides is important to maintaining audience attention. Audiences do not want to simply hear information regurgitated to them. This will bore them, and they will quickly become disinterested in the overall message you are trying to communicate. In such a scenario, you may soon find yourself coming across as unimaginative and lacklustre.

Here is an example of a poor quality visual aid due to a lack of simplicity and focus. Notice how the slide has an excessive amount of content and disjointed ideas, and is generally hard to follow.

FIGURE 2.4: A POORLY DESIGNED PRESENTATION SLIDE

PROJECTED PERFORMANCE OF PROPOSED STRATEGY (CONTINUED)

- PROPOSED CAPITAL EXPENDITURES WILL BE WITHIN FY 2016 – FY 2017 GUIDELINES
- STRATEGY INCREASES THE FIRM'S NEGOTIATING LEVERAGE WITH SUPPLIERS
- PROJECT INTERNAL RATE OF RETURN IS 27.6% (EXCEEDS FIRM'S HURDLE RATE OF 15%)
  - USING PROJECTIONS/COMPETITIVE ASSUMPTIONS OUTLINED IN Q2 2016 STRATEGIC PLANNING SESSION
- PROJECT NET PRESENT VALUE IS $1.3 MILLION (UTILIZING FIRM'S HURDLE RATE OF 15%)
  - ALSO USING PROJECTIONS/COMPETITIVE ASSUMPTIONS OUTLINED IN Q2 2016 STRATEGIC PLANNING SESSION
- CURRENT OPERATIONS GENERAL' MANAGER AND ASSISTANT MANAGER WILL LEAD THE PROJECT INTO Q3 2017
- HISTORICAL SUCCESS OF SIMILAR PROJECTS ON OPERATING EFFICIENCY HAVE HAD AN 82% SUCCESS RATE AS MEASURED BY THE BALANCED SCORECARD (BSC)

Next is an example of a far superior visual aid. The slide is focused and simple. The most pertinent content is clearly emphasized, and there is no extraneous information.

FIGURE 2.5: AN EXAMPLE OF
A WELL-DESIGNED PRESENTATION SLIDE

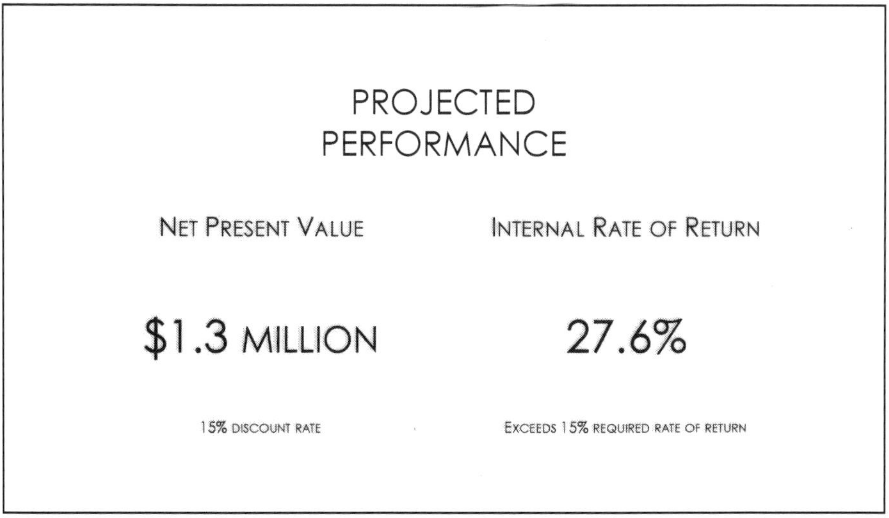

PROJECTED
PERFORMANCE

NET PRESENT VALUE   INTERNAL RATE OF RETURN

$1.3 MILLION   27.6%

15% DISCOUNT RATE   EXCEEDS 15% REQUIRED RATE OF RETURN

Style   Unless you are the President of the United States delivering a State of the Union Address, the best speeches are the ones that are energetic and slightly *conversational*. People love enthusiasm; it's contagious. When you are showing energy and enthusiasm, your audience will share in that energy. Even when an audience is being presented with the same material, the difference in engagement between a passionate speaker and a mechanical speaker will be like night and day. The trait of being conversational has similar impacts. Your speaking style is conversational when you are speaking *with* the audience, rather than *to* the audience. Allowing for audience questions, letting them in on the discussion, and sharing the journey of the speech with them will make them feel involved.

Body Language   Make your body language match the content of your speech. The discussion of a very serious topic such as a criminal investigation, should not involve you gesticulating wildly about in excitement. On the other hand, do not allow yourself to become unduly proper and formal if you are giving a speech about dating. Be sure to be reasonably lively in all circumstances. Make eye contact with various audience members, and never stare at one spot for a protracted period of time.

Audience Note-Taking In this author's opinion, the practice of presenting content to audiences and forcing them to take notes for future reference is an egregious inefficiency. There is a simple way to solve this. Prepare a single-page set of notes that summarizes the presentation's key points. Let the audience know at the start of the presentation that they will each receive this set of notes at the end of the presentation so they may focus their energies on paying attention, rather than hurriedly scribbling down notes. Alternatively, you can consider emailing your notes in digital form to attendees after the meeting. Either of these options will create a much more enjoyable atmosphere for everyone involved, and your audience will retain far more information.

A NOTE ON SOCIAL NETWORKING

Facebook, Twitter, and Instagram are all the rage these days. These forms of social networking are wonderful for exactly that: your social network. Professional networking however, may be a different story. For such purposes, I recommend LinkedIn as the networking medium of choice. LinkedIn is free, and it is much like Facebook, except it is business and career-oriented.

A word of warning regarding your casual networking: Be aware that as part of the hiring process for a new job, and likely throughout the term of your employment, your employer will examine your online presence. This means searching for your name on Facebook, Twitter, and any other online content linked with your name that they can possibly find. As a general recommendation, keep your nonprofessional online content *private*, and make sure no one else can tag you or post photos of you without first getting your permission. Assume that anything online that can be seen will be seen by your employer.

In addition to understanding that many employers monitor your online presence and activities, be aware of the fact that any content you post on Facebook grants the company a license to use it. (For the specific details, refer to the Statement of Rights and Responsibilities that must be accepted upon signing up for the social network.[11]) Even if you delete a post, photo or video from your page, don't assume it means the content has disappeared from Facebook, and remember that it can be used by Facebook for advertising purposes. If you don't want content that could potentially harm your career to come back and haunt you at an inopportune time, think carefully about what you choose to share. Also, make sure your preferences are set not only to notify you if someone else tags you, but also to allow you to approve being tagged in other people's posts.

ROMANTIC RELATIONSHIPS

Because of their emotional intensity, romantic relationships are the most heated, involved, and torrid of all the relationships to be discussed in this chapter. A misstep in this area of your life can lead to absolute personal and emotional ruin. Utmost care must be used when the reader finds themselves in the delicate situation of a romantic relationship.

First and foremost, in a romantic relationship there should never ever be any attempt made to change or control the person one is dating. More specifically, "change" means trying to command the lifestyle or associations the other person enjoys. This possessive attitude is quite common amongst people who claim to be "in love," but in reality it is a self-contradictory stance. For if person A loves person B, then why should person A be trying to change the lifestyle or personality of person B? Would not person A's intentions imply that person B is in fact not their ideal mate? If so, the only logical conclusion is that person A does not in fact love person B, but rather loves their *idealized version* of person B.

The lesson to be drawn here is as follows: love honestly.

CHEATING

For our purposes, we use the common sense definition of the word "cheating": a person becoming romantically or physically involved with someone else without the consent of their partner in their already established relationship. There are no nuances or technicalities to be debated here. Refrain from cheating. It is as simple as that. The reasons against cheating are of a twofold nature, one being the major reason and the other being comparatively minor.

The major reason is that cheating is immoral. The violation of trust and the potential pain you may cause is simply unconscionable. It has been the steadfast position of this author for many years that the only person that the reader can cheat is themselves. By cheating on a significant other, a person has simply shortchanged themselves. They have degraded their moral character, in addition to the emotional impact on their partner.

The second, comparatively minor argument against cheating is the consequences of doing so. If you cheat and have been caught by your significant other, you will face regret, shame, guilt, the potential loss of a relationship, and possibly even social exile by peers who become informed of your actions and have lost respect for you. This reason is minor compared to our first reason on the basis that ethical behaviour should never be pursued simply for reward or avoidance of negative consequences. Rather, ethical behaviour should be pursued for its own sake: a concept we discuss further in Chapter 3. For if we are only behaving "properly" for reward or to avoid punishment, then that is merely a mechanical action rather than a true commitment. In such a scenario, how would that make us any better than animals? Such a person would simply be submitting rather than thinking.

THE IMPORTANCE OF HAVING YOUR OWN LIFE

If you are in a relationship, it is probably safe to say that you enjoy the company of the other person. That this is a positive feeling goes without saying. However, it is worth noting that it is possible to have too much of a good thing. Even casual observation of people's relationships will show a startling number of people who grow to rely totally on their significant other for personal satisfaction, emotional stability, social interaction, and even financial stability.

You must have your own life. This point cannot be stressed enough. Do not allow your significant other to become the very centre of your universe. Doing so can potentially set you up for disaster. As a concrete example, if you were to spend all of your free time with your boyfriend or girlfriend, only to allow your other relationships to atrophy, what would happen if your boyfriend or girlfriend broke up with you? Having allowed your friendships to dwindle, and being without your significant other, loneliness would almost certainly set in. This would be emotionally devastating.

Another significant factor is your own personal growth. Your career, your aspirations, and your goals can only come to full fruition if you anchor *yourself* as your personal centre of gravity. You will be hard pressed to grow into your personal potential if your whole life has been revolving around someone else. Last, but not least, a person who is clingy and not self-sufficient is simply unlikely to be considered as an attractive mate. Who wants to date a person who acts clingy like a child who's unwilling to let go of their mother?

SHOW THE OTHER PERSON SINCERE AND HONEST APPRECIATION

A relationship can often grow "tired." This is especially true after a number of years. By this time, significant others and spouses may tend to start taking each other for granted. Don't let this happen. This was touched upon earlier in our section on familial relationships, but it is worth repeating here. It is often said that people tend to not appreciate something they have in their lives until it is gone. The author's observations match this point of philosophy. Make sure to keep this principle in mind over the years in regards to your significant other or spouse. Think about how life would be different without them and how much they have become a part of you. Give them honest and sincere appreciation. Tell them how you feel and that you don't take them for granted. Make sure they know this. This show of sincerity keeps a relationship strong.

ASKING SOMEONE OUT

There have been many books written on the topic of how to ask someone out, but some of them appear to provide questionable advice. These authors recommend complicated systems and arcane formulas for doing something that is in reality very simple. If you want to hang out with someone to get to know them better, just smile and ask. If you want to date someone, just smile and ask. It's that simple. And in reality, the simple approach tends to yield the best results. Can it be scary? Yes, but all things excellent are as difficult as they are rare. Have confidence in yourself. If the other person says "no," that is the worst thing that can happen. Don't take it personally, and consider it their loss. Dust yourself off and move on. At the very least, you will have tried, and that is much better than having never made a move and wondering what might have been.

Nonetheless, the common concern of arousing attraction from the other person—getting the other person to like you—is legitimate and worth discussing. How is this best done? It's simple. Follow the path laid out in this book toward happiness. This sounds merely like a self-serving statement, but it is nonetheless true. People tend to be most attracted to others who have a sense of direction in their lives. They exude happiness and ambition, and are well put together. They may be early on their path to their dreams, but they know what they want out of life. This is the most attractive type of person.

Nothing is more attractive than accomplishment and aspiration. Think of any famous person you may have a crush on. Would you put them on nearly as high a pedestal in your mind if they were not accomplished and well-regarded in the eyes of the public? Probably not. They would be just another person. It is the level of achievement that the person has risen to that gives them their aura. People chase those who chase their dreams. Strive to fulfill your personal potential, and attraction will take care of itself.

GENERAL INTERPERSONAL SKILLS

1. Smile often. A simple smile boosts everything from first impressions all the way to your apparent level of attractiveness. Smiling is a painless way to feel and spread an extra bit of happiness to the people around you.

2. Try to see things from the other person's viewpoint. When dealing with people, seeing things from the other person's perspective will improve your relations. Having a disagreement? Try to honestly put yourself in the other person's shoes to see how they feel. This way, you can make an honest assessment regarding their argumentative position. This is far better than simply saying, "You're wrong." That's just childish.

Want to encourage action or hard work? Think from the other person's perspective. Simply yelling at people and threatening them to make them work hard will only arouse resentment and arguments. Instead, try thinking from their perspective. What incentive can I give these people to work hard? What will motivate them? What will inspire them to really push themselves? Think in terms of what they want and desire. Give them praise and aspirations to live up to.

3. You can always defer telling someone off until tomorrow. When two people are having a heated argument or disagreement, often times the conversation ends with both sides saying potentially unforgiveable things to each other. This blow-up often kills any possibility of amicable interactions going forward. You become forever enemies. You can save yourself a lot of trouble and anguish by remembering that you can always defer confrontation until tomorrow. You don't lose the right by waiting. Hold your tongue and sleep on it. If you still feel like expressing negativity the next morning, you can still do it. Just wait and see if you still feel that way. It's a lot easier to avoid an emotional blow-up than to mend one. An ounce of prevention is worth a pound of cure.

4. Always do what you say you will do. In life, your word is your bond. If you tell someone you will meet them for dinner at 7 p.m., make every effort to be there on time. If you promise someone you will help them move some furniture to their new house, do it. If you tell someone that you will not reveal their embarrassing secret to anyone else, you'd better take that secret to the grave. If you are someone who chronically does not live up to their word, your lack of integrity can damage not only your personal relationships, but also your professional relationships and your reputation as well. Word will get around fast that you cannot be trusted. Not living up to your word is one of the fastest ways to undermine and damage your relationships.

ACTION STEPS BEFORE READING THE NEXT CHAPTER

TO-DO: INTERPERSONAL SKILLS
- Decide on a new interest or hobby that you can use to meet new people or deepen relationships with those you already know.
- Go online and make all of your social media accounts private and viewable only to your friends.
- Start smiling at people more.

RECOMMENDED FURTHER READINGS ON
INTERPERSONAL SKILLS
- *The Charisma Myth: How Anyone Can Master the Art and Science of Personal Magnetism*, Olivia Fox Cabane
- *How to Win Friends and Influence People*, Dale Carnegie
- *Public Speaking for Success*, Dale Carnegie
- *The Quick & Easy Way to Effective Speaking*, Dale Carnegie
- *The 5 Love Languages: The Secret to Love that Lasts*, Gary Chapman

CHAPTER 3
ETHICAL LIVING

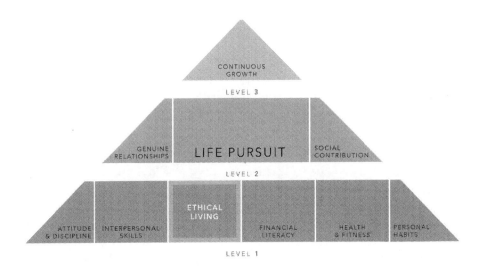

THE PARADIGM OF HAPPINESS

In a logical and progressive fashion, this chapter will examine the importance of both ethical attitudes and ethical behaviour. Together, we will explore the following:

- what ethical behaviour is;
- why we should behave ethically;
- what mental framework we could use for making ethical decisions;
- what common ethical pitfalls to watch out for.

Let it be known, before we get into the meat and potatoes of this discussion, that it is not my intention in writing this chapter to debate the philosophical nuances or technicalities of ethics. What we are concerned with here are practical ethics. This means ethics within an everyday context that readers can truly relate to. As such, this chapter is a succinct essay regarding the development of a practical framework for ethical thinking and does not attempt to make any broad, sweeping changes to the foundation of philosophical ethics. We'll leave that to the university professors.

WHAT IS ETHICAL BEHAVIOUR?

Ethical behaviour is action that adheres to a prescribed set of moral rules.[1] This is a typical dictionary-like definition of the phrase. While such a definition suffices for our immediate purposes, it should be noted that it raises an even greater question than it answers. For we must ask of this definition what set of moral rules is it best to adopt? This is an exceedingly difficult point of contention that we shall attempt to resolve later in this chapter.

WHY SHOULD WE BEHAVE ETHICALLY?

There are many ways to approach the question of why humans should behave ethically within society. Answers will vary from person to person, from time to time, and from society to society. However, this author argues that the core answer is that ethical behaviour is its own justification. In and of itself it is simply the right way to behave. Why? Because as humans we have innate knowledge of what is right and wrong. It is part of the human condition. Albert Einstein once said, "Those who have the privilege to know have the duty to act."[2] As such, human beings are the only animals on this planet that have the intellect to conceive of and understand the concept of ethics. Therefore, we have no excuse, but rather the duty, to act accordingly.

Behaving ethically is the right thing to do simply because it is its own rationalization. It has been argued by biologists such as Richard

Dawkins that a sense of altruism is built into our biology through the evolutionary process of natural selection. The argument goes that altruistic behaviour makes for superior survival characteristics within an organism since, among other things, it allows for the formation of social groups for protection and support.[3] This argument makes great empirical sense and is perhaps the source of the pure and simple righteousness associated with the definition of ethical behaviour with which most people identify.

Let us explore this idea a little further. Let us say that in addition to the axiomatic virtue attached with ethical behaviour, we can make the argument that behaving ethically is in fact the most self-serving mode of conduct possible. Let us draw a comparison to the economic system of free market capitalism. Within broad limits, capitalism redirects and focuses the selfish tendencies of human nature for the greater good. Capitalism does so by giving people the incentives to behave in a certain way. The primary incentive is the profit motive.

All other things being equal, humans desire to earn money and increase their wealth. However, in order to do this a person must offer something beneficial to the rest of society in exchange for this money. If you offer nothing beneficial to society—whether it be goods, services, one's labour, or ideas—then you will not receive any money and your standard of living will diminish. Therefore, the only way to act selfishly and increase your wealth is to offer more and more valuable contributions to the rest of society. In effect, you must be altruistic to be selfish. While this system of economy isn't perfect, there is a subtle brilliance to capitalism that provides motivation for people to endure hardship and labour.

We can draw a parallel between this lesson on economic incentives and ethics. In order to best serve ourselves in life, we must act ethically. As we discussed in the previous chapter, all human beings require at least some degree of companionship and social interaction to maintain their long-term mental equilibrium. Imagine if you and a recent acquaintance have begun to develop a budding friendship, and you enjoy each other's company. While I believe humans are above such purely petty motives, from a somewhat cynical viewpoint your friendship can be seen as a simple relationship of symbiosis, or mutual gain. You are helping each other maintain a healthy mental equilibrium by providing social interaction for one another.

However, imagine that your friend decides that it is in their best interest to start stealing money out of your wallet when you are not looking, with the hope that you will be none the wiser. Through this action your friend has made an unconscious (or perhaps conscious) calculation that they increase their personal benefit by pilfering money from you, in addition to receiving the benefits of your company.

This is a "best of both worlds" situation for your friend in the short term, but sooner or later you find out, or at least suspect, that they are the culprit responsible for your vanishing money. As a result, you stop returning their calls and elect to eliminate this friend from your social circle. In addition, you decide to tell other people in your social circle of your friend's betrayal. Now, your former friend's own social circle begins to dwindle in size as people leave this person's life in droves. Your ex-friend begins to feel lonely, and the quality of their life declines substantially.

You, on the other hand, have maintained your integrity and have not stolen from anyone. As a result, your friends are still fond of you and the portion of your long-term mental health that is derived from the abundance and quality of your social interactions remains unimpaired. From this scenario, you can see that by behaving ethically you have in fact been behaving selfishly. By not stealing from your friends, you have been ensuring the strength of your social position and the psychological nourishment you receive from having friends.

Your former friend who stole from you, however, is having a tough time, to say the least. By behaving in an overtly selfish way, they have, in fact, done nothing but hurt themselves. The very next week, your former friend is also caught stealing from work; consequently, they lose their job and cannot afford to pay the rent. They get kicked out of their apartment, and since they no longer have friends, they have no one to stay with or seek out for support. A year later, they are homeless and living on the street. Such is the life of someone who behaves unethically. Their life will likely be "nasty, brutish, and short" as the English philosopher Thomas Hobbes would say.[4]

From the above discussion, we can conclude that there are no reasonably justifiable grounds to behave unethically. Every human can identify with the intrinsic need for a robust ethical disposition. It produces a self-satisfaction and self-respect that is beyond any material reward. Beyond that, we have demonstrated that the very act of behaving ethically produces tangible benefits. All of this results in one thing: a happier life. And ultimately, that's the point.

DEVELOPING A FRAMEWORK: WHAT IS AND ISN'T ETHICAL?

We now turn to the task of answering the question we proposed at the beginning of this chapter. What is the best set of moral rules to adopt? It is my position that the more specific an ethical framework becomes, the less flexible and enduring it must necessarily be. Thus, it is my intent to propose a framework of how to think about ethical issues in contrast to simply laying down specific hard and fast rules such as "Don't jump the turnstiles in the subway station. That would be immoral."

The prospect of laying down such a set of rules would be flawed for three reasons:

1. The rules would be vast and overly complicated;
2. the rules would be egregiously objectionable or even inapplicable to one or more current cultures or schools of thought; and
3. even cultures that accepted such rules would change over time, thus rendering the rules obsolete.

THE ETHICAL FRAMEWORK EXPLORED

The framework that follows consists of three ethical principles or "tests" that include: 1) The Golden Rule, 2) The Newspaper Test, and 3) Phronesis. May you find these to be simple, universal, and enduring.

Principle 1: The Golden Rule   The Golden Rule is a common theme among many ethical and philosophical frameworks and is usually defined as, "Only treat others in the same way you would like to be treated." The Golden Rule provides a strong foundation for anyone trying to live a more ethical life as it possesses the unique quality of reciprocity. This essentially means putting yourself in someone else's shoes, so to speak. If you are a waiter in a restaurant and are considering serving a customer some soup that you know a line cook has sneezed in, just think: would you want that done to you? Obviously not, so the clear choice is to simply make a new bowl of soup. If you see someone injured and lying on the ground, just think: if that were you, would you want help? Of course you would, so the obvious choice is to help this individual.

So, when faced with a moral dilemma, your first thought should be, "How would I feel if I were on the receiving end of the decision I am about to make?" With this tool, complicated ethical situations and grey areas can be greatly simplified.

While the Golden Rule is powerful, it does have some practical limitations. Some of these limitations are nuanced and are beyond the scope of our discussion here. We are, however, concerned with the rule's limitations when it comes to situations that do not involve another individual or so-called "counterpart." For how can you put yourself in someone else's shoes when your current moral dilemma does not immediately involve anyone but yourself? A simple example is dumping toxic waste in the middle of an open field instead of disposing of it safely. Most people would consider this unethical, but would find difficulty in applying the Golden Rule in coming to this conclusion. To address this, we move to the next pillar of our moral framework.

Principle 2: The Newspaper Test   The Newspaper Test[5] is a thought experiment that covers a broader range of ethical scenarios than the Golden Rule but is arguably less penetrating. From this reasoning, we can determine that it is best to use the two rules in conjunction with one another rather than either one individually. Consider the above scenario where I mentioned dumping toxic waste in an open field, and let us apply our Newspaper Test.

In doing so, we can circumvent the limitations of the Golden Rule test to answer the question, "Is what I'm doing ethical?" Imagine if the action you are about to perform (dumping toxic waste in this case) were to be written about on the front page of every newspaper in the world by a somewhat crass and unkind reporter tomorrow morning. Would you be happy with everyone in the world knowing what you had done? Would that be okay with you? What would your friends and family think? What would the legal authorities think? What would be the consequences?

If the answer to any of those questions is negative, then the Newspaper Test deems that your proposed action is ethically questionable. The lesson is simple. Do not engage in any activity that causes you anxiety when contemplating the prospect of everyone in the world becoming aware of it. Some may argue that the Newspaper Test is overly conservative in dictating what can and cannot be done on ethical grounds because it represents a sort of "worst case scenario" consideration. I find such reasoning to be basically unsound. My experience shows that it is far better to suffer the pain of ethical discipline than to risk suffering the pain of ethical regret.

Principle 3: Phronesis   *Phronesis* is a word of Greek origin that is usually translated as "practical wisdom" or something similar.[6] Phronesis is our third and final ethical principle that we shall use to buttress the previous two. While the Golden Rule and Newspaper Test constitute flexible and practical tools for ethical decision making, they are not perfect. If one thinks hard enough, at least one loophole can be found in practically any test of ethical behaviour. This is where phronesis comes in to complete our three-legged ethical milk stool. Phronesis proposes that as independent critical thinkers, we can use our own judgment, based on experience, to determine what the most ethical course of action is. The idea here is that we will *know* by a combination of instinct, accrued knowledge, and experience what is right and wrong. In essence, phronesis gives power back to the people to make their own decisions. We have already discussed taking responsibility for one's actions, and ultimately that responsibility falls within the province of ethical considerations as well. Use your best judgment. Think independently and have the courage of your convictions.

By combining a prudent application of phronesis with the above tools, a complete system for maintaining ethical conduct begins to emerge. Much of the heart of phronesis is intangible, relying heavily on intuition or "gut feeling" regarding what is right and wrong. In many cases, following this instinct helps to protect against the human tendency to rationalize unethical behaviour. My observation is that many people who commit even the most egregious acts of violence and crime do not consider their actions to be unethical in principle. They come to this conclusion by way of self-deluded rationalization.

CHOOSING YOUR ETHICAL CHARACTER

It is important that the reader be aware of the fact that morality and ethical behaviour are a conscious choice. If you, the reader, possess ethical qualities that you are not proud of, you can choose to behave differently. This may be stating the obvious, particularly in light of the preceding discussion, but becoming explicitly conscious of this fact is an empowering realization. For if we can improve our mental attitudes (as discussed in Chapter 1), what is stopping us from improving our moral fibre? The answer is nothing. Make an active and conscious effort to improve your ethical standards and your self-respect, quality of life, and happiness will only improve.

While I consider ethical substance to be of the highest importance in achieving a happy and fulfilling life, the reader should not accept advice on this matter from the author without question. The best way to think about how, and whether or not, you should behave ethically is by sitting down by yourself, and thinking about it. Think rationally and independently. Use your intelligence. Consider for yourself the reasoning behind what others consider to be ethical conduct, even my reasoning in this book. Wherever you live in the world, question the status quo. Are the moral standards you observe truly in the interests of society at large? Could they be improved? Do not unquestioningly trust the scribblings of some old text on how to behave. You are your own best guidance.

THE DEVELOPMENT OF ETHICAL CHARACTER

Ethical development is something that takes time. If unethical behaviour has become ingrained in your life, you may find it has taken a hold of your psyche like a bad habit; perhaps a bit like smoking. If you find yourself in this situation, you may feel as though your behaviour is not under your control. This will subside with time once a definite mental decision has been made to change your ethical makeup. Implementing meaningful changes to your psyche takes significant time. Do not fret if you are unable to see immediate changes in your behaviour.

First identified by the ancient Greeks, there is a phenomenon in human behavior known as *akrasia*. Akrasia is when a person behaves in a way that is counter to their best judgment. The person knows that Action A is a logical preference over Action B, but the person performs Action B anyway.[7] Akrasia is fundamentally a symptom of a lack of mental self-discipline and is frequently the cause of much unethical behaviour. Keep the three rules of ethical decision making in mind, and remember that acting in an ethical way is in your best interest. You are effectively developing the discipline of trading small, short-term gains for large, long-term gains.

After some effort, you will find yourself graduating from akrasia to cognitive dissonance. Cognitive dissonance is when you hold two opposing thoughts in your mind, unable to reconcile them with each other.[8] Cognitive dissonance is an unpleasant feeling, but it can be a sign that your self-control over your behaviour is beginning to strengthen. The momentum behind Action A and Action B are now more or less equal. You may even find yourself flip-flopping between the two when a relevant situation presents itself. Work with the cognitive dissonance. Use the unpleasant feeling as a motivation to work through the discomfort and grow stronger, much like how a muscle is strengthened when it is consistently subjected to strenuous exercise.

Finally, after a period of continuous effort, your mind will graduate from cognitive dissonance to cognitive resolution. At this stage, your mind develops full control over executive decision making.[9] You begin to see decisions in terms of their long-term consequences, and you will make the choices that give you the greatest happiness and satisfaction. Many people go through their entire lives without developing this ability. And unfortunately, the longer they go with negative habits, the more likely they will remain entrenched. You will see huge positive changes in your life as you progress towards ethical self-control.

COMMON ETHICAL PITFALLS

The human mind is tricky. We often create excuses for behaving in ways that we know are wrong. We build walls of rationalization to defend our unethical behaviours. These pitfalls are as common as they are fallacious. I would like to discuss these pitfalls with you so that you can be prepared. You can think of these as the flipside of the positive rules for ethical behaviour that we outlined at the outset of this chapter.

UNIVERSALITY—EVERYONE ELSE IS DOING IT!

Perhaps the most common of all ethical fallacies is the idea that when everyone does something it becomes justifiable as an action. Whole countries and societies can fall victim to this ethical nemesis. Take illegal file-sharing, for instance, via torrent sites such as The Pirate Bay and others. These sites allow users to download music, movies, software, and other digital files without having to pay for them. In effect, a single individual could purchase a copy of the movie *Interstellar*, for example, share it online, and then every other person in the world could download a copy for free. This, of course, is tantamount to theft, but since it's so widely done, we tend not to think of the act as actually being immoral.

Consider the work of the people who produced this film: the tireless effort and the millions of dollars spent in production. The film itself is an artistic and creative output of many long hours of endeavour and commitment. If the roles were reversed, I doubt that any of us would be happy about people reaping the benefit of our work without our being compensated for it.

There are even more egregious examples of the Universality fallacy being misused as reason for committing heinous acts. For example, consider the imposition of European colonial values on Canada's Aboriginal population during the nineteenth and twentieth centuries. The colonists regarded Aboriginal people and their cultures as inferior, so laws were passed that allowed government agencies to forcibly remove Aboriginal children from their families and communities and send them to residential schools.[10] Tremendous human rights abuses and a legacy of trauma came about as a result of this forced cultural assimilation. Under the guise of nineteenth century colonial thinking on the assimilation of Indigenous persons into the settlers' cultural values and mores, people were led to accept—or ignore—practices that they likely never would have allowed to happen to their own children and communities. The thought process might have been that since Europeans have a tradition of culturally assimilating the local inhabitants of their overseas colonies, it must follow that what we are doing is the right thing. This ultimately led to the Truth and Reconciliation Commission of Canada in 2008, in an effort to right these wrongs.[11]

We probably all fall prey to the Universality fallacy at some point or another in our lives. However, it certainly helps to be aware of it because then we can use that fact to help guard ourselves against this fallacy. Think independently and remember, just because a multitude of other people are committing to an action, it does not mean that they are doing what is justified!

LEGALITY—IF IT'S NOT ILLEGAL, IT MEANS IT'S OKAY!

The Legality Fallacy is used by people to defend their actions as being within the letter of the law and therefore consider their actions as being moral. While it is true that most of the laws we have in North America conform to our general expectations of morality, this is not always the case. Take marital infidelity for instance. There is no law that says you cannot cheat on your spouse (at least in North America), but you would be hard pressed to defend that action as being ethical.

Another example would be the shady dealings of financial institutions and their various agents. Many financial institutions on Wall Street (Bay Street in Canada) deal in ways that are not explicitly illegal but may not be in the best interests of their clients or society at large. These practices include promoting overly aggressive loans (loans to people that effectively become enslaved because they can't possibly ever pay them back) and knowingly selling unwise or risky investments to the public.

The Legality Fallacy is particularly popular because of the lack of consequences for actions that are not illegal. By definition, law enforcement cannot intervene unless a law has actually been broken, or at least there is a suspicion with probable cause that a law may be broken. The readers of this book, ever aspiring to be better and more positive contributors to society, should seek to hold themselves to even more stringent standards than simply following the law. Combine law abidance with the Ethical Framework offered above and prosper!

CONSEQUENTIALISM–THE END JUSTIFIES THE MEANS!

Consequentialism is the fallacy of believing an act is not wrong because the result of the action did not end up hurting anyone, or at the very least the outcome ended up being better than expected. As an example, imagine you had the idea of breaking into a neighbour's house and stealing their property. After jimmying the door open and rifling through their belongings, you discover that they are a terrorist. You find fake passports, automatic weapons, blocks of explosives, and terrorist manifestos. Even worse, you find a written plan to attack your City Hall tomorrow. You leave with your loot and drop an anonymous tip with the authorities. The would-be terrorist is caught before they can act on their heinous plans.

The fact that you saved City Hall from a terrorist attack, as fortunate as that is, does not mean that your act of theft is somehow justified. Thinking otherwise may put you on a dangerous, slippery slope. People's intentions behind their actions, regardless of their ultimate outcome, are important factors in the determination of the ethical nature of a decision. It takes a strong person to admit to both themselves and others that outcomes do not in themselves justify means. You are that strong person.

There are many more ethical fallacies out there in addition to the three listed above, but these three are by far the most common. We must continue to think critically about our actions and do everything we can to constantly strengthen our moral fibre over time. As we get older, we tend to be entrusted with more and more responsibilities at work, in the community, and within our family life. This gives us ever greater temptations to abuse the power that comes with these responsibilities. None of us will ever be perfect, but it is our duty to grow our moral discipline in tandem with the growth in these responsibilities.

Here is one story about my own ethical growth. During the spring of 1999, I was ten years old. To this day, I vividly remember a conversation I once had with my father, after school, regarding one of his friends, whom we'll call Dale. It was a blazingly hot day, with the sun beating down on anyone that dared to venture out of the shade. I had trekked from the elementary school I was attending to my house, dodging the swarms of gnats along the way. I turned the corner to my house and saw my father working on his truck in the driveway. Even from a distance, I could see tenseness in the lines of his body.

"Hi, Dad," I said, with childish irreverence.

"Hey, Kiddo," He brightened up a bit upon noticing my presence.

"Do you need any help with anything?" I said, hoping the answer was in the negative.

"Yeah, do you mind steadying this bench for me?"

"Sure."

After a few minutes of working, I built up the nerve to ask him what was wrong. "Dad, is something the matter?"

"Well," he took a protracted pause. Something about his face told me he was trying to stop himself from overcomplicating his explanation. "Son, you are a good kid. I've just got to let you know, there's a lot of people in the world who aren't as nice as you. There are a lot of people in this world who will try and take advantage of you."

"What do you mean?" I laughed, not seeing where his comment was headed.

"So I've got this friend, Dale. For the past couple of years, we've been meeting for lunch just about every Thursday. He's one of my former coworkers from when I used to work at the railway yard. We've been close friends for years."

"Oh, that's cool." I said, in low tones.

"Anyway, about two weeks ago, Dale asked me if I had a spare set of tires he could buy off me to replace the balding ones on his truck. We agreed on a price of eighty bucks. He's a friend. I didn't want to overcharge him."

He paused again, and turned away from the truck so that he was now facing me. "I gave him the tires, and he said he'd pay me next week when we met again for lunch. That was over a month ago now. Since then, we haven't had lunch or even seen each other. He hasn't even bothered to call me."

His tone of voice turned subtly, so that he now sounded almost wounded.

"You've got to figure that to him the value of my friendship was only worth about eighty bucks."

He turned away again and continued working. And he never saw Dale ever again.

Interestingly, this incident didn't make much impression on me when it first happened. It was only later, by degrees, that the conversation seemed to take on significance. My mind at the time, childish as it was, didn't really believe that people could be so shallow. I thought, "Who would seriously give up a lifelong friend for eighty dollars?" However, the incident would come back to me regularly through the ensuing years, a constant reminder that our adherence to ethical principles is like the planting of a tree that we later come back to for shade. We truly do reap what we sow.

As I entered high school and eventually university, the same shameful side of human nature that my dad experienced did show itself in both my experiences and that of my family and friends. Even then, I still thought that people would become more mature as time went on. Unfortunately, this simply isn't true for many people. What happens to many, frighteningly, is that their methods for practicing deviance simply become more clandestine. While my father may not have been an Einstein or a Rockefeller, as I grew up it became clear that he had a substance of character that few people in the world have. It is lessons such as this that I will be forever grateful for.

Don't be another Dale.

ACTION STEPS BEFORE READING THE NEXT CHAPTER

TO-DO: ETHICAL LIVING

- On a sticky note, write down the three ethical rules discussed in this chapter (The Golden Rule, The Newspaper Test, and Phronesis), and put them in a place where you will see them often, such as a corkboard or journal.
- Think about whether you have been living your life in an ethical way. Are there behaviours you can improve?
- Think about what ethical fallacies you may be using as rationalizations in your life; pledge to diminish their use.

FURTHER RECOMMENDED READINGS ON ETHICAL LIVING

- *Nicomachean Ethics*, Aristotle
- *The Theory of Moral Sentiments*, Adam Smith
- *Meditations*, Marcus Aurelius

CHAPTER 4
FINANCIAL LITERACY

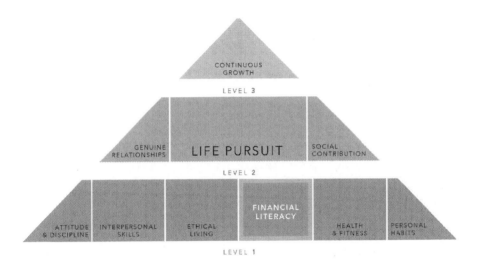

THE PARADIGM OF HAPPINESS

D espite the universally unquestioned importance of financial literacy in the twenty-first century, for one reason or another, society at large has deemed it unworthy of inclusion in nearly all public school teaching curricula. This book seeks to help remedy this problem with a chapter dedicated to supplying basic guidance in all things financial. The chapter has been divided into three major sections in addition to this introduction: 1) attitudes, 2) budgeting, and 3) investing.

The fundamentals of personal finance are still a mystery to an alarmingly large proportion of the population.[1] This ignorance even applies to those who are otherwise very well educated. A proper handling of money matters serves as a basic pillar of happiness in modern society. This is especially true after considering that financial problems represent a major cause of depression, anxiety, divorce, and even suicide.[2,3] Throughout this chapter, I shall seek to recast money as a constructive rather than destructive component of everyday life.

ATTITUDES

It has been an often-quoted maxim that money can't buy happiness. This author absolutely agrees with this statement—with one small caveat that may seem contradictory in its implications. While money itself cannot buy happiness, it nonetheless constitutes *a basic pillar or component* of happiness for just about anyone living within an industrialized nation.

To illustrate this point, consider the following. Classical economic theory works on a basic assertion: an efficient economy seeks to produce the highest possible amount of goods and services for society in which the benefits of producing these goods and services outweigh the costs. Doing so supposedly creates happiness, or at least economic "utility."[4] To the extent that we are able to produce more desirable goods and services within this framework, we as a society are better off.

At face value, there is, of course, some legitimacy in this way of thinking. If a homeless person who was half-starving to death were to be given a square meal and a warm set of clothes, this turn of events would undoubtedly make them happier. To this extent, the predictions of the theory correspond very well with reality. It is in this sense that money and wealth provide a very tangible foundation to human happiness. For how can a person be happy when they are starving or without a home in which to live? For all practical intents and purposes, money is required to meet our basic needs.

The catch is that this economic wealth, desirable as it may be, is not immune to the ever-present law of diminishing returns. Economists have realized this, and have integrated this into their models.[5] Wealth can only improve happiness by so much. However, there is an additional fundamental issue that has not been taken into account: the difference between the utility obtained by satisfying *needs*, and the utility generated by satisfying *wants*. When money is obtained for use in satisfying needs, it has a very real and tangible effect on bolstering real happiness. However, once a person's basic needs are met, an increase in wealth or income is then often spent on *wants*. The "happiness" derived from obtaining these wants is a form of false utility. It is a kind of false happiness that does little to improve real emotional well-being. This is the real meaning behind the aphorism "money can't buy happiness."

Some economists, sociologists, and academics are just becoming cognizant of the limiting qualities of this happiness-through-wealth doctrine. As such, new approaches for developing and catalyzing happiness must be adopted. This book is a prime example of such a new approach. It is plain to the reader by now that I have no enthusiasm for materialism. Let me state my position on the issue categorically: indulging in materialism and buying things that you do not need will not make you happier in life. In fact, such indulgence is likely to have the opposite effect as the resulting drain on cash resources serves as a point of great financial difficulty for many. This anti-materialistic stance forms the foundation of my attitude towards money generally.

Taking this argument to its logical conclusion, it stands to reason that any money you do not immediately need should be saved and invested to cover *future* needs. Remember that within The Paradigm of Happiness, money forms a foundational pillar of Level 1. A relative abundance of money saved from the invisible claws of materialistic desires can be used as a resource for career goals and personal aspirations. On the other hand, a financial attitude generally characterized by squandering money will serve only to hinder the reader from progressing to Level 2 of The Paradigm. By extension, this spendthrift behaviour also means personally obstructing oneself from reaching the ultimate bonanza of Level 3, and, I fear, will destine the reader to a life of emotional dissatisfaction.

Money today can be considered as a fundamental enabler. The stone hand-axe was once the basic tool of choice for our ancestors such as *Homo ergaster* and *Homo erectus*.[6] In our modern society, money has now been adopted to fulfill this most critical role. The intelligent handling of personal finance has literally become a basic survival skill.

We begin our task of honing our financial skills by examining the two primary principles of sound personal finance:

1. Budgeting: spending less than you make to create savings
2. Investing: using those savings to buy assets

We shall proceed with an analysis of each principle individually.

BUDGETING: SPEND LESS THAN YOU MAKE TO CREATE SAVINGS

The purpose of a budget is to ensure long term financial stability and efficiency on the part of the budgeter. The primary indicator of successful budgeting is the degree to which an individual has managed to spend less money than they have earned within a given interval of time. An alternative method of arriving at this indicator would be to measure the proportion of savings a person has managed to accrue relative to income within a given interval of time. The greater the ratio of savings to income, the more successful the budget has proved itself to be.

The simplest and most effective way to ensure that personal expenses do not exceed income is the so-called "pay-yourself-first" strategy. Such a strategy involves earmarking a certain portion, say 10 percent, of every pay cheque towards savings. The rest of the funds can then be spent as the individual deems appropriate. By saving first and spending last, the prudent person has almost completely mitigated their risk of overspending. The operative word is 'almost' since this strategy does not explicitly address the dangers of credit—a topic that we shall deal with shortly.

Many, if not most, banks offer preauthorized contribution plans that are tailored specifically for this pay-yourself first strategy. Such a plan instates the regular withdrawal of a preset amount of funds at predetermined intervals from one's savings account. The funds are then transferred to a separate account to be invested in assets. The specific process of setting up a preauthorized contribution plan will be covered later in the investing section of this chapter in. For the purposes of the current section on budgeting, we will continue our discussion on the premise that a preauthorized contribution plan has already been implemented by the reader.

The basic essence of a personal budget can be distilled down into a simple arithmetic equation:

$$\text{Income} - (\text{Compulsory Savings} + \text{Expenses}) = \text{Surplus}$$

Below, I have provided an illustration of a basic application of this equation:

FIGURE 4.1: A HYPOTHETICAL MONTHLY BUDGET SHOWING A SURPLUS

———— MONTHLY BUDGET ————

Gross Income	$4,167
After Tax Income	$3,283
Savings (10%)	$328
Income Available for Expenses	$2,955
Expenses (Fixed)	
Mortgage/Rent/Property Tax[7]	$475
Transportation	$570
Insurance Payments[8]	$100
Internet	$40
Cable	$15
Cell Phone	$60
Electricity	$100
Gas/Heating	$80
Debt Payments (Credit Cards, Loans, Etc.)	$100
Expenses (Variable)	
Food/Groceries	$800
Interests/Hobbies	$100
Fitness	$40
Entertainment	$100
Clothing	$100
Other	$100
Total Expenses	$2,780
Surplus	$175

This hypothetical budget contains a typical salary for a person with a postsecondary credential and three years of experience. We make an immediate compulsory deduction of 10 percent for savings, in keeping with our pay-yourself-first rule. Fixed and variable costs are then substracted from the remaining income. Fixed costs are those which cannot be negotiated or changed on a typical month-by-month basis. By contrast, variable costs are discretionary, and are usually the best place to begin cutting expenses if a budget is overrun. The final line in the budget is the surplus. This specifies the amount of funds remaining after both compulsory savings and expenses are deducted. With the budget balanced, the budgeter is free to allocate the surplus funds towards whatever purposes they deem appropriate, such as additional savings or debt repayment.

Personal budgets can be constructed with an unlimited degree of detail, either digitally or on paper. I leave it to the reader to decide what level of granularity suits them best. A more detailed breakdown of expenses and sources of income may lead to small advantages in budgeting, but if it is too detailed and complicated it might feel too burdensome or overwhelming and readers will give up tracking their spending.

I recommend that the reader follow my basic model for budgeting as a satisfactory compromise between simplicity and comprehensiveness. With the increasing ubiquity of computers on a worldwide basis, there is also a question of whether such a budget should be kept on a computer or in a physical book. I can offer no useful recommendation on the superiority of one over the other. Ultimately, the decision hinges on personal preference.

In constructing the budget, the first step will be to identify and compile all of your personal sources of income. This not only includes money from your job but also any income on the side such as, say, music gigs or a home-based business. This sum will be put into the income portion of the budget. The next task will be to compile all monthly expenses. This will likely be a somewhat more complicated process compared to accounting for income since the sources of monthly expenses are usually much more varied than the sources of income. To assist in this process, it is often helpful to collect and review all of your personal bills and financial statements.

This data will give you a clear picture of where exactly your cash is going.

Assign each of your expenses to their appropriate categories and subtract them from your income. If the amount remaining exceeds 10 percent of your net income, you are golden. This is the portion you will earmark for your compulsory savings. If on the other hand, the remaining balance is less than 10 percent, check to see if it falls within the threshold of 5 percent. If so, this amount will be sufficient for now, but I would advise trying to find ways to cut costs until the larger 10 percent margin is met.

As mentioned above, the most fruitful area for the pursuit of cost-cutting will be in the variable expenses category. If car payments and fuel costs are particularly burdensome, consider taking public transportation more often. If entertainment costs are particularly high, consider staying in more often. It is vitally important for your financial stability, and ultimately your own personal happiness, that your budget balances. Beyond cutting expenses, the reader also has the option of supplementing their personal income. This is usually accomplished by either 1) working extra hours at your current job or business, or 2) procuring new sources of income such as a second job.

An additional consideration stems from the difficult problem of deciding how much money to allocate to debt repayment. As every individual's personal situation differs drastically, the prospect of offering specific recommendations on the subject is beyond the scope of this book. I do think, however, that two largely universal rules can aid greatly in this type of decision. First, it is usually better to pay off debt sooner rather than later. This means paying considerably more than the minimum payment. By retiring debts sooner rather than later, the borrower will substantially reduce both their financial and psychological burden. This point is especially true when the accumulation of interest on the debt is considered. In the case of credit cards, some interest rates can even exceed 25 percent. At such a rate, the principal amount owed would double in less than three years.

My second rule is that the repayment of debt—however large—should never take precedence over the accumulation of at least *some* regular savings. If the reader's debt servicing burden is particularly large, then they may be inclined to reduce the proportion of their income dedicated to savings from 10 percent to, say, 5 percent or even 3 percent. Regardless of the percentage chosen, some savings will be needed for potential emergencies, which always seem to crop up at the most inopportune times. Without such an emergency fund, the reader would instead be forced to resort to more borrowing during times of crisis, thus exacerbating their already considerable hardship.

If debt proves to be especially overwhelming, an additional option would be for the borrower to contact a credit counselling agency for help. These agencies are often nonprofit and can greatly assist in the management or consolidation of debt. A quick Google search for such organizations within your city should yield many results.

Once your budget is completed, it is then your mandate to ensure that your monthly spending conforms to your budget's prescription. Log all of your month's purchases into a blank version of your budget and compare the final tally at month's end to your model budget. Changes in personal circumstances may justify changes to the budget in the future, but above all, be sure your budget balances.

Credit Cards   There exists a popular and quite valid distinction in the minds of the public between so-called "good debt" and "bad debt." Good debt usually refers to money borrowed for use in purchasing necessities or assets such as a college education (a student loan, for example) or a home (a mortgage). Bad debt, by comparison, is typically money borrowed for buying non-essential goods and services. Obviously, the biggest culprit that causes bad debt is credit cards. Easy money coupled with high interest rates has led many people to financial ruin. In an effort to mitigate the dangers of credit cards and similar forms of consumer credit, I suggest three guiding rules regarding their use.

First, treat every credit card purchase as if it were cash. This means logging credit card purchases into your monthly budget as a regular deduction from income. Let it be known that credit cards are in no way a form of free money. This point may seem obvious, but in practice, the concept has been lost on many people. Second, only use credit cards for payment when there is no other option available. If you are making a clothing purchase at a shopping mall, use debit or cash. If you are shopping online however, a credit card may be your only choice. Finally, never let a credit card balance "carry" from month to month. Doing so will subject you to exorbitant interest charges. Perhaps worse still is that not paying off your credit cards may start you on a slippery slope towards bona fide credit card enslavement.

FIGURE 4.2: BUDGETING DOESN'T HAVE TO BE A BORE. WORKING OUT A SOUND FINANCIAL PLAN WITH YOUR SIGNIFICANT OTHER CAN BE A GENUINE BONDING EXPERIENCE.

INVESTING: USING SAVINGS TO BUY ASSETS

Upon developing a workable budget and savings program, we now turn to the question of what to do with the compulsory savings we accumulate. To maximize the utility of those savings, the most logical course of action is to invest the money. Investing is the act of expending money now with the reasonable expectation of receiving even more money later on. Alternatively, it is the deferral of current consumption (spending), in order to consume more in the future.

What the above discussion ultimately means is that money makes more money. In this way, the reader is able to use investment vehicles to generate income outside of regular work or employment. These vehicles are otherwise known as passive income. By earning this extra income, we have additional means to support ourselves and our life goals. Investing our savings makes immanent sense in growing our financial resources and reducing our future burdens—especially in retirement.

So what exactly does the aspiring investor actually invest their money in? Investment mediums are known as assets. Typical assets include real estate, stocks, bonds, and commodities. They are deemed assets because they all possess financial value. I recommend, as a general rule, that readers focus their investment efforts on stocks and bonds for their portfolio. An investment policy divided amongst these two asset classes provides the best balance between both safety of principal and an adequate return. Let us briefly discuss the nuances of each and examine why together they constitute an optimal investment strategy.

Stocks, otherwise known as shares, refer to ownership certificates in publicly traded companies. This means that upon buying stock in a soft drink company, for example, the investor literally owns part of the company. Thanks to the ubiquity of online brokerage accounts, stocks can be held by investors at a very low cost and traded amongst speculators at lightning speed.

Stocks are typically purchased with two profit factors in mind: (1) the prospect of a rising share price via an increase in value of the underlying company, and (2) regular dividend payments. (Dividends are portions of corporate profits paid out to stockholders at regular intervals and can be thought of as a kind of interest earned on your shares.) Most leading companies, the so-called "blue chips," have a long record of rising dividends.

Compared to stocks, bonds are somewhat less prominent in the everyday consciousness of the public mind. Bonds are actually very simple financial instruments. A bond is nothing more than a loan contract. When money is loaned by a creditor to a debtor, they are, for all practical intents and purposes, always expecting to be paid back. So, upon receiving the funds, the debtor issues a contract that specifies their financial obligation to the creditor in exchange for the money.[9] This contract is a bond. In effect, when buying a bond, the true nature of the purchase is the lending of money.

Bond holders seek to profit primarily from the regular interest payments made on the debt that is owed to them. This is very much similar to the interest paid on a mortgage or a credit card bill. These payments are made on a semi-annual basis and are referred to as "coupons" in financial jargon. An additional point of consideration is the bond's maturity date. This is the date on which the principal amount on the loan is due to be repaid. Maturity dates for bonds can range from several weeks to several decades. Bonds can be bought from many different types of entities such as municipalities and corporations. For the purposes of our hypothetical portfolio, we shall be purchasing government bonds.

Stocks and bonds in combination form an ideal investment portfolio. Stocks have the favourable characteristics of being very high return assets over significant periods of time with *reasonable* stability to boot. Even with dividends excluded, a single dollar invested in the Dow Jones Industrial Average at the beginning of the twentieth century would have increased 175-fold by the end of the twentieth century, from 66 points to 11,497 points.[10] Since stocks are productive assets (ownership interests in companies), their long-term increases in value are generally justified. The ever-increasing capacity of businesses as a whole in producing everyday goods and services forms the backbone of this value.[11]

While stocks are great assets for constituting the growth portion of an investment portfolio, it is true that stock prices can be volatile in the short run. Because of the volatile nature of stocks, I recommend that stocks be balanced out by a significant bond component in the investor's portfolio. The long-term returns of government bonds pale in comparison to stocks, but the true strength of bonds lies in their superior safety of principal. They can maintain their investment merit even during major stock market downturns.[12]

Consider a scenario in which an investor was forced to withdraw a significant sum of money from their savings because of a medical emergency during the market crash of 2008–2009. (Murphy's Law would almost ensure such a thing would happen.) During this period, the overall stock market had lost half its value. However, any individual who had significant funds invested in, say, a government bond index fund would have been able to sell those holdings at full, or near full, value to cover their emergency expenses. (A concept known as bond laddering, which is built into many such funds, is also partly responsible for this stability.)[13] Any other investor purely holding stocks would have been forced to sell their holdings at rock bottom prices, thus forfeiting much of their initial principal.

A 50 percent/50 percent allocation between these two investment mediums of stocks and bonds is the most prudent option for most investors. This policy is simple, effective, and provides a satisfactory balance between savings preservation and overall investment growth. An additional portfolio consideration is a concept known as rebalancing. Over long time horizons, the overall balance of your portfolio will deviate significantly from the initial 50 percent/50 percent arrangement. As the years pass, the stock component will likely outstrip the growth of the bond component. It is also entirely possible, particularly in short-term scenarios, that the stock component can suffer a sudden sharp decline in value via a market crash. To both counter and take advantage of these fluctuations, I recommend a regular practice of rebalancing to restore this 50 percent/50 percent ratio when it has been disturbed by as much as 10 percent from its equilibrium.[14]

As an example, if the stock component increased to 60 percent of the portfolio, the investor would proceed to sell off one-sixth of the stock component. They would then use these funds to purchase bonds. Not only does this practice maintain portfolio balance, it has the added benefit of automatically purchasing stocks when they have declined to attractive prices, and selling them when they have advanced to potentially unjustifiable highs. This can improve the investor's overall returns over the course of many years.

It is imperative that the reader not see stock market fluctuations as a negative factor in their investments, but rather, as a tool to be used to their advantage. Stock market fluctuations frequently produce unduly low prices that represent prudent buying opportunities. By the same token, they just as often offer unduly high prices, ripe for shrewd selling.

A final point regarding our 50 percent/50 percent portfolio policy is the psychological comfort it provides. During periods of stock market optimism and rising prices, the investor can enjoy quiet satisfaction from their gains.[15] By contrast, investors can derive emotional solace from the stability of their bond holdings during periods of market depression. The cornerstone of this investment approach is the replacement of guesswork with sound financial discipline.

The Benefits of Prudent Investing   As touched upon previously, the recommended mode of investing is dependent on a "preauthorized contribution plan" that makes regular withdrawals of funds from the investor's account at set intervals. Some banks will refer to this as a "preauthorized contribution plan", as I have, whereas others may refer to it as a "preauthorized purchase plan" or something very similar.

While we have specified stocks and bonds as our assets of choice, the exact vehicle we shall be using to invest in them is known as a mutual fund. Mutual funds come in two basic varieties, actively managed and passively managed. As the name suggests, actively managed funds have an actual portfolio manager picking and choosing what assets to buy and sell. By contrast, passively managed funds mechanically follow a market index with no significant human intervention at all. These passive funds are often referred to as index funds. Due to their automated nature, index funds possess the enormous advantage of charging lower fees.

The most common justification mutual fund managers make for charging higher fees is their claim of superior skill in selecting investments. The idea is that they can pick specific stocks or other assets that will earn above average returns, and thus more than compensate for their higher fees compared to index funds. Undoubtedly, there are some money managers who can do this on a consistent basis. Is this a valid justification for selecting an exceptional manager to invest your funds?

The answer is yes, but within that answer lie two fundamental problems. The first is that very few mutual fund managers are actually able to outperform their benchmarks. According to the Princeton economist and author Burton Malkiel roughly two-thirds of actively managed mutual funds lag behind their index-fund counterparts in any given rolling three to five-year time period.[16] This puts investors at an immediate disadvantage in their quest to pick winners. The odds of an actively managed fund outperforming its index-fund counterpart continue to dwindle as successive years in a fund's record are analyzed.[17]

The second problem is that in selecting a money manager, the past record is in no way a reliable criterion for projecting future performance. It may seem plausible to conclude that managers who have outperformed their benchmarks and "beaten the odds" for a number of years are safe choices. However, there is no way to separate those who possess potentially superior skill from those who may just be lucky. Success in the past is in no way indicative of success in the future. It may very well be that a long period of outperforming benchmarks has made the manager "due" for a period of equally unusual underperformance. John Bogle, founder of The Vanguard Group–an American mutual fund company–refers to this phenomenon as reversion to the mean.[18]

The primary reason fund managers end up underperforming is the high fees they charge for their experience and education—particularly over long time horizons.[19]

It is vitally important that the reader not make the mistake of underestimating the significance of mutual fund fees. A difference as little as 1 percent in management fees between one fund and another can very easily mean the loss or gain of hundreds of thousands of dollars over time.

I will illustrate the importance of this point with an example. Consider the following scenario. Suppose we have a pair of 25-year-old twin sisters, Miriah and Alicia, who both decide to invest $10,000 each in the stock market for a total of $20,000. Miriah decides to commit her money to an index fund and earns an average of 9.5 percent per year (the historical rate of return with dividends[20]), compounding annually. Since the fund requires no active management, she is charged a modest 0.5 percent annual fee. This reduces her overall return to 9 percent. By contrast, Alicia decides that her best option is to turn her funds over to the hands of a professional who also achieves a 9.5 percent average annual return. The enterprising money manager charges her a 1.5 percent fee that reduces her overall return to 8 percent. Both sisters are sensible and resolve to keep their funds invested until retirement at the age of 65. This affords compound mathematics exactly 40 years to grow their respective nest eggs. The result:

Miriah's total funds after 40 years:
$314,094 (without a money manager)

Alicia's total funds after 40 years:
$217,245 (with a money manager)

The results never fail to impress. The old and famous declaration of compound interest being the eighth wonder of the world goes unchallenged.[21] With a difference as small as 1 percent in fees, we find that upon retirement, Miriah has accumulated $96,849 more than Alicia. This example not only serves to illustrate the power of compound interest, but also the destructive power of professional fees in reducing your wealth. In this scenario, we have posited a 1.5 percent fee for the actively managed fund, but it should be noted that many funds charge rates *much* higher than this.

However, a much more positive reflection from this exercise is the fact that both sisters, regardless of fees, have accumulated great wealth, considering their modest initial investment. Even better is the fact that in all likelihood you, the reader, are likely to have far more than $10,000 to invest over the course of your lifetime. This is an empowering realization indeed.

If there should remain any doubt in the reader's mind regarding the astuteness of indexed investing, consider what Warren Buffett—the world's greatest investor—had to say about it: "The best way [for most people to invest] is to just buy a low-cost index fund and keep buying it regularly over time, because you'll be buying into a wonderful industry, which in effect is all of American industry."[22]

It is the steadfast position of the author that reasonable caution and prudence will mitigate the meaningful risks associated with investing. Both historical evidence and conservative reasoning strongly suggest that the long-term probability of losing money in the stock market via the strategy outlined above is almost nil.[23] The real point to be made is that the risk of investing in the stock market pales in comparison with the risk of *not* investing.

This risk stems from inflation, which refers to the general trend of rising prices throughout the world economy year after year.[24] Inflation is effectively a form of tax. However, unlike income tax, this "tax" (inflation) does not entail any reduction in the number of dollars owned by you. Rather, inflation reduces the *value* of each individual dollar as opposed to reducing the *number* of dollars.[25] In essence, the destructive power of inflation is rooted in its invisibility; silently robbing consumers of their purchasing power year after year.[26] A dollar in the reader's pocket is destined to be worth less tomorrow than it is today.

Armed with a framework for intelligent investing, however, the reader not only has a chance of keeping up with inflation over the years, but even outpacing it significantly. By contrast, money that is not invested will earn a 0 percent return, and the crippling effects of inflation will guarantee a loss in purchasing power. A dollar at the beginning of the twentieth century required more than 20 dollars at the century's end simply to match its value.[27] Indeed, the risks associated with not investing are formidable.

Furthermore, without the power of investing and compound interest, not only will the reader's dollars lose value over time, but it will be difficult—next to impossible—for the average income earner to save an adequate amount of money for retirement. This fact is particularly alarming in light of the steady increases in the average human life span throughout modern history.[28] Every additional year a person lives constitutes an additional year of associated living expenses that must be paid for from somewhere.

Putting the Investment Plan into Action   I have outlined both the strategy for an all-purpose investment policy and the reasoning behind it. The next step will be to determine which financial institution you will choose to manage your investments. The number of choices and the criteria for choosing (location, service, etc.) are both immense. The primary deciding factor on the part of the reader should be the amount of costs—fees and expense ratios—that are charged by the institution.

For Canadians, I recommend investing with one of the largest of the "Big Five" banks because they have the greatest economies of scale, which allows them to charge lower expense ratios and offer longer branch hours. Should the reader live outside of Canada, or perhaps desire to exercise their own judgment, a simple Google search for the names of familiar neighbourhood banks should yield their websites. Upon finding a bank the reader is comfortable with, they should query the website's search bar for the phrase "index funds." Once a list of the bank's index funds has been found, the reader should look for two in particular. The first will be called a Government Bond Index Fund. The other will be called a [name of your country or region] Equity Index Fund. This would, for example, be called a 'Canadian Equity Index Fund' in Canada, or a 'U.S. Equity Index Fund' in the USA.

Having found the two relevant index funds, click on them. This will lead the reader to a web page detailing the fund's history, performance, and expenses. Two items are of particular interest to us here. The first is the fund's load (transaction cost), and the second is its management expense ratio (ongoing cost). The minimum standard for investment for both our funds entails the following: (1) absolutely no loads under any circumstances, and (2) a management expense ratio of no more than 1 percent. Due to the size difference in the scale of the two countries' economies, Canadians may find the search for funds meeting such criteria somewhat more difficult than their American counterparts. Again, the larger Canadian financial institutions will be more likely to meet our aforementioned cost goals.

At this point, we have acquired an initial indication of the fund's suitability for our purposes. However, our investigation must go further to confirm this initial impression. Some financial institutions do not display the full details of their fund's expenses up front, and instead elect to disclose the full fee structure only in the fund's prospectus. (The prospectus is a document detailing a fund's most intricate aspects.). The fund's web page should contain a link to the prospectus, usually in PDF form. A viewing of the prospectus may reveal extra fees that were not disclosed on the web page. As an example, a bank may list the management fee (which is not the same thing as management expense ratio) on the fund's web page, but leave other expenses such as the TER (trading expense ratio) for disclosure only in the prospectus. When sorting through the maze of numbers, look for *total* or *net expenses* in the prospectus as a true figure for the fees being charged.

Tiresome as this exercise may be, I make no apologies for it. I will reiterate that it is imperative the reader guard against paying any loads and more than a 1 percent management expense ratio. Shopping for the best deal is highly recommended: the lower the costs, the better.

After finding two suitable funds, our next step is to call the chosen financial institution to book an appointment. The appropriate phone number will be available on the company's website. Ask to make an appointment with a financial advisor regarding investment in the bank's mutual funds. Additionally, ask what kind of documents you will need to bring to the session. These may include an income tax return, driver's license, or additional documents, depending on whether you already have an account with the institution in question. Finally, ask how long such an appointment is likely to last and plan accordingly.

Upon meeting with a financial advisor, there are six key points that must be articulated in the conversation:

1. "I would like to start investing in the following index funds: *a government bond index fund*, and an *[name of your country or region] equity index fund* that tracks an internationally recognized equity index such as the Standard & Poor's (S&P) 500 for America or the Toronto Stock Exchange (TSX) Composite for Canada."

2. "I want both funds to have no load fees or switching costs, and total expense ratios of less than 1 percent each."

3. "I would like to invest money at regular intervals with your

bank's preauthorized contribution plan. I would like to split my regular contribution at an even 50/50 ratio between these two funds."

4. "I would like you to help me maximize my personal tax benefits with any tax free and tax deferred savings accounts I may be eligible for."

5. "Based on my personal situation (income, age, personal goals, etc.), how much money should I be contributing to my investments? How often should I be contributing?"

6. "I plan on revisiting the bank once every summer (the time of year when most people receive their tax returns) to have you help me decide:
   a) whether to rebalance my portfolio back to a 50/50 ratio if the benefits outweigh any potential tax liability or transaction costs;
   b) what to do with my tax return money (if any);
   c) how to maximize my tax benefits for the coming year; and
   d) how much and how often to contribute to my investments in the coming year."

If the advisor, or the bank as a whole, fails to cater to any of these six key points, feel free to get up and walk away. Remember that as an investor with the bank, you are purchasing their products. You are the customer. As such, the investor has every right to expect that their needs will be met by the bank. Do not compromise. Trust your instincts. If something "smells fishy," such as the bank's representative being vague about costs, don't hesitate to walk away. However, if all six points on the list above are satisfied, your task of setting up an investment plan is complete.

As point six on the list specifies, I highly recommend that readers make an annual visit to the bank's financial planner to "tune up" their investment portfolio. While forgoing this visit will most likely not entail a significant downside, regularly rebalancing your portfolio can help to improve long term investment gains by shifting more money into stocks when they are attractively priced and shifting money out of them when they may be overpriced.

FIGURE 4.3: SITTING DOWN WITH A FINANCIAL ADVISOR AT THE BANK CAN DO WONDERS FOR YOUR FINANCIAL WELL-BEING. HOWEVER, NEVER HESITATE TO QUESTION WHY THE ADVISOR IS RECOMMENDING ONE TYPE OF INVESTMENT PRODUCT OVER ANOTHER.

The Suitability of Our Investment Policy and Potential Alternatives   The investment plan I have outlined is a conservative, all-purpose, auto-pilot program that should deliver reasonable results over the years, with a minimum of effort. It is, however, just a single strategy. The reader is free to tweak the suggested strategy, such as by allocating half the stock component of the portfolio to international equities for greater diversification. In this section, I articulate two more possible variations to the proposed investment policy.

A 75 percent/25 percent ratio between stocks and bonds respectively

Instead of 50 percent/50 percent, a 75 percent/25 percent ratio between stocks and bonds may be a prudent choice for some people. For example, if investors already have a significant sum of savings relative to personal income, a 25 percent allocation to bonds as a "rainy day" portion of the portfolio may be sufficient. A particularly young investor with a time horizon of decades to ride out the market's ups and downs may also find the 75 percent/25 percent plan to suit them better with its greater growth potential.

A 25 percent/75 percent ratio between stocks and bonds respectively

A 25 percent/75 percent ratio between stocks and bonds may prove to be the optimal allocation of funds for some investors. For instance, a prospective new homeowner who is saving to make a down payment on a house would likely prefer the safe-haven of stability found in bonds over stocks. Or perhaps consider the needs of a 60-year-old school teacher on the cusp of retirement. They are looking forward to a leisurely life of golfing and bridge in Florida in just five short years. They will need to rely on their savings as a steady source of income very soon. At this age, the preservation of funds takes precedence over the prospects of amazing growth.

Above all, remember that venturing into the uncharted waters of self-directed investment policy should not be made before conducting an extensive and honest assessment of your ability to successfully, prudently, and confidently take on an investment strategy independently. Read, research, and consult with experts before making drastic changes to your portfolio. Enthusiasm and excitement may be prerequisites for success in many endeavours in life, but such virtues may be indistinguishable from hindrances in the world of investment when they are not tempered by scrutiny.

Additional Considerations   Some readers may very well find themselves alarmed when reading the various prospectuses of government bond funds. Many such funds—despite their names—may hold a small portion of high grade corporate bonds or mortgages in their portfolios in addition to government securities. This is not an uncommon practice in the industry and should not cause concern if the amount is modest (say, no more than 20 percent).

The astute reader may also point out that pursuing the investment policy outlined in this chapter could potentially have been made a simpler affair with the use of target date funds or balanced funds. Balanced funds typically allocate the investor's portfolio between stocks and bonds, as we have done above. The difference, however, is that instead of investing in two separate funds—one for each asset—both purchases are done with a single fund. Target date funds operate in a similar manner, but the allocation of the fund's assets between bonds and stocks is changed over time in order to arrive at an optimal allocation by the target date, which is usually the investor's retirement age.[29]

These alternatives are worthy of consideration. However, two separate index funds, in aggregate, typically carry much lower expenses than either balanced or target date funds. This obviously depends on the time and place in question, but this has certainly been true in the case of Canada at the time of this writing in 2017. Secondly, your tax-benefitted savings accounts nullify much of the potential tax burden in transferring money from one fund to the other in the strategy I have proposed. This can mitigate the potential costs involved in portfolio rebalancing. Finally, investing in two separate funds gives the investor greater control over their money than any single fund solution could possibly provide. Having two index funds allows the investor to allocate and reallocate their money as personal circumstances dictate. By contrast, a single fund would force the investor to accept whatever ratio was given to them.

If you are investing outside of a tax-benefitted account and want to rebalance without triggering a tax liability, consider rebalancing simply by directing more of the new money you will be investing in the coming year into the fund that has fallen behind. This will allow you to bring your total portfolio back up to your target allocation without having to sell anything. However, in the end, don't overemphasize or fret too much about rebalancing. For instance, John Bogle, the legendary founder of The Vanguard Group, says that rebalancing may not even be necessary.[30] What's far more important is that you are saving and investing at all. If you do end up deciding to go with a balanced fund or target date fund instead, just make sure you do everything you can to minimize costs.[31]

In this chapter, I have encouraged Canadian readers to invest with larger financial institutions as they will tend to have the most locations, lower expense ratios, and longer operating hours. However, there are other financial institutions that also meet these criteria. For investors in the USA, fund providers such as the previously mentioned Vanguard (recommended by influential investors such as Warren Buffett) are extremely popular for similar reasons, although there are many suitable options.

CLOSING THOUGHTS

The reader should now be equipped with the basic tools necessary for the careful management of their personal finances. Remember that while money cannot buy happiness, it nonetheless constitutes a key pillar in supporting the reader's personal goals and aspirations. I will conclude this chapter with the reiteration of some important financial principles.

The first principle is that consumerism, and the purchase of material goods, does not make a person happier. Personal achievements, healthy relationships, and the act of giving back to society are what make people happy.

The second principle is that money is best viewed pragmatically as a tool for survival: to meet your needs for food, clothing, comfortable living, and so on.

The third principle is that savings should be grown through the investment of assets. This allows you to put your money to work for you, and it can help to mitigate the crippling effects of inflation.

The fourth principle is that when seeking help from financial advisors, stick with those of only the highest reputation and distinction. In life, whenever money is involved, it is all too easy to fall prey to the unscrupulous.

The fifth and final principle is to have confidence in your own abilities and instincts. If your judgment has deemed a particular course of action to be in your best interests, follow it. If something about a potential investment opportunity smells fishy, avoid it. Trust yourself above all else.

ACTION STEPS BEFORE READING THE NEXT CHAPTER

TO-DO: FINANCIAL LITERACY
- Assemble your own monthly budget using the example budget presented at the beginning of this chapter.
- Go online and decide which financial institution you want to invest with, based on fees, locations, operating hours, and availability of investment options.
- Call a branch of the financial institution you have chosen and book an appointment with a financial advisor/planner.

RECOMMENDED READINGS FOR FURTHER FINANCIAL EDUCATION
- *Debt-Free Forever: Take Control of Your Money and Your Life*, Gail Vaz-Oxlade
- *MONEY Master the Game: 7 Simple Steps to Financial Freedom*, Tony Robbins
- *Fail-Safe Investing: Lifelong Financial Security in 30 Minutes*, Harry Browne
- *The Little Book of Common Sense Investing: The Only Way to Guarantee Your Fair Share of Stock Market Returns*, John C. Bogle
- *The Millionaire Next Door: The Surprising Secrets of America's Wealthy*, Thomas J. Stanley, William D. Danko

CHAPTER 5
HEALTH AND FITNESS

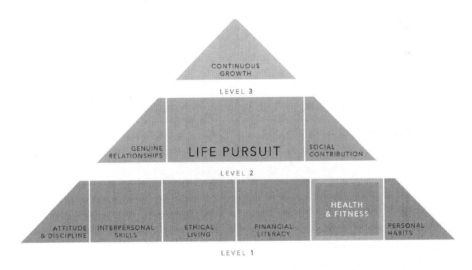

THE PARADIGM OF HAPPINESS

In this chapter, I'm going to be covering the three basic pillars of overall health and well-being: nutrition, exercise, and mental health. Obviously, an individual must have some measure of good health to be happy. Without a healthy body and mind, it would be impossible for us to advance upwards in The Paradigm of Happiness. Being healthy is the foundation for everything we enjoy and take for granted in life.

Without proper nutrition, exercise, and mental well-being, we may find ourselves overweight, prone to sickness, lacking energy, and worst of all, facing a shortened lifespan. Of course, by healthy, I'm referring to the traditional definition of having a fully functional and efficient body, conditioned by positive lifestyle habits. This book does not subscribe to health indicators and practices that are not generally supported by empirical research.

NUTRITION

There's a good chance that you're probably not eating a perfectly healthy diet on a day-to-day basis, and you know what? That's okay. Society's not-so-well-kept secret is that nobody does. And that, my friend, is a very powerful realization. Think about it this way: If I told you that the ultimate goal was to eat a perfectly healthy diet—right down to the precise servings of a specific food group you need on a daily basis—that wouldn't be too appealing, would it? Your diet would be monotonous and darn near impossible to maintain in a modern lifestyle with its surprise lunches, birthday dinners, hectic schedules, late night study sessions, and the like. The truth is that if you were to strive for perfection in your diet, especially if you were to demand that perfection immediately, your failure would be practically guaranteed. You'd give up because it simply isn't realistic. I know I would.

On the other hand, a far more practical approach would be to start slowly, and make small positive changes to your diet over time. As well as making changes over time, you need to accept the fact that you are human, and no human is perfect. The idea that you are going to be able to consistently maintain a 100 percent healthy diet over the course of years, or even just months, is pure fantasy. The long-term goal is to eat as many ideal foods as is practical, while reducing the foods that don't benefit you. *However*, that does not mean you have to be perfect and eliminate foods that you enjoy in order to be healthy. This is life, and sometimes making the most of the time you have on this planet means sharing a tub of ice cream with your romantic partner while cuddling on the couch and watching a movie. Don't let those cravings derail you. They're perfectly normal. Remember that every healthy food choice counts, and that *occasionally* treating yourself to ice cream or potato chips does not in any way mean a diet failure.

When you strive for diet perfection, especially through sudden changes to eating habits, what tends to happen is that you become discouraged because the abrupt change is simply untenable. It's a huge change, and you've had no opportunity to work your way up to it. As a result, you become demoralized and give up.

What sounds better to you? A mostly healthy but imperfect diet that you ease yourself into gradually, or a perfect diet that lasts three days and that you ultimately give up on? *I know which one I'd choose.*

Ultimately, what is most important is that you have the right attitude toward food. What is food? What is its purpose? Food is for both your body's nourishment and your psychological enjoyment, but having said this, it's important to strike the right balance between these two benefits. Certainly, we want to eat foods that are good for the body, but to eat only certain foods strictly on the merit of their health benefits is no way to live. On the other hand, eating food strictly for enjoyment's sake—or worst of all, binge eating—is not going to serve us any better.

Remember: eat to live, don't live to eat.

WHAT IS THE IDEAL DIET?

First things first: It's important to realize that meals *can* be both delicious and nutritious. Eating healthfully does not require a sacrifice in taste. Another important thing to remember is that the pleasure of great-tasting food is part of the eating experience as it improves personal morale. Taste is certainly important. You know what kind of foods satisfy your taste buds, but how do you decide what foods—and how much of each food group—should be on your plate at each meal, or where to find this information?

One place to start researching nutritional guidelines are government websites on health and nutrition. For example, the United States Department of Agriculture updated and republished its nutritional guidelines in 2011 as ChooseMyPlate.gov.[1] Here's what the USDA's MyPlate proportions look like:

FIGURE 5.1: THE USDA'S CHOOSEMYPLATE.GOV GRAPHIC

The USDA's ChooseMyPlate.gov guidelines seem reasonable. Every major food group is included, and fruits and vegetables together constitute 50 percent of the overall diet (30 percent from vegetables, 20 percent from fruit).[2] According to this model, protein from a variety of sources should make up 20 percent of one's diet. Grains should make up the remaining 30 percent of one's diet, and half of that should be from whole grain sources.[3] The USDA nutritional guidelines also recommend including one serving of low-fat milk or yogurt with each of the three main meals, for a maximum of three servings of dairy each day.[4] Furthermore, although not shown in the ChooseMyPlate graphic, information elsewhere on the website discusses the need to include some healthy fats and oils in the diet (with calories from saturated fats not exceeding 10 percent per day).[5] Also, the model addresses the importance of maintaining an active lifestyle in order to sustain good health.[6]

Overall, the USDA's ChooseMyPlate.gov guidelines appear to represent a balanced diet. However, researchers and nutritionists at Harvard University's T.H. Chan School of Public Health allege that the ChooseMyPlate.gov guidelines are still problematic because (1) the guidelines still reflect nutritional ideologies that are not necessarily reflected in more recent studies on nutrition and health; and (2) food industry lobbyists' interests and concerns may have influenced the final decisions about the types foods and recommended serving sizes included in the guidelines.[7]

In response to the alleged shortcoming of the USDA's nutrition guidelines set out in the ChooseMyPlate.gov model, the Harvard-based researchers mentioned above designed and published a healthier set of nutrition guidelines, along with a graphic representation of serving sizes by food group, shown below[8]:

FIGURE 5.2: HARVARD'S NUTRITIONAL GUIDELINES ARE WELL-SUPPORTED BY EMPIRICAL RESEARCH

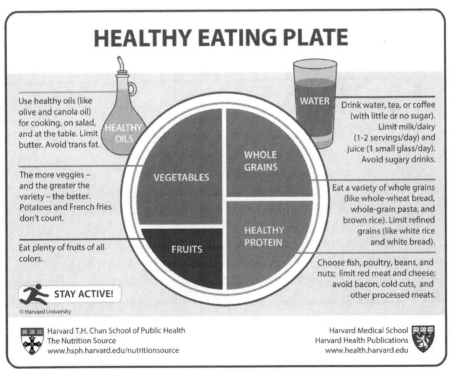

Excerpted from the Harvard School of Public Health, 2011. © 2011. Harvard University. Updated 2011 www.health.harvard.edu. Reproduced by permission.

While both the USDA and Harvard guidelines are similar, they have some differences. The key recommendations from the Harvard-based set of nutritional guidelines are as follows.

1. Drink water as your beverage of choice.
2. Remember that vegetables and fruits should take up half the space on your plate; proteins and grains should each take up 25 percent of the space on your plate.
3. Choose whole grains over refined grains. When shopping, be sure to look at the ingredients list for grain foods to be sure they are whole grains. The first ingredient listed should be whole wheat, whole oats, whole rye, whole grain corn, brown rice, wild rice, barley, bulgur, or oats.
4. Include healthy oils such as canola and olive as a regular part of your diet.
5. Opt for healthier protein sources such as legumes, poultry, or fish that is high in omega-3 fatty acids, rather red and processed meat.
6. Limit dairy to two servings per day (for adults). Harvard's nutritional guidelines recommend that we also look to other sources of food to meet our nutritional need for calcium.[9] The empirical evidence on the health benefits of dairy for people who are not lactose intolerant is mixed and too complex to discuss in this book.

DECONSTRUCTING THE HARVARD GUIDELINES

Ideally, vegetables should be the largest part of your diet, comprising almost one-third (30 percent) of your daily nutritional value. Eating a diet with lots of nutrient-rich vegetables has been shown time and again to lower your risk of everything from chronic indigestion to all kinds of cancer. The important thing is to go for variety. The benefits of eating a variety of veggies are two-fold: (1) it will prevent you from getting bored, and (2) your nutritional intake will be more well-rounded and complete.

The easiest way to make sure you're getting a sufficient range of vegetables is to eat a wide variety of vegetables from across the colour spectrum—green, dark green, orange, red—as often as possible. The more the colours differ, the more they are likely to be different in their health benefits.[10]

Fruit is almost as healthy for the body as vegetables; however, there are a couple of potential drawbacks with fruit. First, some fruits have a lot of natural sugar in them and second, they tend to be quite carbohydrate-rich. It is because of these two considerations that the nutritional guidelines developed by the Harvard researchers recommend a slightly lower proportion of fruit (20 percent) to vegetables (30 percent) in the diet. It should be noted, however, that the sugars and carbohydrates found in fruit are much healthier than those found in processed foods. Aim for variety in the kinds of fruit you eat, as well. Again, the simplest rule for variety is in the colour. The greater the variety of fruits you eat, the greater the nutritional diversity you will be getting.[11]

Fifty percent of your diet coming from fruits and vegetables may seem like a lot, but decades of research has only strengthened the argument that these foodstuffs are real life miracle foods.[12] This makes plenty of sense when you consider that the diet of our ancestors was largely plant-based until just a few million years ago. We have evolved to not just benefit from, but *need* a high intake of plant matter.[13]

Eating whole grains as opposed to refined grains provides us with many health benefits. A whole grain is considered whole because it has all three of its major components—the germ, the bran, and the endosperm—intact. This ultimately results in having a much higher nutritional value compared to refined grains, which only contain the starchy endosperm. In addition to being more nutritionally dense, eating whole grains has been linked to a reduction in risk factors for Type 2 diabetes, cardiovascular disease, and coronary heart disease.[14] It is important to make sure that your daily grain consumption consists of mostly whole grains.

Admittedly, the phrase "healthy protein" in and of itself is very ambiguous, so let's clear up some confusion here. Some healthy protein choices include poultry, fish, beans, and even some vegetables such as lentils.[15] Studies have shown that one egg per day consumption is safe for most individuals, unless you are at particular risk for diabetes.[16] Common unhealthy protein choices typically include beef, pork, and processed meats such as hot dogs, cold cuts, and bacon. What are the primary differences between the healthy and unhealthy choices? The unhealthy varieties of protein tend to contain much higher quantities of saturated fat, salt, and added contents for flavouring and preservation. Studies have shown that these protein choices put people at considerably higher risk for cancer, diabetes, and heart disease.[17]

Moving on to oils and fats, there is indeed a difference between healthy and unhealthy varieties. Healthy oils are typically plant-based such as soy, canola, sunflower, and olive. Their unhealthy counterparts on the other hand would be butter, hydrogenated, and partially hydrogenated oils.

Fat in foods have been blamed for increasing our waistlines for many years. However, there are many different types of dietary fats, and not all fats are created equal. The worst offenders are trans fats and saturated fats, while the so-called "good" fats are monounsaturated and polyunsaturated.[18]

As you can imagine, the mix of fats and oils consumed matters more than the total amount when it comes to maintaining a healthy diet. Sources of good fats include, omega-3 fatty acids found in fatty fish, tofu, walnuts, canola oil, flaxseeds, and flaxseed oil. Mono- and polyunsaturated fats can be found in foods such as avocados, nuts and seeds, olives and olive oils, vegetable oils such as sunflower oil, and peanut butter.[19] Trans fats and some varieties of saturated fats are bad for your health due to their linkage to heart disease, stroke, and some cancers. Trans fats are typically found in fried foods and commercially prepared foods such as potato chips, pastries, hydrogenated and partially hydrogenated oils and some chocolate bars. Saturated fats are found in coconut and palm oil and some dairy products (high fat cheeses, cream, full-fat milk, butter, and ice cream).[20]

Finally, the most basic form of sustenance for the body next to air is water. Water makes up the balance of your body by mass, and is critical to normal functioning from head to toe.[21] These critical functions include everything from lubricating your joints to cooling you down through perspiration. Frequent water consumption also tends to help control weight as it reduces hunger pangs with a feeling of fullness. If you can't drink eight glasses in a day, at least drink as much as you can. An easy way to increase your water consumption is not to buy alternative beverages. When you're in the grocery store, skip the sodas and juices. You'll save money, and by the time you get home, you'll be pretty much forced to drink water.

WHAT TO DO IF YOU HAVE FOOD SENSITIVITIES

There are two types of food sensitivities: allergies and intolerances. Food intolerances are generally defined as the body's inability to fully digest a particular type of food, which induces a slow reaction on the part of the sufferer.[22] Food allergies, on the other hand, tend to be immediate and severe when the afflicted person eats an offending food because the person's immune system responds to the food as a perceived threat.[23] The results can sometimes even be fatal. Because of the fast and obvious reaction, food allergies are easier to diagnose. Food intolerances are often more problematic to identify precisely *because* they don't cause immediate, severe reactions.

Two of the most common food sensitivities are caused by a gluten intolerance and lactose intolerance, respectively. Because their symptoms are common to many disorders, these food sensitivities often remain undiagnosed.

Celiac disease is an inherited autoimmune disorder characterized by an intolerance to gluten, a protein found in certain grains such as wheat, rye, barley, and oats. According to the University of Chicago's Celiac Disease Center, common symptoms of this autoimmune disorder include abdominal pain, cramps, fatigue, and diarrhea; in extreme cases, symptoms might also include vomiting, nausea, bloating and constipation.[24]

Lactose Intolerance is the inability to digest or fully digest lactose, a particular type of sugar found in milk products, due to insufficient amounts of the digestive enzyme lactase in the small intestine. According to the University of Chicago Medicine's online health library, common symptoms of lactose intolerance include experiencing bloating, gas, cramps, nausea or diarrhea after consuming dairy products.

What's that, you say? You don't have a food sensitivity? It's possible, but don't be so sure. Many people don't know they have a food sensitivity simply because they have been living with that sensitivity and the aggravating inflammation that accompanies it for their entire lives and therefore think it's normal. If you don't have anything to compare your current state of well-being with, then it's difficult, at best, to tell whether you are truly healthy or not.

So, how do you find out if you have a food sensitivity? Many people often reach for the obvious idea of systematically cutting out foods that may be the cause of some health detriments and then monitoring changes in the body. This may be the right idea, but it's important to never self-diagnose yourself when it comes to any kind of health or diet issues. Call your family doctor and schedule an appointment. Tell them that you would like to be tested for food sensitivities. Your doctor will ask you a few questions and likely give you a referral to a specialist who will do a thorough examination. For true intolerances that are difficult to detect, it is indeed likely that your specialist will ask you to systematically cut food groups out of your diet and keep a diary of your eating habits and symptoms.

So why couldn't you just do this yourself? There are three reasons why you should not attempt a self-diagnosis through a do-it-yourself elimination diet. Without consulting a health professional you may: 1) inadvertently cut out foods that are important sources of nutrition to your body; 2) fail to cut out all the foods within the offending food group; and 3) unintentionally create false positive or false negative results due to an unconscious bias.

So why are we going to all this trouble? Remember that the whole goal of our time together here is to find ways to maximize your happiness in life. By diagnosing food sensitivities and cutting out foods to which your body reacts negatively, you can have more energy, look better, feel better, and be healthier overall. Your quality of life can improve very tangibly. It goes without saying that being healthy and feeling good are prerequisites to happiness. Beyond the immediate benefits of recognizing food sensitivities, continuing to eat foods that you are sensitive to can lead to the development of all kinds of degenerative diseases later in life. For instance, celiac disease sufferers are at a significantly increased risk for development of gastrointestinal tract cancers if they continue to eat gluten throughout their lives, all the while unaware of their intolerance.[25]

After your tests are complete, your specialist will give you the results for any foods you have sensitivities to. Depending on the specialist (if they are good), they will give you a full diet plan to accommodate your sensitivities. If not, then at the very least they should be able to offer you nutritional substitutes for the foods you need to avoid.

HOW MUCH AND HOW OFTEN SHOULD I BE EATING?

You should generally aim to eat three to five reasonably portioned meals every day. There will certainly be occasions when this will be impractical. After all, sometimes dinner parties can last for hours. But for the most part, try to eat three meals and two snacks, evenly spaced throughout the day, as regularly as possible. Here's a general rule: when eating, don't eat until you're absolutely full. Just eat enough so that you are not hungry anymore. This will satiate your appetite, but will also prevent you from becoming sleepy from overeating. Also, keep in mind that the stomach needs time to feel full. After eating food, your body takes about 10 to 20 minutes to register the feeling of satiety.

With regard to portion sizes, the *Dairy Council of California*[26] has a wonderful comparison chart that allows people to easily gauge portion sizes using nothing but their hands as measuring tools.

FIGURE 5.3: THE DAIRY COUNCIL OF CALIFORNIA'S INTUITIVE MEASUREMENT SYSTEM UTILIZES NOTHING BUT YOUR HANDS

Serving-Size Comparison Chart

FOOD	SYMBOL	COMPARISON	SERVING SIZE
Milk & Milk Products			
Cheese (string cheese) 	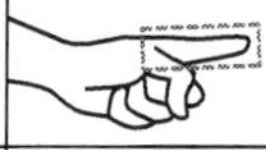	Pointer finger	1½ ounces
Milk and yogurt (glass of milk) 		One fist	1 cup
Vegetables			
Cooked carrots 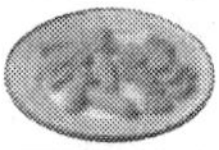		One fist	1 cup
Salad (bowl of salad) 		Two fists	2 cups
Fruits			
Apple 		One fist	1 medium
Canned peaches 		One fist	1 cup
Grains, Breads & Cereals			
Dry cereal (bowl of cereal) 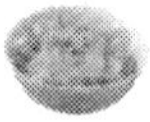		One fist	1 cup
Noodles, rice, oatmeal (bowl of noodles) 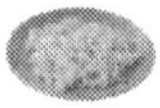		Handful	½ cup
Slice of whole wheat bread 	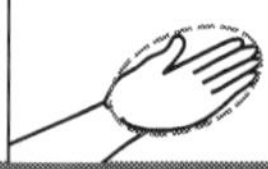	Flat hand	1 slice
Meat, Beans & Nuts			
Chicken, beef, fish, pork (chicken breast) 		Palm	3 ounces
Peanut butter (spoon of peanut butter) 		Thumb	1 tablespoon

Again, we are trying to strike a balance between being rigorous and being practical. I could recommend that you portion out all your meals and servings using precise kitchen implements, but doing so would quickly become discouraging. By using your hands to determine portion sizes, you are more likely to stick with portioning plans.

Now that we have a convenient way of measuring out portions, it would be prudent to have a dietary plan that sets some guidelines for a healthy daily intake of calories. In particular, the amount of calories from protein, sugar, sodium, fibre, and calories as a proportion of total daily calories is important. The ideal combination of these dietary elements should be determined by a visit to your family doctor or registered dietician.

Finding a reasonable approach to tracking calories is of particular concern to many people. This is understandable as calories represent the energy the body receives from food, and a constant surplus of calories over daily energy expenditure leads to weight gain. Again, while a visit to your doctor is the best practice, a basic chart of the average recommended calorie intake for people of various ages and both genders can provide some general guidelines. Here are charts provided by Health Canada.

FIGURE 5.4: HEALTH CANADA'S SUGGESTED DAILY CALORIE INTAKE FOR MALES BY AGE, SEX, AND ACTIVITY LEVEL[27]

Males (Calories Per Day)

Age	Sedentary Lifestyle[1]	Low Activity Lifestyle[2]	High Activity Lifestyle[3]
2 – 3 years	1100	1350	1500
4 – 5 years	1250	1450	1650
6 – 7 years	1400	1600	1800
8 – 9 years	1500	1750	2000
10 – 11 years	1700	2000	2300
12 – 13 years	1900	2250	2600
14 – 16 years	2300	2700	3100
17 – 18 years	2450	2900	3300
19 – 30 years	2500	2700	3000
31 – 50 years	2350	2600	2900
51 – 70 years	2150	2350	2650
71 years +	2000	2200	2500

FIGURE 5.5: HEALTH CANADA'S SUGGESTED DAILY CALORIE INTAKE FOR FEMALES BY AGE, SEX, AND ACTIVITY LEVEL[28]

Females (Calories Per Day)			
Age	Sedentary Lifestyle[1]	Low Activity Lifestyle[2]	High Activity Lifestyle[3]
2 – 3 years	1100	1250	1400
4 – 5 years	1200	1350	1500
6 – 7 years	1300	1500	1700
8 – 9 years	1400	1600	1850
10 – 11 years	1500	1800	2050
12 – 13 years	1700	2000	2250
14 – 16 years	1750	2100	2350
17 – 18 years	1750	2100	2400
19 – 30 years	1900	2100	2350
31 – 50 years	1800	2000	2250
51 – 70 years	1650	1850	2100
71 years +	1550	1750	2000

[1] Sedentary: Your typical daily routine requires little physical movement (e.g., sitting for long periods, using a computer, relying primarily on motorized transportation) and you accumulate little physical activity in your leisure time.

[2] Low Activity: Your typical daily routine involves some physical activity (e.g., walking to bus, mowing the lawn, shoveling snow) and you accumulate some additional physical activity in your leisure time.

[3] High Activity: Your typical daily tasks involve some physical activity and you accumulate at least 2 ½ hours of moderate- to vigorous-intensity aerobic physical activity each week. Moderate- to vigorous-physical activity will make you breathe harder and your heart beat faster.

Broadly speaking, in practice each of the different activity levels would look like this:

Sedentary Lifestyle: Your daily activities require a minimal amount of physical exertion. This description would fit someone who works in an office environment during the day, and does not engage in sports or gym workouts in their spare time.

Low Activity Lifestyle: An average day might include walking or biking to work at an office job. You engage in some light exertion in your spare time, such as playing the occasional game of ultimate frisbee or soccer.

High Activity Lifestyle: You bike or walk to work to your job on a daily basis. In addition, you regularly do intense weight training and cardiovascular exercise such as running at your local gym in your spare time.

Be sure to include variety in your overall diet. A simple example would be combining complex carbohydrates from bread (or a gluten-free alternative) with the lean protein of turkey (or a vegetarian equivalent) in a sandwich. Strive for variety within every food group. As a concrete example, eating fruit is great, but only ever eating the same fruit is not only boring but nutritionally incomplete. Remember, an easy way to getting nutritional variety with fruits and vegetables is to eat a diverse combination of different coloured fruits or vegetables together in order to get much needed vitamin and nutrient diversity.

Of our three to five recommended meals a day, take extra care to be sure you never miss breakfast. It's cliché to say that breakfast is the most important meal of the day, but it's true. Empirical studies have shown that breakfast eaters tend to eat fewer calories in total during the day, have better productivity in both school and work, and have better health later in life.[29]

I know it's difficult, and at times even bothersome, but try your best to drink the recommended eight cups of water every day. Keeping hydrated will aid in maintaining the health of everything in your body. Perhaps best of all, keeping your body flushed with water can help prevent painful kidney stones from developing later in life![30]

If you're having trouble maintaining healthy snacking habits, here's a tip: keep healthy snacks such as fresh fruit or dehydrated fruit in sight. A bowl full of fruit on your kitchen table should suffice. Another great option is keeping precut and washed veggies with low calorie dip ready to go in the fridge. Raw nuts are also a healthy option for those who are not allergic to them.

THINGS TO AVOID

This goes without saying, but avoid excessive alcohol consumption. Binge drinking can do all sorts of nasty things to your body, such as increasing your risk of heart disease, stroke, and liver disease, not to mention potentially putting a hole in your pocketbook over time. Let's face it: being drunk on a regular basis isn't exactly dignified anyway.

While popular opinion suggests that moderate alcohol consumption can actually be good for health, the evidence is not so cut-and-dried. As an example, research conducted by the *American Journal of Public Health* suggests that there is a statistically significant link between moderate alcohol consumption (one-and-a-half drinks per day) and deaths by cancer. As the *American Journal of Public Health* states quite succinctly, "(1) alcohol is a known carcinogen, (2) cancer risk increases considerably at high levels, but there is no safe level at which there is no cancer risk."[31]

One should also try to limit excessive consumption of calorie-dense foods with little nutritional value such as candy bars and chocolate. Foods containing refined sugar, flour, and products with high levels of saturated and trans fats should be eaten only rarely as special "treats."

FOR THOSE OF YOU WHO *HATE* FRUITS AND VEGETABLES

There are probably a lot of you out there who absolutely hate fruits and vegetables. This is unfortunate since, as discussed before, a healthy diet will include lots of these miracle foods. There is, however, a way to get a large serving of fruits and vegetables into your diet without having to eat them whole. The solution: buy yourself a juicer. Juicers can be found in most department stores for less than $100. Its purpose is to separate the liquid from the fibre in fruits and vegetables to create delicious juices. Just about any combination works as long it includes at least one piece of sweet fruit like an apple or pear.

With a juicer, you get most of the nutrition you would have obtained from eating raw fruits and vegetables, with the exception of the fibre content in the pulp. This is probably the biggest knock against juicing: you lose some nutritional content in the juicing process, and not having the fibre means that the sugar from fruit will hit your bloodstream faster than otherwise. Nonetheless, juicing has many benefits. Since drinking a glass of carrot, orange, and/or celery juice is easier and perhaps more appealing than eating all of those things whole, it is very likely you will end up getting more fruit and vegetable nutrition in the end. Furthermore, fresh fruit and vegetable juice is just plain delicious.

I'll reiterate that another simple trick to increase your fruit intake is to simply keep those healthy foods in sight. Put a large bowl of fruit, such as apples or bananas, on your kitchen counter or the centre of your dining room table so the fruit in it can be eaten on impulse. Fruits like oranges or kiwis that must be peeled first might dissuade you from eating them.

Dehydrated fruit makes a convenient and portable snack when you're on the go and want something healthy to munch on (although it is important to remember that they are high in sugar compared to fresh fruit). Raisins, dried apricots, and dried cranberries are among the most popular dried fruit snacks. Dehydrated fruits make a particularly great snack when eaten as a replacement for unhealthy alternatives such as potato chips and chocolate bars.

One of the biggest problems with fruits and vegetables is that they tend to spoil quickly compared to processed foods. This spoilage can, in some ways, be interpreted as a positive sign. These foods wilt and spoil because they are fresh. By contrast, processed foods may last longer, but that is because they are usually made from refined flour and sugar and have various preservatives added to them so they last much longer. Once when I was a teenager, I was cleaning out our family's fridge when I found a slice of processed cheese that had slipped down the back of the lowest shelf. I unwrapped the cheese and sniffed it. It was perfectly fine. No mould at all, either.

I knew for a fact that cheese had to have been nearly a year old. The fact that processed food just never seems to go bad speaks volumes about its nutritional value.

There is still, however, the pesky problem of how to get our fruits and veggies to last longer. This is especially true if we want to enjoy them during off-season months. The easiest solutions are canning and freezing. Canned fruit salads in particular are very convenient. Just make sure to buy only those that are packed in water instead of syrup in order to avoid unnecessary added sugars. As for frozen fruits and vegetables, you can find all kinds of vegetable medleys in the freezer aisle of your local grocery store. Go ahead and experiment!

LET'S GO SHOPPING

So now that we have some idea of what we should be eating, let's take a look at what kinds of foods should be on our shopping list for our trip to the grocery store. We'll also discuss how to pick out the right products. Note that those with special dietary considerations may shop and eat somewhat differently from most people.

Since we know the rough proportions for each of the food groups that we should be eating, it follows that we should be buying roughly the same proportions of food during our weekly grocery shopping trip. The following is a sample list of the types of foods you should be aiming for. Of course, this is not a hard and fast list that you must follow but merely an example. Feel free to omit or add appropriate foods to the list as desired.

Vegetables, Beans, Legumes   Buy these fresh from the produce section. Most of these will go into meals such as stir fries and salads.
- Bell Peppers
- Carrots
- Cucumber
- Boxed salad (pre-mixed leafy greens)
- Broccoli
- String beans
- Potatoes
- Lentils (These will typically be found in the dry goods aisle.)

Fruit, Berries, Melons   Buy these fresh from the produce section, when in season. Most of these can simply be eaten raw.

- Apples
- Oranges
- Bananas
- Tomatoes
- Strawberries
- Blueberries
- Pears
- Cantaloupe
- Honeydew
- Watermelon

Meats/Protein   Beware of cold cuts, hot dogs and the like that have high levels of sodium content. Remember that according to the American Heart Association the maximum recommended intake of sodium for the average adult is 2,300mg.[32]

- Frozen or fresh chicken breast
- Fish fillet (Fresh or frozen; salmon and halibut are great choices.)
- Lean cuts of meat. (Limit bacon.)
- Eggs

Grains   Opt for products made with 100 percent whole grains. Besides the overt labelling, you will know whether the product you are buying really contains 100 percent whole grains if the phrase 'whole grain' appears as the first item on the ingredients list. Keep in mind that gluten-free whole grain options are readily available in grocery stores as well.

- Whole grain pasta of your choice
- Whole grain bread
- Breakfast cereal (Look at the nutrition information on the cereal box and aim to purchase a cereal that contains at least 3 grams of fibre per serving, no more than 240mg of sodium per serving, and no more than 7g of sugar per serving. Examples that fit the bill include bran flakes and toasted oat cereals.)
- Regular instant or quick-cooking oatmeal

Dairy
- Grated cheese for salads
- Low-fat milk (Purchase sparingly; soy milk and almond milk make fantastic alternatives.)
- Yogurt

Beverages   Do your best to avoid soft drinks and other sugary beverages. Diabetes is no joke!
- The best choice of beverage is water: water is (practically) free, rehydrates the body efficiently, does not contain sugars, and helps to reduce hunger pangs.
- Soy milk and almond milk are good alternatives to regular milk. They taste great, possess "good" fats of the omega-3 and omega-6 varieties, and also contain protein.
- If you must buy milk, stick with skim or 1-percent milk.
- And again, do your best to avoid soft drinks—even the diet ones. You will be eating healthier and saving money while you're at it!

Condiments
- Salad dressing of your choice for boxed salads
- Dip for vegetable platters and snacks. (Note that many commercially prepared salad dressings are full of sugars and unhealthy fats. Read the labels!)

The following are some ridiculously simple and healthy meal ideas that I promise you will enjoy.

BREAKFAST

One-Minute Breakfast: Apple and Peanut Butter Quick Fix

Ingredients:
- 1 apple
- Peanut butter or preferred nut butter

Instructions:
- Cut apple into manageable slices for finger food.
- Generously spread peanut butter on the apple slices.
- Serve with two 8-ounce glasses of water.

FIGURE 5.6: ONE-MINUTE HEALTHY BREAKFAST (APPLE SLICES & NUT BUTTER)[33]

LUNCH

Protein Packed Garden Greens Salad

Ingredients:

- 1 serving of your favourite mixed greens (boxed or pre-mixed is fine)
- 8 oz. chicken breast (consider removing the skin for reduced saturated fat intake)
- 1 piece of your favourite whole fruit
- Low calorie salad dressing based on oil and vinegar such as Balsamic Vinaigrette (creamy salad dressings tend to have higher calorie and fat content)
- Serve with a large glass of water

Instructions:

- Season chicken breast as desired. (Salt, pepper, and garlic powder are good options.)
- Grill chicken breast on medium-high grill or grill pan until just cooked through; turn occasionally. (A small electric grill works nicely as well.)
- Cut cooked chicken breast into strips.
- Add chicken breast strips into large bowl with greens and salad dressing. Add other accoutrements (such as shredded cheese) as desired and toss thoroughly but gently.
- Serve with side of whole fruit and glass of water.

FIGURE 5.7: PROTEIN PACKED GARDEN GREENS SALAD[34]

DINNER

Gooey Grilled Cheese Goodness Do grilled cheese sandwiches scream sophisticated? No. Are they fun and easy? Yes. If you need a quick and simple dinner after work, this is an often overlooked option.

Ingredients:
- 2 slices of whole grain bread
- Butter
- 1 slice of cheese of your choice; just large enough to cover the surface of the bread (mild cheddar or American are good choices)

Instructions:
- Butter one side of each slice of bread.
- Place the cheese between the two slices of bread with the buttered sides facing outwards.
- Place the sandwich in a skillet over medium heat and toast the sandwich for about five minutes per side.
- Serve immediately, while the cheese is still gooey.

FIGURE 5.8: GRILLED CHEESE IS A SIMPLE
BUT SATISFYING COMFORT FOOD

SNACKS

We all need a healthy snack now and then. The following are five guilt-free, healthy options that will allow you to satiate your hunger until your next meal!

1. **Dehydrated Fruit** Dehydrated fruit can make a phenomenal snack that is highly portable, reasonably healthy, and will not spoil if stored properly. (Remember, though, that dried fruit is high in sugar.)
2. **Yogurt** A staple in the North American diet, yogurt makes a good substitute for ice cream and other indulgences.
3. **Raw Fruit** Chomping on a crispy apple or juicy orange is one of life's simple pleasures.
4. **Celery Sticks and Peanut Butter** Wash a couple of celery sticks and cut off the bottoms. Apply peanut butter into the "nook" of the celery and serve!
5. **Whole Grain Toast** Two pieces of whole grain toast with a small helping of butter (or nut butter) for taste make an excellent snack with a minimum of fuss.

BATCH COOKING

While this will be covered in more detail in a future chapter, it's worth mentioning here that one of the easiest ways to reduce cooking time and increase overall efficiency is batch cooking. Batch cooking is the process of cooking large portions of food for, say, a couple days in advance so that you don't have to prepare every meal on a case by case basis. This preplanning has four primary advantages:

1. It generally enables healthier eating as you are not scrambling to produce meals on an ad hoc basis. It will also reduce your tendency to gravitate towards unhealthier snack foods.
2. It tends to produce more reasonable portion sizes.
3. It saves time.
4. It reduces stress during particularly busy periods of your life.

Consider a fairly common dish such as chicken stir-fry. Cooking a few extra servings would take almost no extra time at all, yet would yield several extra meals that you subsequently would not have to cook. The active cooking time might be 15 minutes, so the amount of time you will have saved is 15 minutes times the number of extra meals you have made. You can simply take the extra servings, put them in some plastic or glass food containers and either refrigerate or freeze them, depending on how long into the future you're prepping them for.

Of course, the one disadvantage to batch cooking is that storing the food in the refrigerator and freezer means that not all of the meals you eat will be truly fresh. Naturally you wouldn't want to eat leftovers for *every* meal, but it is appropriate as a time saver as you see fit. A blend of immediate cooking and batch cooking is a suitable approach for most people.

BATCH-COOK FRIENDLY MEALS

The meal options we have discussed above for breakfast, lunch, and dinner are designed for maximum simplicity and efficiency. They also have something of a built-in bias towards immediate serving, and aren't really built for batch cooking. With the preceding discussion in mind, what follows is a recipe that is batch cooking friendly. While I have provided one sample recipe below, other recipes can be found in Appendix 1. Consider cooking a large batch of food on Sunday so that you have lunch for the whole week. Since these meals are intended to be self-contained and portable, they include as many of the major macronutrients as possible.

The Simple Trio   This is a quick and easy batch cooking combination that actually requires minimal cooking. In an effort to capture the major macronutrients that should be part of your meal with a minimum of fuss, I have elected to choose brown rice, turkey sausages, and mixed vegetables. What makes this meal especially easy? The turkey sausages and mixed vegetables can easily be found in frozen and bulk form at your local grocery store. I've chosen turkey as the meat of choice because it is a lean protein that is low in saturated fat, particularly compared to pork.

Ingredients:
- Frozen pre-cooked turkey sausages
- Frozen mixed vegetables (A medley of vegetables including broccoli, carrots, cauliflower, etc.; any brand is fine.)
- Brown rice

Instructions:
This recipe makes a business week's worth of lunches (5 meals).
1. Pour approximately 1½ cups of brown rice into a large bowl and rinse to clean out any sediment.
2. Pour the washed rice into your rice cooker, fill with water until all the rice is just submerged, and set the rice cooker to cook.
3. Once the rice is cooked, pour equal portions of the rice into five separate plastic food containers. Spread out the rice in the containers to create a "bed."
4. Allow the rice to cool.
5. Place three to four of the frozen sausages onto the bed of rice.
6. Place the desired amount of frozen veggies onto the bed of rice. As vegetables are low in calories and high in nutrients, feel free to be a little generous in your portions.
7. Place lids on each plastic food container and place in the freezer. Make sure to put a label on the container that states the contents, the date frozen, and the "use by" date.
8. From a frozen state, heat in microwave for five minutes to prepare. Less cooking time will be required if food has been thawed.

I encourage you to check out the additional batch cooking recipes at the end of Appendix 1. I chose to include these meals because they are generally amenable to freezing, which allows them to keep longer than meals that can only be refrigerated. If you are in doubt, consult the the Food and Drug Administration's (FDA) website[35] for guidelines on how long various foods can be stored safely.

If you follow a typical 9 a.m. to 5 p.m. work schedule, consider moving tomorrow's lunch out of the freezer and into the fridge to begin defrosting the night before. The lunch will continue to defrost throughout the morning. Come lunch-time, your meal will require minimal reheating.

Observant readers will notice that our proposed meal combination contains one major source of complex carbohydrates, high quality protein, and a medley of vegetables. This allows the entree to cover the major nutritional bases simply and effectively. However, if you would like to supplement any of these meals with more substance, adding an individual yogurt cup or piece of fruit rounds out the meal nicely. Feel free to create your own weekly batch-cooked meals with my recipes as a guideline.

In a pinch, frozen and prepackaged meals can work in place of batch cooking. This will likely cost more money and making healthy choices may be more difficult, but there is an advantage in the time and effort saved. The University of South Florida has written a guide for how to choose frozen dinners. According to the University of South Florida, the major components of their recommendations include looking for meals that are 300–500 calorie servings; contain 10–18 grams of fat and have less than 600 milligrams of sodium. In addition, frozen dinners should contain 10–20 grams of protein, less than 4 grams of saturated fat, at least 5 grams of fibre, and should have a balance between the major food groups.[36]

A FEW FINAL TIPS ON NUTRITION

1. Any food group can be unhealthy when it is processed—even fruits or vegetables—so avoid over-processed food.
2. When eating at a restaurant, remember that you are the customer. You don't have to just accept what's on the menu and hope for the best. Ask the server about the ingredients in a dish before ordering it. Ask for changes in the dish if one of the ingredients or cooking processes raises a red flag.
3. Don't force yourself to finish meals. All this does is lighten your wallet, fatten your waistline, and make you feel sluggish. Ask your server to pack up the remaining food in a take-out container, and use the leftovers the next day.
4. The impact of alcohol consumption on health should always be taken seriously, but there is a particular risk for individuals

whose skin flushes red when drinking alcohol. Empirical studies suggest that such a reaction to alcohol intake is indicative of an inability to digest it properly and is common amongst East Asian populations. According to the researchers Brooks, Enoch, Goldman, et al., the evidence suggests that those who experience this reaction are at a much higher risk of cancer if they consume alcohol regularly.[37]

5. Seriously consider purchasing a food scale to more easily assess how much food you are eating and to follow recipes more accurately. Many people are surprised at how much or how little food is in one serving of fruits and vegetables, or how much food is really in one serving of poultry or red meat.

6. Getting a set of stackable food containers is an absolute must for controlling the portions for your meals or for batch cooking. A decent set from your local grocery store will not set you back by much and will be of great benefit.

EXERCISE

We will now consider the second pillar of health: exercise. Exercise is an activity requiring physical effort with a goal to either maintain or improve your health and fitness. Exercise has many specific benefits including improved mood, better sleeping, increased energy, weight loss, and reduced chances of developing just about every known disease. Aside from the health benefits, though, let's face it: exercise can also make us look better. At face value that may seem shallow, but it's a legitimately important benefit to consider. Improved physical appearance will give you more self-confidence and naturally make you more attractive to a potential mate. We've all been told to look for inner beauty in others, and while that is important, the truth is that physical compatibility is just as important as personal compatibility.

Putting value on appearances isn't really as shallow as it is alleged to be. Physical attraction to another's body is usually because of implicit signs of the person's health and vibrancy. Additionally, when someone is fit, it is a sign that the person has their act together, and genuinely cares about keeping their body healthy and well maintained. Physical attractiveness goes beyond mere appearances. Furthermore, it's been proven empirically that people who are more physically attractive are more likely to be approached positively at work, school, and in their social lives.

Here's what champion body builder and former California governor Arnold Schwarzenegger had to say about body building and exercise in the *Encyclopedia of Modern Body Building*:

> "You'll find, as I did, that building muscle builds you up in every part of your life. What you learn here will affect everything else that you do in your life... I know I can succeed in anything I choose, and I know this because I understand what it takes to sacrifice, struggle, persist, and eventually overcome an obstacle."[38]

YOUR BODY AND YOU: PREVAILING ATTITUDES

First things first: In today's world, there is clearly a problem of perception when it comes to the ideal body. What is beauty? What is desirability? What is achievable? How much of what we see in magazines and TV is real?

One could make the argument that this is a perception problem, and the pressure to be beautiful is more prevalent among women than men. There may be some truth to this argument; however, there is a similarly growing trend amongst men and boys as well.[39] There is increasing pressure to look a certain way and to have a certain body. The persistent message and pressure from the beauty and fashion industries that is delivered by mass media is that unless you look a certain way, you are ugly and perhaps even a failure in life.

For my female readers, just remember that the stick-thin, Photoshopped appearance of models, actresses, and celebrities is not only pernicious, but for the most part, not healthy at all. Beyond that, it's not practical. The ideal of a supposedly perfect body that has been pushed on us by media is, for the most part, nothing but a fantasy. Go ahead, search the names of various celebrities and models and append the phrase "without make up" or "without Photoshop" to their names; see what results you get. You might be surprised by the pictures you see.

Promoting this type of unrealistic ideal of the female form is not limited to women and young adults. Even children are exposed to it. The very act of playing with Barbie dolls at a young age has only made the impractical ideal of the female body more deeply implanted in the minds of young girls.[40]

The truth is that nobody's body is perfect. And you know what? That's okay! The truth is that we are *all* imperfect, and that is what makes us human. Being healthy and fit may be one thing, but if you want to be happy, you must accept that your body is, well, human. Humanity is the quintessential embodiment of imperfection! It is this very imperfection that gives you and your body both character and uniqueness.

Additionally, you have to realize that no two bodies are ever going to be identical. As such, it follows that even if a perfect body you saw in a magazine was real, it just wouldn't be realistic to assume that your body should look exactly the same way.

Let me reiterate, you must accept your body for what it is—with all the great things it can do. You and your body are incredible; do not let anyone, not even those close to you, ever convince you to believe otherwise.

One point to consider is that weight and size do not necessarily reflect health or wellness. Being above average size or girth doesn't automatically mean you're unhealthy. The flip side to this concept is that being skinnier or more muscular doesn't necessarily mean you are healthier. For instance, the desire to be skinnier can lead to anorexia—a dangerous physical condition that results in an emaciated body and the internal organs shutting down. (This disorder often—but not always—develops in people who have trauma histories; e.g., the individuals were victims of childhood abuse or sexual abuse/assault, or witnessed or experienced domestic violence.[41]) In a similar vein, an excessive desire to be well-muscled and "buff" can often lead to the use of steroids—a class of drugs that can have severe consequences.

There is a powerful series of documentary videos, posted on social media and YouTube, called *Killing Us Softly*.[42] This series of documentaries, created by Jean Kilbourne, aptly communicates the absurd and dangerous beauty ideals communicated through advertising in the mass media. I highly recommend that the reader take the time to watch it.

"Love yourself, accept yourself, forgive yourself and be good to yourself, because without you the rest of us are without a source of many wonderful things."[43]
Leo F. Buscaglia

LET'S GET TECHNICAL

There are three basic forms of exercise, and any good exercise program will incorporate all three of them to varying degrees. The three basic forms of exercise are:

1. Aerobic: long duration/low intensity exercise that primarily challenges the heart and lungs such as jogging or stair climbing.
2. Anaerobic: short duration/high intensity exercise that primarily challenges individual muscle groups such as the biceps or quadriceps. Exercises that fall into this group would include biceps curls with free weights or even sprinting.
3. Stretching: intentional elongation of a muscle or muscle group in order to improve tissue elasticity and prevent potential injury. An example would be the splits or bending down and touching your toes to stretch your hamstrings and calf muscles.

Opinions may differ, but from this author's perspective, aerobic exercise is the most important of this activity trio. If I had to choose one form of activity while discarding the others for the rest of my life, it would be aerobic exercise. While jogging every day won't necessarily give you chiseled abs or a v-shaped torso, the most important organs—the heart and the lungs—will be getting a workout. Additionally, the overall health of the body improves as calories are burned, and increased oxygen and blood flow will circulate throughout the body.

WHAT ARE YOUR EXERCISE GOALS?

People exercise for different reasons. Some want to lose weight, while others want to gain muscle mass. Some want to compete in the Olympics, others just want to look good naked! What this book provides is a recommended general exercise program for improving your overall health, in addition to improving the function, and overall appearance of the body. I would love to be able to cover all possible workout programs with you—to give you a complete guide from marathon training to becoming a professional boxer—but such detail is beyond the scope of this book. Note that you should consult your doctor before starting any new exercise program.

EXERCISE OPTIONS

First, let's identify your options for where you can exercise. For most people there are three options:

1. Home gym
2. Gym membership
3. Sports club

Whichever one of these options you choose, the important thing is that you pay sufficient attention to the three basic pillars of fitness (aerobic, anaerobic, and stretching) that we discussed earlier. Let's talk about how a typical person would cover all three bases with our exercise options.

Home Gym

Aerobic Exercise Methods:
- Jogging or running around your neighbourhood
- Jump rope for indoor aerobic exercise during colder seasons
- Hitting a punching bag
- Purchase a treadmill for home use
- Stair climbing

Anaerobic Exercise Methods:
- Push-ups
- Incline push-ups

- Sit-ups/crunches
- V-sits
- Squats
- Calf raises
- Lunges
- Reverse lunges
- Pull-up bar

Stretching Methods:
- Splits
- Quadriceps stretch
- Triceps stretch
- Hamstring stretch
- Pectoral stretch
- Deltoid stretches

Gym Membership   Having a gym membership is the luxury approach to exercising. At the gym, you will have all the equipment you need to do any type of exercise, usually in a multitude of different ways. Naturally the trade-off will be increased cost associated with any gym membership. Most gym passes cost about $30 to $50 a month. You may be able to get advice from fitness trainers who are on staff as well.

Sports Club   For many readers, joining a sports club may be the best choice for satisfying their exercise needs. The difference between going to the gym for exercise and joining a sports club is that playing sports is generally more fun, *and* more affordable – an especially important consideration for students and others who are not working. Having fun is unbelievably important to making regular exercise a life-long habit.

Go to your local recreation centre, or if you're still in school check out your school's programs for teams and clubs to join. Most sports teams will give you a great work out. The best part of all is that for a large portion of the time, you may not even realize that you are exercising, burning calories, and working your muscles! As a rule of thumb, if you are practicing your sport on a regular basis (at least four times a week) and are feeling quite winded, you are probably getting a good work out and you can leave it at that.

A PROPOSED EXERCISE REGIMEN

The following is a general exercise program that will meet the fitness needs and time constraints of most individuals at minimal cost:

Number of sessions: 4–7 per week
Time: 1 hour
Structure: 5 minutes of stretching, 20 minutes of aerobic exercise, 30 minutes of anaerobic exercise, 5-minute cool down and stretching

This exercise formula covers all three basic pillars of fitness. It is very simple, requires no expensive equipment, and takes little time. Without question, it aims in the right direction, and it allows for great flexibility regarding personal resources. Let us further expand on this fitness regimen and see how a typical person would execute this program under each of our three proposed exercise options.

Example Home Gym Program
Five-minute warm up stretching routine:
- Hamstring stretch
- Triceps stretch
- Deltoid Stretch
- Quadriceps stretch
- Calf stretch

We begin our home gym session with some stretches to improve the elasticity of our major muscle groups and to help prevent possible injury. Let's walk through the entire workout together as follows.

FIGURE 5.9: EXERCISE #1 - HAMSTRING STRETCH

Instructions: Sit on the ground with your legs straight out in front of you and bend forward, reaching for your toes with the tips of your fingers. Continue to bend forward as the stretch goes on. You should feel the stretch at the back of both legs. Hold for 30 to 60 seconds.

FIGURE 5.9.1: EXERCISE #2 - TRICEPS STRETCH

Instructions: Place your arm with elbow bent behind your head. Use your opposite arm to provide gentle pressure on the elbow to assist with the stretch. You should feel the stretch in your upper arm. Hold for 30 to 60 seconds.

FIGURE 5.9.2: EXERCISE #3 - DELTOID STRETCH

Instructions: Hold one arm out straight, across your chest. Use your opposite arm to apply gentle pressure to your elbow and upper arm to assist with the stretch. You should feel the stretch in your shoulder. Hold for 30 to 60 seconds.

FIGURE 5.9.3: EXERCISE #4 - QUADRICEPS STRETCH

Instructions: Stand with one leg bent backwards. Grasp the foot of the raised leg with the opposite hand and hold for 30 to 60 seconds. You should feel the stretch in your upper leg.

FIGURE 5.9.4: EXERCISE #5 - CALF STRETCH

Instructions: Stand with one leg in front of the other and lean your weight forward onto the front leg. Ensure the heels of both feet on are on the ground. You should feel the stretch in your back leg.

20 minutes of aerobic exercise:
- 10 minutes of jump rope
- 10 minutes of jogging/running

FIGURE 5.9.5: EXERCISE #6 - 10 MINUTES OF JUMP ROPE

Instructions: Stand with your feet slightly closer than shoulder width apart and time your jumps with the revolution of the jump rope. Remember that the jumping motion is accomplished with the feet and not with the knees.

FIGURE 5.9.6: EXERCISE #7 - 10 MINUTES OF JOGGING/RUNNING

30 minutes of anaerobic exercise (rest for 30 to 60 seconds between sets):
- Push-ups; 4 sets of 25 reps or till exhaustion
- Crunches; 4 sets of 25 reps or till exhaustion
- Squats; 4 sets of 25 reps or till exhaustion
- V-sits; 4 sets of 25 reps or till exhaustion
- Calf raises; 4 sets of 25 reps or till exhaustion

FIGURE 5.9.7 A-B: EXERCISE #8 - PUSH-UPS

Instructions: Lie in a prone position with your weight supported by your hands and the toes of your feet. Ensure that your hands are shoulder-width apart and your feet are placed close together. Lift your body weight via a straightening of your arms. Lower your body back down until the space between your chest and the floor is approximately the width of a fist. This exercise engages the pectoral and triceps muscle groups; you can place your hands closer or further apart to change the angle of the exercise.

FIGURE 5.9.8 A-B: EXERCISE #9 - CRUNCHES

Instructions: This exercise engages the abdominal muscles. Lie flat on your back with your hands behind your head and your knees bent. Contract your abdominals as you lift your upper torso off the mat. Lower your upper torso back down to the starting position to complete the movement. Notice how the lower back does not leave the mat, even at the peak of the movement.

FIGURE 5.9.9 A-B: EXERCISE #10 - SQUATS

Instructions: This exercise engages the quadriceps. Stand with your feet shoulder width apart and your toes pointed slightly outwards. Place your hands together and in front of you. Slowly lower your body weight, then return to a standing position. The depth of the squat determines the level of difficulty. You can vary the width of the stance to change the angle of the exercise.

FIGURE 5.9.10 A-B: EXERCISE #11 - V-SITS

Instructions: Lie flat on your back with your hands behind your head. Simultaneously lift your torso and legs off the mat so that your body forms a 'V' shape. Try to keep your knees straight during the motion. Return to the starting position to complete the motion. This exercise engages the abdominals; the lower abdominals are more emphasized relative to crunches.

FIGURE 5.9.11 A-B: EXERCISE #12 - CALF RAISES

Instructions: This exercise engages the calf muscles. You may find that the calf muscles typically need many repetitions to get a complete workout. Stand on a stair step or platform with your heels hanging off the edge. Hold on to a bannister or support for balance. Slowly lower your body weight so that your heels are lower than the platform you are standing on. Slowly lift your body in the same manner for a complete repetition.

Five-minute cool down stretching routine (Refer back to the warm up section of this workout for a recap of these stretches.):
- Hamstring stretch
- Triceps stretch
- Deltoid stretch
- Quadriceps stretch
- Calf stretch

Home workout complete!

Example Gym Membership Workout Program   Here we will walk through a workout at the gym in the same manner we did for a home gym workout above.

Five-minute warm up stretching routine:

- Pectoral stretch
- Hamstring stretch
- Triceps stretch
- Deltoid stretch
- Quadriceps stretch

FIGURE 5.9.12: STRETCH #1 AT THE GYM - PECTORAL STRETCH

Instructions: Stand with your hand grasping a pole or door frame. Turn your body so that you are facing away from the support. The greater the turn, the greater the stretch. You should feel the stretch in your chest. Hold for 30 to 60 seconds.

FIGURE 5.9.13: STRETCH #2 AT THE GYM - HAMSTRING STRETCH

Instructions: Sit on the ground with your legs straight out in front of you and bend forward, reaching for your toes with the tips of your fingers. Continue to bend forward progressively more as the stretch goes on. You should feel the stretch at the back of both legs. Hold for 30 to 60 seconds.

FIGURE 5.9.14: STRETCH #3 AT THE GYM - TRICEPS STRETCH

Instructions: Place one arm, elbow bent, behind your head. Use your opposite arm to provide gentle pressure on the elbow to assist with the stretch. You should feel the stretch in your upper arm. Hold for 30 to 60 seconds.

FIGURE 5.9.15: STRETCH #4 AT THE GYM - DELTOID STRETCH

Instructions: Cross your straightened arm in front of your chest. Use your opposite arm to apply gentle pressure to your elbow and upper arm in order to assist with the stretch. You should feel the stretch in your shoulder. Hold for 30 to 60 seconds.

FIGURE 5.9.16: STRETCH #5 AT THE GYM - QUADRICEPS STRETCH

Instructions: Stand with one leg raised and bent backwards. Grasp the heel of your raised leg with the opposite hand. You should feel the stretch in your upper leg. Hold for 30 to 60 seconds.

20 minutes of aerobic exercise:
- 20 minutes of stair climber OR
- 20 minutes of jogging/running on treadmill

FIGURE 5.9.17: EXERCISE #6 AT THE GYM - STAIR CLIMBER

FIGURE 5.9.18: EXERCISE #7 AT THE GYM - JOGGING/RUNNING ON TREADMILL

30 minutes of anaerobic exercise (rest for 30 to 60 seconds between sets):
- Abdominal pull-down; 3 to 4 sets of 10−15 reps
- Triceps pull-down; 3 to 4 sets of 10−15 reps
- Pectoral fly; 3 to 4 sets of 10−15 reps
- Biceps curl; 3 to 4 sets of 10−15 reps
- Leg press; 3 to 4 sets of 10−reps
- Lat pull-down; 3 to 4 sets of 10−15 reps

FIGURE 5.9.19 A-B: EXERCISE #8 AT THE GYM - ABDOMINAL PULLDOWN

Instructions: This exercise engages the abdominals. Using a rope pulley attachment, kneel in front of, but facing away from, a pulley machine, with the arm of the pulley extended 45 degrees upwards. Lower your torso and contract your abdominals with your arms grasping the rope from around your shoulders. Return to the starting position to complete the motion. Note: there should be minimal movement of the lower back relative to the upper back.

FIGURE 5.9.20 A-B: EXERCISE #9 AT THE GYM - TRICEPS PULLDOWN

Instructions: This exercise engages the triceps muscles. Attach a revolving straight bar (pictured) to a pulley, adjusted to a near vertical position. With your elbows fixed in place at your sides, pull down on the bar with your palms facing downwards. Return to the starting position to complete the movement. Keeping the elbow fixed in place during the movement ensures maximum effectiveness.

FIGURE 5.9.21 A-B: EXERCISE #10 AT THE GYM - PECTORAL FLY

Instructions: This exercise engages the pectoral muscles. Using your gym's pectoral fly machine, adjust the height so that your arms are chest level when grasping the handles of the arms. With your elbows slightly bent, move the arms so that your hands meet in the middle. Actively contract your pectoral muscles, particularly at the peak of the movement to ensure maximum effectiveness.

FIGURE 5.9.22 A-B: EXERCISE #11 AT THE GYM -
BICEPS CURL

Instructions: This exercise engages the biceps muscles. In a seated position, keep your arm fixed against your knee and lift a free weight up and towards your torso. Bend at the elbow and actively contract your biceps during the motion.

FIGURE 5.9.23 A-B: EXERCISE #12 AT THE GYM - LEG PRESS

Instructions: This exercise engages the quadriceps muscle group. Adjust your gym's leg press machine so that your knees start out at an approximately 90-degree angle. Place your feet approximately shoulder width apart. Using mostly your heels, engage your quadriceps muscles to push on the platform. Be careful not to lock your knees at the peak of the motion, as this risks injury.

FIGURE 5.9.24 A-B: EXERCISE #13 AT THE GYM - LAT PULLDOWN

Instructions: This exercise engages the latissimus dorsi muscles. Using your gym's lat pull-down machine, attach the wide bar to the pulley. Adjust the knee pads so that your body won't rise off the seat during the exercise. Place your hands on the bar with the palms forward and wider than shoulder width apart. Pull the bar downward, with your back slightly curved and chest projected forward at the peak of the motion. As you lower the bar past your chin, squeeze your shoulder blades together.

Five-minute cool down stretching routine (Refer back to the warm up section of this workout for a recap of these stretches.):

- Pectoral stretch
- Hamstring stretch
- Triceps stretch
- Deltoid stretch
- Quadriceps stretch

Gym workout complete!

There are countless different exercise programs out there that you can adopt, and no single guide could possibly cover them all. Go to your local library and pick out some exercise books that look interesting to you. There are many books that deal with specific circumstances that may apply to you as well, such as if you are pregnant, have disabilities or are elderly. Ask for workout routines from your friends who are knowledgeable about exercise. Even Internet forums such as the popular /r/Fitness Subreddit on www.reddit.com are invaluable sources of information.[44] Use a simple notepad to compile different workouts that you would like to try, and don't ever hesitate to carefully attempt something new!

Maintaining variety in your exercise routine and constantly challenging yourself guarantees that you will not grow bored of working out. The program I have provided for you here is a base to start from, but over time you will discover which kinds of exercises you enjoy more than others. You will also discover which kinds of exercise give you better results than others. This author enjoys running immensely and finds it very effective for weight management. Experiment and see what works best for you.

ADDITIONAL EXERCISES

Appendix 2 contains examples of additional exercises that can be mixed and matched with the exercises in the sample routines outlined above.

Sports Club   Specific workouts will of course vary by the type of sport. Just make certain that your program covers all three of the main pillars of physical fitness discussed earlier. If you are unsure, consult your coach or trainer.

This concludes a basic workout program that will meet the needs for both general fitness and health for most individuals. Be sure to consult your doctor before embarking on any exercise program. This proves particularly true for the very young and the elderly. Various methods of exercise to cover the three main pillars of fitness have been offered. I recommend alternating between these different types of exercise in order to stave off monotony. Be creative! Invent new workouts. Change your schedule! Look up new exercise methods from YouTube or from other books.

SLEEP

A final point of consideration is the unsung hero of productivity and health: sleep. Make sure you get enough of it. Many captains of industry and would-be success stories brag about how little sleep they get by with. It's true that those who want to be successful need to get off their butts and get working, but underestimating the importance of sleep is an unbelievable folly. Empirical studies have unequivocally shown that getting less than six to eight hours of sleep for protracted periods of time can lead to all kinds of problems, ranging from weight gain and decreased mental acuity to an increased propensity for heart disease and dementia.[45]

You may think that creating more available time by running on little to no sleep makes you a trooper and more productive, but the truth is that someone who has had sufficient sleep is likely to get more done in the long run as they will be far more effective performers. Pulling all-nighters may occasionally be inevitable, but chronic sleep deprivation is both self-defeating and potentially deadly.[46]

Make sure you get enough sleep!

Far from too little sleep, some individuals suffer from the opposite problem of getting too much sleep. Just as there are negative health effects associated with sleep deprivation, getting too much sleep is not good for one's health either. There is growing evidence that sleeping longer than nine hours a night can have negative impacts on health as well. Again, sleeping within a range of six to eight hours per night is optimal for the typical individual.[47]

Of course, there will be hectic periods of your life when getting a full eight hours of sleep will not be practical. In such cases, research shows that taking a nap during the day can significantly counteract the impact of sleep deprivation.[48] In these situations, any sleep is better than no sleep. A 20 to 30 minute nap is usually sufficient as a restorative measure for your energy level and alertness.

MEASUREMENT: THE UNSUNG HERO OF PROGRESS

In order to maximize your progress in your fitness journey, it's important to measure certain key indicators. Your weight on the scale is the most obvious indicator. Most people who are looking to improve their fitness and appearance will likely want the number on their scale to be going down, rather than up. Certainly, being overweight is, on the whole, a bigger problem for North Americans than being underweight. A falling number on the scale usually means a reduction in body fat—definitely a positive sign. However, we need to get a little more precise about this number. Of course, whether or not the number you see on the scale is too high or too low depends on other factors such as height, gender, age, and muscle mass.

As always, consulting your doctor and getting a physical exam is better than reading any book. A physician or specialist will have access to all kinds of precise tools, such as skin fold calipers, that you will likely not have at home; additionally, a specialist will have greater experience in handling specialized instruments and tools. Finally, a specialist will be able to interpret test results with a trained eye, particularly as there are many variables that can skew the results of health-related examinations.

Nonetheless there are many helpful key measurements that can be performed at home, and doing them on our own will allow you to perform them at your convenience. The first of these is the Body Mass Index (BMI) test. Your BMI score is a modified ratio of your weight to your height and is calculated utilizing the following formula.[49]

$$BMI = weight(kg)/height(m)^2$$

Using nothing more than a simple bathroom scale and a tape measure we can calculate your BMI. The Government of Canada has published guidelines on interpreting your BMI score as follows:

FIGURE 5.10: HEALTH RISK CLASSIFICATION ACCORDING TO BODY MASS INDEX (BMI)[50]

Classification	BMI Category (kg/m^2)	Risk of Developing Health Problems
Underweight	< 18.5	Increased
Normal Weight	18.5 - 24.9	Least
Overweight	25.0 - 29.9	Increased
Obese Class 1	30.0 - 34.9	High
Obese Class 2	35.0 - 39.9	Very High
Obese Class 3	> = 40.0	Extremely High

Keep in mind that these ranges are approximations only and should therefore be interpreted with caution. For starters, the BMI classification system isn't designed for people who are under 18 years old or for those who are pregnant. Furthermore, results can be skewed by those whose body types are statistical outliers—including those who are exceptionally tall or elite level athletes who have a lot of muscle mass.

As you exercise more and eat an improved diet, keep track of changes in your BMI over time. A BMI that is above the 'normal weight' classification but is decreasing will, generally, be a desirable trend. The opposite will be true for someone whose BMI is below 'normal weight' but trending upwards. You can use your BMI score in conjunction with the calorie budgeting and exercise tools we discussed earlier to determine where you should focus your efforts. As a simple example, if your BMI is too high, look to reduce your calorie consumption and increase your weekly amounts of aerobic exercise. Your BMI score is an invaluable tool in providing a general overview of the current state of your health and fitness.

The next tool I would like to discuss is a rather simple one—the measuring tape. Using a standard measuring tape, you can keep track of changes in the circumference of various parts of your body in order to determine your progress. It's a low-tech tool, but an effective one. Have you been working on increasing mass in your biceps or pectoral muscles? The measuring tape will be a far more objective tool than simply looking in the mirror. Do you want to see if your waist has shrunk due to a reduction in body fat? Again, the measuring tape will help to prevent distortions caused by a full stomach or a shrunken pair of pants. Just make sure that when you're measuring the same part of your body over time that you really do have the measuring tape on the same spot. Letting the measuring tape drift will distort your results!

MENTAL HEALTH

YOUR MIND AND YOUR BODY

First and foremost, it is important for you to be happy about your body. You must love and accept yourself for who and what you are. You are beautiful no matter what anyone says to the contrary. The purpose of this chapter has been to persuade you into adopting a healthier lifestyle, but an added bonus is that it can help you to look and feel more attractive. Good nutrition—combined with a robust exercise program—will practically guarantee good weight loss and muscle toning results. It is imperative that you realize such results require hard work and dedication to the task. Bulimia, anorexia, and steroid use are no substitutes for the healthy habits and work-out strategies described in this chapter. In fact, the former two are recognized as mental health disorders. All things excellent are as difficult as they are rare, and achieving six-pack abs is no exception. Love yourself and your body, and enjoy the never-ending journey of self-improvement.

YOUR LOCUS OF CONTROL

There are essentially two types of mental attitudes people adopt in their approach to the world: these two mental attitudes are the internal locus and external locus of control. The essential difference is in regards to the level of control that an individual believes they have over events and circumstance in their life.[51]

People with a strong internal locus of control believe that their life circumstances are influenced or shaped through their own decisions, effort, and behavior. These individuals accept that they are responsible for directing their lives. People with a strong external locus of control believe that their life circumstances are controlled by external events such as fate, luck, God, or powerful other beings.[52] In a sense, it is as if these people allow life to push them around.

There is some evidence to suggest that individuals with an internal locus of control are more likely to end up with happy and satisfying results with the events of their lives as they unfold.[53] It is true that everyone in life is dealt at least a slightly different hand; however, it is in the best interest of your happiness and well-being to do the best with what you have been given in life.

WHERE DOES GOOD MENTAL HEALTH COME FROM?

At its core, good mental health comes from ascending the levels of The Paradigm of Happiness. The Paradigm of Happiness is a model that distills all the salient factors that are relevant to living a fulfilling and successful life. When we live lives that are constructive rather than destructive, we are more likely to experience greater levels of emotional satisfaction and happiness. Our thoughts and actions affect our mental health. In turn, our mental health has bearing on our future actions. This relationship between thoughts, emotions, actions and mental health builds into a feedback loop that can be used to reinforce both positive and negative life choices.

SOME EXERCISES FOR POSITIVE MENTAL HEALTH

1. Reflection   Western society in particular is very concerned with activity and the idea of "keeping busy." However, what's lost due to the non-stop activities is time to truly think, time to simply reflect, collect our thoughts, and plan ahead. Set aside 15 to 20 minutes every day or so to simply sit down, stare out the window and think. This personal time is invaluable. This time allows you to gather your thoughts and see your whole life and direction through a clearer perspective–a wider vantage point. You will have many epiphanies and perhaps even life changing thoughts simply by sitting and thinking. Letting your mind wander can do wonders.

2. Meditation   Although reflection and meditation appear to be similar activities, meditation is nonetheless distinctly different from reflection. Meditation is the practice of letting your mind clear itself so that you think of nothing. Absolutely nothing. Your mind needs rest just like every other part of your body. Unfortunately, not many people get that kind of mental rest. To meditate, sit down in a quiet environment, close your eyes, and relax. Don't think. It's harder than it sounds. Just relax. Focus on something internal that is either constant or rhythmic. This can be your breathing, the traditional "om" sound, or any other kind of cadence you prefer. I prefer to focus on my breathing. Keep your eyes closed and relax like this for fifteen minutes to half an hour, focusing only on the rhythmic action of your breathing. The goal of the exercise is to quiet your mind.

When you first attempt meditation you will likely find that you simply can't get your mind to quiet down. Incessant random thoughts will enter your head. Everything from what you should eat for your next meal to what your best friend from elementary school is up to right now will pop into your consciousness (this is sometimes referred to as "monkey mind"). Before you know it, you will have forgotten about your breathing altogether. Don't give up, though. After a few weeks of practice you will soon find that your mind begins to slow down and quiet down. Anxieties and pressures of the day begin to leave you. You will find yourself more collected. Your thoughts will be more orderly. Your concentration improves. This is the point of meditation: to learn to control and quiet your own mind.

3. Low Intensity Cardiovascular Exercise   The aerobic exercise we discussed earlier can have the added advantage of being highly meditative—as long as it is a relatively low-intensity exercise such as walking or leisurely swimming. When doing cardio, the brain experiences increased blood flow and oxygenation, which allows for clearer thinking. This along with the repetitive action of exercise allows the mind to wander and relax. Some of your best creative ideas can come from doing exercise.

MENTAL ILLNESS

Mental health disorders such as anxiety disorders, depression, and anorexia are notorious for going undiagnosed and untreated, and are often referred to as silent illnesses for this very reason.[54] Some specific types of mental health disorders include obsessive compulsive disorder, social anxiety, bipolar disorder, and alcohol/ substance abuse. If you or anyone around you starts to display symptoms related to mental health disorders such as anxiety; depression; or anorexia, call a help line and seek medical attention immediately.

Although it is beyond the scope of this book to describe specific symptoms, the Canadian Mental Health Association (CMHA) notes that changes in emotions (e.g., feeling sad, hopeless or angry), thoughts (e.g., difficulty concentrating, comments that reflect low self-esteem or self-blame), behaviours (e.g., sleeping and eating more or less than usual, becoming withdrawn, reacting more strongly to events) and physical health (e.g., experiencing more aches and pains, fatigue) are clues that someone might be experiencing a mood disorder.[55]

To learn more about these kinds of mental health challenges and where to get help, consult a reputable organization such as the Canadian Mental Health Association or an equivalent organization if you live outside of Canada.[56]

SOME LAST THOUGHTS ON GENERAL HEALTH

This should go without saying, but heavy drinking, smoking, and using illicit drugs (or misusing prescription medications) are three behaviours that can ruin your health and your life. For some individuals, experimental or recreational use of alcohol, tobacco or illicit drugs can quickly spiral into both physical or psychological dependence on these substances and serious health issues. Ideally, it is best to avoid drugs and tobacco and be prudent about alcohol consumption as reducing or quitting use of these substances requires tremendous self-discipline and commitment.

I invite readers to engage in a little thought experiment with me. Imagine for a moment that at the age of 18 you were given a free car by an anonymous benefactor. As you can imagine, there is a catch. The catch is that this is the only car you can possibly own for the rest of your entire life. You're never going to be able to own another one, no matter how much money you earn. Now, if you knew that this was the only car you were ever going to own, you would certainly take excellent care of it. You would read the manual multiple times over. You would change the oil and rotate the tires regularly. You would take care of any scratches or dings that developed. You would be sure not to drive it too hard.

Your body is like this car: It is the only one that you will ever have for your entire life. Many people don't treat their body that way, however. They abuse their bodies and neglect their health. Much like with the car, you want to do everything you can to keep it in tip top shape. That means eating the right foods, avoiding substances that damage the body, taking care of injuries, and getting regular exercise. Remember, you only get one body for your entire life!

ACTION STEPS BEFORE READING THE NEXT CHAPTER

TO-DO: HEALTH AND FITNESS
- Use the nutritional guidelines in this chapter to write down a list of healthy foods to buy when you next visit the grocery store.
- Write down on your calendar what times of the week you will dedicate to exercise (see Chapter 6 for more on time management).
- Meditate for 10 minutes before proceeding to the next chapter.

RECOMMENDED READING

RECOMMENDED FURTHER READING ON NUTRITION
- *Nutrition Almanac: Fight Disease, Boost Immunity, and Slow the Effects of Aging,* John Kirschmann

RECOMMENDED FURTHER READING ON EXERCISE
- *The New Encyclopedia of Modern Bodybuilding,* Arnold Schwarzenegger
- *The Art of Expressing the Human Body,* Bruce Lee, John Little

RECOMMENDED FURTHER READING ON MENTAL HEALTH
- *How to Stop Worrying and Start Living,* Dale Carnegie
- *A Natural Approach to Mental Wellness: Japanese Psychology and the Skills We Need for Psychological and Spiritual Health,* Gregg Krech

CHAPTER 6
PERSONAL HABITS

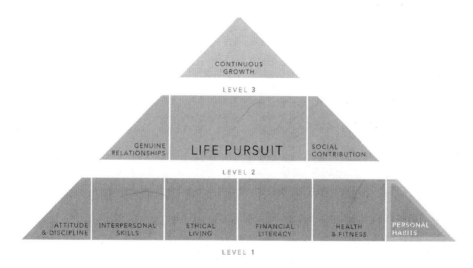

THE PARADIGM OF HAPPINESS

Nobody plans to fail, but many fail to plan. The purpose of this chapter is to develop a robust framework for decision making, personal planning, organizational skills, and effective daily routines. How many readers can truly deny that having a greater sense of rhyme and reason to their daily schedules would reduce their personal stress, and thus increase their overall satisfaction with life? This chapter serves to tie together all of the topics covered in the previous five chapters, such as exercise habits and social endeavours, into a cohesive whole. This newly minted organizational paradigm will then serve as a perfect springboard to the next levels of The Paradigm of Happiness, which will be covered in the upcoming chapters of this book.

TIME MANAGEMENT

Time is the world's most precious non-renewable resource. Even for the most powerful, wealthy, and well connected individuals, there is no way to replenish this inexorably scarce commodity. Here I shall propose a simple self-management system consisting of two primary tools to maximize your effective use of time:

1. A to-do list
2. A calendar

These two tools are ubiquitous and exist in both electronic and paper forms. I leave it to the reader to decide which medium best suits them. Both the to-do list and calendar are most powerful when used together rather than individually. In my system, I use the to-do list, formatted as either bullet points or numbered items, to record all the tasks that are important to complete but are *not* time specific. I use the calendar, on the other hand, to record and assign deadlines to important tasks that are scheduled for specific times.

As a simple example, a dentist appointment would obviously qualify as a time-specific event, so it would be added to the reader's calendar. By way of contrast, a self-assigned task such as cleaning one's room would not normally be considered time sensitive, so it would be noted on the to-do list as an item to be completed at the reader's convenience.

In effect, the calendar provides some basic structure for your day. You are then free to check off items on your to-do list during your free blocks of time. If all of our daily tasks were simply written on a to-do list, the result would be chaos. Conversely, if those same tasks were all solidified within a specific time frame on a calendar, the consequence would be an unrealistically rigid schedule. In my personal life, I have found that the most sensible approach makes use of both tools. Here is a sample pairing of a to-do list (Figure 6.1) and calendar (Figure 6.2) for illustration.

FIGURE 6.1: A SAMPLE TO-DO LIST OF ITEMS THAT ARE NOT TIME-SENSITIVE OR TIME-SPECIFIC

To-Do List

- 0 Completed
- ○ Clean room
- ○ Call Grandma about her meat loaf recipe
- ○ Do dishes
- ○ Rotate tires on car
- ○ Practice monologue for acting class

FIGURE 6.2: AN EXAMPLE OF A CALENDAR WITH SCHEDULED EVENTS

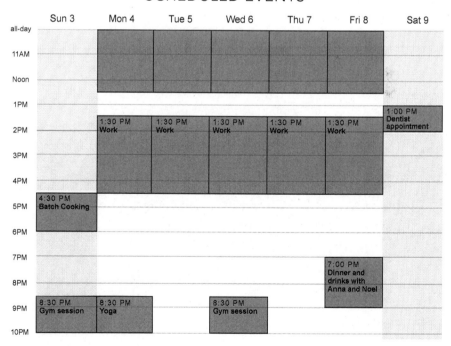

As you can see from these examples, activities scheduled for specific dates or hours, such as work, gym classes, and social appointments with others, are logged into specific time blocks within the calendar. The empty spaces represent time that has not been reserved for anything specific. It is within these empty spaces that we can tackle the tasks on our to-do list. This combination of rigidity and fluidity gives us the ability to be both punctual and flexible at the same time.

You can also see that I have reserved Sunday afternoons for cooking lunch in large batches for the coming work week (refer to Chapter 5 for our discussion on healthy eating). In order for food to remain fresh throughout an entire week, remember to cook foods that can be readily frozen without a loss in taste when defrosted. Some dishes that I could have made include lasagna, soup, chili, samosas, stew, meat loaf, or one of the recipes recommended in the previous chapter. These are all foods that keep well when frozen. While many of these meals should be accompanied by a side of vegetables, remember to *not* freeze leafy greens.

After cooking a large batch of your food of choice, take five BPA-free plastic food containers (one for each day of the work week) and place a meal's worth of the food into each one, along with your chosen vegetables. You might also want to make a label for each container to indicate the date on which the food was cooked. You have now pre-cooked an entire week's worth of lunches. This provides our readers with the following benefits:

1. It saves time: It only requires one cooking session to prepare a week's worth of lunches.
2. It ensures portion control: This can aid in the maintenance of a healthy weight.
3. It saves money: Pre-cooked lunches can help to prevent costly meals eaten out at restaurants.
4. It reduces stress.

It is important to be goal-oriented when making a schedule. It is not enough to simply write down everything that one plans to do, or has an appointment for. Be sure that upon committing to an appointment, a dinner date, a study session, or whatever the activity may be, that the event is of true benefit and utility. Having an organized schedule around activities that do not benefit you is no better than not having a schedule at all. Police yourself and be goal-oriented. Ensure that all the activities you spend your precious time on are contributing to your life goals. (Refer back to our relevant discussion on Personal Constitutions in Chapter 1.)

HOW TO MINIMIZE TIME WASTING

In addition to planning to-do lists and calendar appointments, there is an additional tool the reader can employ in order to minimize procrastination: time tracking. Time tracking is a strategy that involves entering your daily activities for each hour into your calendar as a way of enforcing accountability. The idea behind such a strategy is to make individuals extremely cognizant of their recent actions. As an example, someone who has spent the past 60 minutes doing nothing but browsing Facebook will be made acutely aware that they have not been doing anything productive. By making time-wasting activities more apparent, we are not only able to weed out inefficiencies in our schedules, but also motivate ourselves to work more effectively.

The calendar below shows an example of this strategy in action. Notice that there are entries for appointments and activities that were planned, and additional entries for those same time slots for what I actually ended up doing during that time. Accountability allows us to put our actual day-to-day activities in perspective.

FIGURE 6.3: AN EXAMPLE OF A WEEKLY CALENDAR WITH BOTH PLANNED AND ACTUAL ACTIVITIES

	Sun 3	Mon 4	Tue 5	Wed 6	Thu 7	Fri 8	Sat 9
all-day	Lunch with Dad						
1PM	Drive Home	12:30 PM Lunch at work & call Grandma about meatloaf recipe	12:30 PM Lunch at work & read book				1:00 PM Dentist appointment
2PM	1:30 PM Read Book	1:30 PM Work / 1:30 PM Work	1:30 PM Work / 1:30 PM Work	1:30 PM Work	1:30 PM Work	1:30 PM Work	
3PM							
4PM	3:15 PM Rotate tires on car						
5PM	4:15 PM Batch Cooking / 4:30 PM Batch Cooking	Drive Home	Drive Home				
6PM	6:00 PM Dinner with Family	5:15 PM Browse Facebook and news / Dinner	Shower / 5:45 PM Dinner				
7PM	Dishes	6:45 PM Watch TV	6:30 PM Browse Facebook and Instagram			7:00 PM Dinner and drinks with Anna and Noel	
8PM	7:15 PM Watch TV						
	Drive to Gym	Drive to Yoga					
9PM	8:45 PM Gym session / 8:30 PM Gym session	6:30 PM Yoga / 6:30 PM Yoga		6:30 PM Gym session			
10PM	Drive Home	Drive Home					
11PM	Shower & brush teeth / 11:00 PM Read in bed	10:15 PM Practice monologue for acting class / 11:15 PM Browse Internet					
12AM							

On the calendar shown in Figure 6.3, planned activities are in light grey and *actual* activities are in dark grey. This allows us to make a direct visual comparison between what was planned and what was *done*. This is a very powerful tool. We can already see how this person decided to allocate their time to complete tasks on the to-do list. On Sunday, when they created this schedule, they rotated the tires on the car and did the dishes. The following day they called Grandma about her meat loaf recipe. So far, so good.

We can also see where there are some inefficiencies in this person's schedule. This individual has a bad habit of idly browsing the Internet and watching TV, particularly in the evening. This is understandable as most people experience something of an energy slump upon arriving home after a long day at work. Nonetheless, it becomes clear from our time tracking exercise that this is an area where the person could use their time more effectively and be more productive. Now that they are aware of this idle time, they can devise strategies to try to avoid time-wasting activities. Perhaps they could enlist their significant other or a close friend to keep them in check after work. Or, maybe they can block off this time specifically for family activities. Such commitment can really help to prevent time wasting.

ADDITIONAL ASPECTS OF TIME MANAGEMENT

It is sound advice to dedicate the beginning of every week, a few moments perhaps, to quickly review the calendar contents of the upcoming seven days. Giving yourself this bird's eye view of the future may take as little as a minute or two, but it can do wonders for your organization as you internalize upcoming events. In addition, you may find that taking a few moments every evening just before bed to review the next day's events has similar benefits. You will find that your mind will begin to intuitively fill in the blanks spots of your calendar with items from your to-do list. Anyone's overall productivity should increase markedly by adopting this system.

The reader will also find that combining a robust planning framework with the motivation and positive mental attitude fostered in will provide further impressive gains in productivity and achievement. A determined and inspired individual with a well-polished schedule is unlikely to fall short of their aspirations. This represents an even greater achievement than you may think.

Remember to guard your time jealously. Time truly is your most valuable resource and is indifferent to your feelings toward it. You are spending time every second of every day regardless of whether you want to savour it or accelerate it. Whatever time has passed cannot be recovered, so always be aware of how you are utilizing it. Do this by keeping your personal goals in mind. Think to yourself, "Is what I'm doing right now benefitting me in any way, or is it hurting me? Is this really helping me accomplish my objectives?" Be particularly wary of time sinks. These are tasks that by their nature take up inordinately long amounts of time with little to no benefit to you in return. These tasks are varied and can include anything from video game and television addiction to those tiring, bureaucracy-filled business meetings where nothing really gets done. Trust your instinct. You will know from a very distinct sense of apprehension at

FORREST WONG

the back of your mind that what you're doing is a waste of time. Try to minimize your involvement with such activities.

Commute time is an especially large time sink for many people. It is particularly troubling because it is so easily justifiable. It is also practically impossible (not to mention dangerous) to attempt to be productive while driving. As a result, that travel time ends up being nothing but a personal encumbrance. Do your best to try to cut down on time spent commuting to different places. Use the planning tools covered earlier in this chapter to improve personal efficiency by combining multiple errands into a single trip. You will save both time and money. If driving is an unavoidably large part of your daily routine, try downloading audio books such as those I have suggested at the end of this chapter (or other titles that resonate with you), and use your driving time to listen to them. If you primarily ride public transit, feel free to read the physical book. This will at least help to maximize the utility of your limited time. Think critically about how you can make better use of idle time and use those valuable minutes for more productive activities throughout the day. For instance, the batch cooking techniques described earlier in this book can be of great help. The rewards are worth the effort as the savings add up quickly.

Finally, viewing a motivational video at the beginning of every day helps to fuel your mind. Numerous motivational videos that value high productivity can be found online for free on YouTube. Simply querying "motivational video" will yield many results. It has often been said that motivation doesn't last, much like bathing; hence, the reason it's important to watch a video every day. Starting your day off with a motivational message can help to spur on your productivity and energy.

SECONDARY PLANNING TOOLS

In addition to the primary planning tools presented above, there are many secondary planning tools that can prove useful for personal projects or work related goals. The first of these is the Linear Progress Indicator, a chart that can easily be made in spreadsheet/ chart software.

Linear Progress Indicator   This simple tool consists of a chart that plots the progress a person or team has made on a task on the y-axis (vertical line) against time on the x-axis (horizontal line). Figure 6.4 is an example of a Linear Progress Indicator for a hypothetical project. The project has a one-year deadline, and the team has drawn a projected progress line represented in dark grey. This line is what the team will be "competing" against when pursuing the project. Their actual progress will be tracked using a light grey line.

FIGURE 6.4: EXAMPLE OF A LINEAR PROGRESS INDICATOR SHOWING THE IDEAL OR PROJECTED PROGRESS OVER TIME

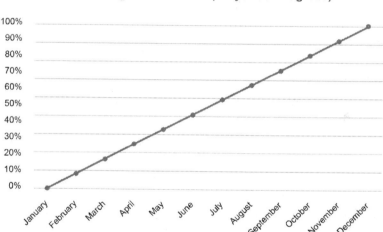

Linear Progress Indicator (Projected Progress)

If the team stays perfectly on schedule and makes progress on their task, the line marking their progress will match the dark grey line, and this would be a roughly one-to-one relationship between progress and time. However, if the team's progress has lagged behind this benchmark, the line tracking their progress will be below the dark grey line. By contrast, if they are ahead of schedule, the line tracking their progress will be above the dark grey line. The Linear Progress indicator allows the user to determine, at a quick glance, the progress they have made on a project or task relative to the time they have left. Very useful!

Figure 6.5 is an example of what the Linear Progress Indicator would look like if the team fell behind schedule and caught up in the final months of the year-long project. Their projection is outlined in dark grey and their actual progress in light grey.

FIGURE 6.5: EXAMPLE OF A LINEAR PROGRESS INDICATOR SHOWING ACTUAL VERSUS PROJECTED PROGRESS

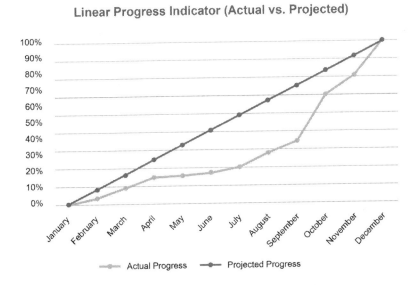

Figure 6.6 is an example of what the Linear Progress Indicator would look like if the team started and finished the project ahead of schedule. Again, projected progress is outlined in dark grey while actual progress is outlined in light grey.

FIGURE 6.6: AN EXAMPLE OF A PROJECT THAT IS AHEAD OF SCHEDULE

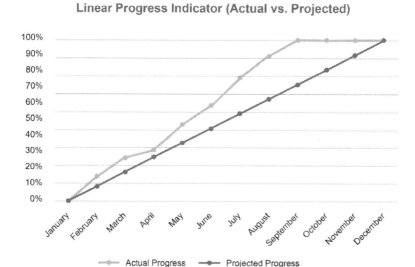

Linear Progress Indicator charts can easily be created by hand, on paper, or digitally via spreadsheet software such as Excel. Choose what works best for you!

Stagger Chart   The Stagger Chart is a forecasting and planning tool that is commonly used in business management, but its usefulness is not limited to giant corporations. The following is an example of how a Stagger Chart works.

Let's say one day we decide to open our own business selling artisanal cookies from home. Our profit in this venture will depend entirely upon the number of cookies we sell. Before long, we start to get a sense of what our future orders will look like based on social media shares, word of mouth, and our website hits. We start forecasting what our cookie orders might look like for the next 90 days and write it down accordingly. (See Figure 6.7) As each month passes, our past predictions are compared with our more recent predictions, and eventually our actual results.

FIGURE 6.7: AN EXAMPLE MONTHLY FORECAST OF ORDERS FOR ARTISANAL COOKIES IN A STAGGER CHART

2016 — *Forecast for the Month of:*

Forecast Made in the Month of:	Jan	Feb	Mar	Apr	May	June	July	Aug	Sept	Oct	Nov	Dec
Jan	25	27	39									
Feb	*24	24	35	42								
Mar		*20	13	41	24							
Apr			*10	63	43	37						
May				*54	45	33	48					
June					*42	48	37	41				
July						*40	54	50	33			
Aug							*47	50	45	35		
Sept								*45	41	30	29	
Oct												
Nov												
Dec												

On a month-by-month basis, results and new predictions are entered into the chart. Updates and changes to forecasts are made monthly, with final results posted in the ensuing months. This tool allows us to compare forecasts with actual results and to predict whether project completion deadlines will be met or missed. The columns show the months of the year we are forecasting. The rows show which month the forecast was actually made. As the forecasts are updated, we accrue a useful historical record.

You can see in Figure 6.7 that our forecasts during the year have been consistently higher than the actual result for the relevant month. This is valuable information because it tells us that our forecasting technique needs some work. Perhaps better sources of data could be used, or a kind of "loss allowance" could be implemented that could make our future forecasts more accurate.

Without such a chart, it would be far more difficult to see the contrast between our predictions and actual outcomes.

Stagger Charts can be used as a forecasting tool for practically any project. Use your imagination! They can be used for small time scales such as hours, or large time scales such as years. For example, we might forecast that we will accomplish two hours of work per day on a personal project, based on our other commitments. If we find that we seem to consistently fall short of this goal over protracted periods of time, then we can investigate why we're falling behind schedule and solve the problem.

PERSONAL ORGANIZATION

CLEANING AND ORGANIZING YOUR HOME

Personal organization is vital to becoming as effective and efficient as possible in your day-to-day endeavours. Beyond improving your work flow and reducing your personal stress, having a clean and tidy living area will improve your social and romantic interactions. Imagine the indelible impression it would leave in the mind of a new romantic partner upon seeing stains and mildew in your bathroom, or smelling dirty socks and underwear in your bedroom. Such a sight would be highly unpleasant to say the least. Furthermore, an unkempt home can be depressing for *you*.

So, the immediate order of business is to clean and organize your home. There are three key pillars to this project:

1. going through your possessions and throwing out anything you no longer need or want,
2. cleaning your living area, and
3. organizing whatever is left.

Clearing your Space   Throwing unwanted or unneeded items out of the house can give your home an entirely new look by letting the "air" back in. Start in your bedroom. Are there books from high school sitting on your shelf that you know you will never read again? Donate them. Are there empty pizza boxes and pop cans lying around in your room? Put them in the recycling and garbage, of course. Are there clothes in your closet that don't fit anymore? Donate those, too.

Move to your living areas, look around closely, and repeat the same process you used in your bedroom. Be brutally honest about what you see. Do not burden yourself with anything you do not truly want or need. Throw it out, donate it, or recycle it. When these areas are done, move to your kitchen. Depending on how disciplined you are about disposing of food that is past its expiry date, this may be the most unpleasant part of the project. Search through your cupboards, shelves, and your fridge. Check for freshness and use-by dates and throw out anything you know you will not eat. You may notice afterwards that the smell in your kitchen and dining areas has suddenly improved. Round up everything you plan on throwing out, and take it all to your curbside trash bin. Step 1 of the project is complete.

Cleaning your Space   Moving on to Step 2, you must now clean your home. Before beginning, check to see that you have ample cleaning supplies such as rags, a mop, a broom, dust pan, glass cleaner, gloves, a vacuum cleaner, and general purpose cleaning fluid available. If you do not have a vacuum cleaner and do not wish to spend money obtaining one, try to borrow one from a friend.

Begin cleaning right now. Do not delay. The longer house work is delayed, the more likely it will never be completed at all. Maintaining momentum and progress is paramount. Start with the area in your home that most desperately needs cleaning. For most houses this is either the bathroom or the kitchen.

In the bathroom, scrub the area around the base of the toilet. Scum builds up very quickly there. Scrub your shower walls and doors free of any grime. Wipe down your mirror, and remove any hair that may be clogging your drains. In the kitchen, grease that permeates through the air from cooking will find its way on to almost every surface and make it sticky to the touch. Try to wipe down as many exposed kitchen surfaces as you can safely reach. Be sure to clean the inside of your microwave oven as well.

Once these areas of your home have been cleaned, the rest of your house will likely be comparatively easy. Vacuum the bedrooms, and sweep and mop the floors of your living areas and hallways. Wipe down any hardwood furniture and dusty light fixtures that are within relatively easy reach. Finally, wash your sheets, pillow cases, and any dirty laundry that has accumulated.

Organizing your Space   Let us now move to Step 3, organizing your home. As you begin, remember that this organizational project is intended to improve your personal efficiency and effectiveness, above all else. First, create a work space. This will be the home base that supports your productivity. Make this space a kind of "temple." It is the central place for your work. A dedicated room is best, but having this space integrated with your bedroom will suffice if space is limited. The "feel" of the room should be both comfortable and energetic.

A single desk with drawers or a separate filing cabinet will be enough for most people. However, I recommend getting two desks, if possible. One should be reserved for paper work while the other will be for your computer and printer. A single large "L" shaped desk is also great for these purposes. Make sure there is ample lighting. A bright, overhead light and a desk lamp will allow for variability, depending on the time of day and your mood. Buy some stationery and office supplies for your new office.

FIGURE 6.8: AN EXAMPLE OF A WELL-ORGANIZED OFFICE WITH AN "L" SHAPED DESK FOR PRODUCTIVITY

You may want to consider purchasing a large whiteboard to place on your wall. I have found such a tool to be highly useful for planning and brainstorming. You might want to put your to-do list on this board. If you have a physical calendar, secure it to the wall right next to the whiteboard. When it comes to digital productivity, strongly consider purchasing multiple computer monitors for your computers as this can vastly improve your productivity and comfort when working. Set up two trays, labeled "in" and "out" to keep workloads manageable. Finally, invest in a comfortable chair. It is highly unlikely that you will regret purchasing an adjustable office chair with an especially comfortable seat.

Your kitchen should be the next place that you organize. The key here is to make the kitchen a place to create and store nutritious, fast, and healthy meals. Allocate dedicated spaces in both your freezer and fridge for "batch cooked" meals packed in plastic food containers. Put meals that are not going to be consumed within the next 48 hours in their dedicated section of the freezer, while meals that *are* going to be consumed within the next 48 hours should be put in their dedicated section of the fridge. This allows for a simple system for storing pre-cooked, portion-controlled meals.

FIGURE 6.9: AN EXAMPLE OF A WELL-ORGANIZED FREEZER WITH BATCH-COOKED MEALS

Place a bowl of fruit on your kitchen table or other easily accessible place. This will make it easier to ensure you are eating the recommended daily servings of fruit.

FIGURE 6.10: KEEPING HEALTHY FOODS IN PLAIN VIEW WILL ENCOURAGE FREQUENT CONSUMPTION

In your bedroom, be sure to make the bed every day and organize your clothing according to function. For example, you might want to store all of your professional clothes in your closet, whereas your casual clothing, underwear and socks, and gym clothes could be stored in separate drawers in your dresser. Keep a laundry basket nearby for clothes that need to be washed. Wash your clothing as soon as there is enough in the laundry basket to constitute a single load. Try not to procrastinate as the more errands and chores tend to pile up, the less likely we are to do them.

Keep your keys and personal items in a dedicated spot in a tray or bowl near your front door. Keep a pen and pad of paper for grocery lists nearby, as well. Make sure your bathroom is well stocked with toiletries such as toothpaste, floss, mouthwash, and the like, and be sure to keep them neatly organized. Finally, once you are organized, do not let useless household items accumulate within your home in the future. Recycle, donate, give away, and throw away anything that you do not need anymore. The accumulation of clutter can be insidious.

PERSONAL HABITS

According to Warren Buffett, a wealthy U.S. philanthropist whom I'll discuss in more detail later, "The chains of habit are too light to be felt until they are too heavy to be broken."[1] While true, far too many observers interpret this quote as being negative—usually with some vague picture of alcoholism or gambling addiction in their minds. While this is certainly a valid interpretation, there are far more positive interpretations to be drawn from this piece of sage advice: Good habits are just as hard to break as bad habits.

In this section of the book, I would like to suggest adopting a number of personal habits that will likely pay huge dividends to the reader later in life. In fact, success in life can simply be considered as the accumulation of many small positive habits that form a collection which is much greater than the sum of its parts.

PERSONAL HYGIENE

Let us begin with a consideration of personal hygiene habits. The need for good hygiene seems obvious, but the reader can probably think of one or two people they have encountered who don't seem to share this belief. In addition to the personal satisfaction that comes from general cleanliness, good hygiene can positively affect everything in your life from romance to obtaining employment. A superb resume can easily be marred by a disheveled and unkempt appearance.

Twenty to thirty minutes of daily attention to personal hygiene and grooming can go a long way. Think of it as performing "maintenance" on your body, like you would on your home. These maintenance activities include regular showering, keeping nails trimmed, flossing, and getting regular checkups at the dentist. This small expenditure of time and energy into your hygiene and personal appearance is a good investment. Both your short and long-term physical and mental well-being will be improved.

FASHION[1]

In addition to hygiene, let us now consider personal appearance. Let's first look at your wardrobe. The types of different attire that a person can wear are practically limitless, but for our purposes we will categorize the different kinds of attire into five distinct styles: business, business casual, formal, semi-formal, and casual. I will also consider men's and women's fashion separately. Let's begin with some fashion principles.

Clinton Kelly, of *What Not to Wear* fame, tells us that there are three universal principles to all fashion and style:

1. Fit: Wear clothes that are neither too big nor too small.
2. Proportion: Wear outfits and accessories that complement or "even out" the relative size of various parts of your body.
3. Appropriateness: Do *not* wear your pajamas to a job interview. *Do* wear a suit.[2]

FASHION FOR MEN

Men's Business Wear   Suits are important for job interviews, formal occasions that crop up from time to time, and meetings. Every adult and youth should have a suit at his disposal. Be aware that properly tailored suits can't simply be bought in a quick flash when needed. Fitting and alteration takes time. Every man will find a type of suit that is most appropriate for him. Certain patterns, styles, and colours flatter some body types and skin tones more than others. Get fitted for a suit at your local men's clothing store, have it altered, and have a suit in reserve.

Having a suit tailored will significantly improve its appearance and comfort. Few men will find a suit off the rack that is a perfect fit for them. However, tailoring does cost extra money. If push comes to shove, and an off the rack suit is the only choice, be sure to try on many options for the best possible fit, as fit will impact the suit's appearance as much, possibly more, as material and workmanship.

When it comes to suits, you typically get what you pay for up to about mid-range pricing, which usually means paying up to

[1]   I would like to thank my friend and fashion maven, Dana Soviala, for providing much of the information for the fashion section of this book.

$1,000 for a full suit. However, even $500 can buy you a very decent suit these days. Prices above the $1,000 threshold start to give significantly diminished returns, both in terms of appearance and comfort. There's no need to pay more when the value isn't there.

When shopping for a suit, notice the difference in the "feel" of the various price ranges in terms of fabric and stitching. Ask a sales associate to let you try on a few jackets, and notice the differences in how they feel. In terms of fabric, the general hierarchy is that polyester suits are of the lowest quality, cotton is mid-range, and wool is the highest quality. Keep this in mind when looking around, especially if someone is trying to sell you a polyester suit for $2,000!

As always, when shopping for anything expensive, go to multiple stores and seek multiple options before spending your hard-earned money.

If you can only have one suit, make sure to select a charcoal-coloured suit. Charcoal is a sort of "catch all" colour that will be appropriate for the greatest variety of social events and will work with the greatest variety of colour combinations of shirts and ties. Make sure your shoes always match your belt. Your tie colour should complement your shirt colour, but the two do not have to match.

FIGURE 6.11: AN EXAMPLE OF WELL-FITTED MEN'S BUSINESS ATTIRE

Men's Formal Wear   When it comes to extremely formal occasions such as weddings, these events usually demand a tuxedo, not a suit. The primary difference between the two is that a tuxedo will be worn with a bowtie instead of a necktie, and the jacket itself will typically have some satin. In addition, tuxedos are almost exclusively black or white in colour. The difference in social implication is even greater as tuxedos are usually only worn in special circumstances, such as a prom. In fact, most people wear tuxedos so infrequently that it makes more sense to simply rent one for the occasion. The time, expense, and effort of keeping a tuxedo in reserve in your personal wardrobe is usually not worth bearing for the small number of times you will wear it.

FIGURE 6.12: TUXEDOS ARE THE CHOICE OF ATTIRE FOR THE MOST FORMAL OF OCCASIONS

Men's Business Casual Wear   You should have at least three to four business casual outfits in your wardrobe—more if you wear them to work often. The tough part about business casual (for both men and women), is that it does not have a hard and fast definition. However, an easy way to think of it is to take your business outfit and remove or modify certain elements in order to increase the degree of casualness. For instance, simply removing the tie and blazer from your full suit would then leave you with a business casual look. Or, you can leave on a tie of muted colour (or not wear a tie at all), and put a sweater vest over your dress shirt. This sweater vest/dress shirt combination also works nicely with a pair of jeans. Sweater vests are the friend of the frequent business casual wearer. Keep the sweater vest patterns simple and avoid busy patterns if possible.

FIGURE 6.13: BUSINESS CASUAL APPAREL FOR WORK IS PREFERRED BY MANY MILLENNIALS

Men's Semi-Formal Wear   Semi-formal wear is tricky because much like business casual, it does not have a hard and fast definition. Furthermore, people have a tendency to underdress when asked to attend an event that is semi-formal. There are a few key points to remember here. The first is that if given the choice, it is usually better to overdress than underdress. So, if you want to err on the side of caution when attending that semi-formal get-together next weekend, just wear a full suit. It's much better than the alternative of being the one person looking a bit too casual. Second, the easiest way to think about semi-formal is that it is usually just your business outfit with some modifications. Take your business suit and simply remove your tie, this will usually suffice for semi-formal. Wearing a tie is certainly acceptable, but make sure it's an understated tie.

If the event is being held in the daytime, such as an outdoor party, avoid wearing dark-coloured suits as this will make you look too grave. Lighter-coloured suits will suggest a more casual look, and are more suited for daytime wear. If you only have one matching set of dress pants and blazer, you can accomplish this by wearing a white dress shirt or lighter-coloured shoes—with a belt that matches your shoes, of course.

Men's Casual Wear   This is your everyday outfit: the kind of outfit you put on to go to the mall or to the movies—unless you're on a date! Men's casual outfits do not command the same type of head-turning as a suit would, but there are certainly instances in life in which you do not want to overdress. (Tuxedo at the grocery store, anyone?) Casual outfits have the largest number of fashionably acceptable combinations. For men, this could be as simple a combination as a pair of well-fitting jeans and t-shirt. If you wanted to step up your casual game, a combination of a polo shirt and khakis work nicely together. An additional combination that is very common and very fashionable is jeans, a white t-shirt, and an unbuttoned dress shirt over top. Some of these nicer combinations are referred to as *smart casual*.

FIGURE 6.14: SEMI-FORMAL ATTIRE IS VERY VERSATILE
AND IS APPROPRIATE FOR A VARIETY OF WORK
AND SOCIAL SITUATIONS

FIGURE 6.15: DRESSING CASUAL DOESN'T NEED
TO MEAN DRESSING DRAB

Some final tips for men. What you wear is just as important as how you wear it. There are some basic principles that all men who want to look their best should follow:

1. Wash and iron your clothing. Even nice pieces of clothing can make you look drab if they have not been well maintained.
2. Match your grooming to your audience. In the professional world of business, having a shorter haircut and being clean-shaven is generally recommended. Know your audience!
3. Err on the side of caution. Always opt for looking overdressed rather than underdressed.

FASHION FOR WOMEN

Fashion choices for women are more complicated than men's fashion choices. As a whole, the fashion industry treats women's fashion cyclically. What is in style today is not in style five years from now, but often comes back in style a decade later. We have gone from short-length skirts, to longer skirts, back to short-length skirts. We have gone from fitted jeans to loose-fitting, back to fitted jeans again. A cynic might suspect that a constantly changing fashion cycle is simply a strategy the apparel industry employs in order to increase consumption by the public. Whatever the reason, the fashion world for women is filled with vicissitudes.

The best way to overcome this hurdle is to invest a significant portion of your wardrobe budget into items that are classic and timeless. For formal wear this might include the "little black dress," and for business wear this would include a skirt suit or trousers and jacket in a neutral colour. Pieces like this will be understated and not go out of style easily.

This isn't to say that purchasing "fashionista" pieces for your wardrobe isn't a good idea—far from it. It's just that some thought should be put into how long an outfit can stay relevant in an ever-changing world of fashion. New pieces should also be relevant to your existing wardrobe. Does the piece you're considering match some of the clothes you currently own so you can create a well-coordinated outfit?

I also recommend that the reader consider care of the garment when purchasing it. Certain pieces of clothing will require much more delicate cleaning routines than, say, a pair of jeans that can be casually tossed in the wash. Dry cleaning in particular can be cumbersome (and expensive). At-home dry cleaning kits marketed under recognizable brand names do exist to ease the burden. Ask in-store sales associates about the garment specifics mentioned above.

Women's Business Wear   Unlike men, women have a few more options when it comes to dressing appropriately for a business environment. Options include blazers, pencil skirts, pantsuits, sheath dresses, and more. Nonetheless, in keeping with the above philosophy regarding timeless pieces, the most important investment is a basic suit. If you are to buy only one, aim for a charcoal- or navy-coloured suit. If you want, black may suffice as well, but some may find it a little too severe. While it is possible to purchase off the rack suits, getting your suit fitted and tailored for your body will improve its appearance tremendously. Pantyhose or tights should be worn with the skirt suit as well, as this is a boost to professionalism.

A white, pink, or blue blouse makes a great top to wear under the suit. This can be with front buttons or without. Under certain circumstances, a nice t-shirt can even be worn under your jacket, but this is only when you are *sure* that you won't be taking the jacket off in a professional setting.

FIGURE 6.16: LOOK BOTH PROFESSIONAL AND CHIC AT ONCE WITH A SKIRT SUIT

Women's Business Casual Wear   Women's business casual is just about the most confusing thing in the world of fashion. There is debate about what this term even means. To put it as succinctly as possible, the author's view is that it means dressed up, but not *too* dressed up. Clear as mud, right? There are countless ways to dress in a business casual style. The truth is, the definition of business casual will vary slightly from setting to setting. If you are told to dress business casual in the workplace, check out what the other women are wearing and adjust accordingly. This will narrow down the range of options to a manageable size.

A typical business casual outfit for women might consist of dark pants or khakis along with a nice long-sleeved buttoned shirt. Another option would be, say, pants and a blazer, or a nice pencil skirt with a blouse.

FIGURE 6.17: BUSINESS CASUAL IS A WAY OF DRESSING UP, BUT IN A SLIGHTLY MUTED MANNER

Women's Formal Wear   When dressing formally for a nice dinner event, the act of dressing up is in many ways an act of consideration towards your host. Your attire thrusts you into a sense of occasion that really elevates the evening from the ordinary to the extraordinary. Depending on the type of event (and how your host is dressing), something along the lines of a long gown could work. However, the "little black dress" may also be appropriate. Recall what was said earlier about the little black dress being timeless. It's an outfit that will work in most formal situations and is a safe "go-to" item.

FIGURE 6.18: THE "LITTLE BLACK DRESS" IS A CLASSIC

Women's Semi-Formal Wear   The little black dress is appropriate for this type of occasion as well. (I did say it was versatile, didn't I?) Since it's semi-formal wear, spicing up the outfit with some fun or festive jewelry is appropriate. Beyond the standard-bearer of the little black dress, cocktail dresses are a solid choice too. As a general rule, just remember that with semi-formal you don't have to dress as "severely" as you would when dressing formally.

FIGURE 6.19: SEMI-FORMAL OCCASIONS ARE THE TIME TO HAVE A LITTLE MORE FUN WITH YOUR OUTFIT

Women's Casual Wear   This is the fashion genre where the options can really open up, but again, we want to stick with pieces that are timeless and will work in many situations. This not only simplifies your wardrobe but can save you lots of money in the long run. Start with having at least one pair of well-fitting, high-quality jeans. This can be the basis for a multitude of different outfits and styles. Jeans that are slightly dressy, in a relatively dark hue will add elegance to your figure. Hypothetically, if this were to be your only pair of jeans, don't buy them pre-ripped or torn! A second pair of jeans for doing outdoorsy activities can be lighter in colour and looser in fit. This is the pair of jeans that can be pre-torn (if that's your thing).

Building on this foundation, completing the outfit can be as simple as throwing on your favourite t-shirt and seasonally appropriate shoes and you're off! A comfortable blouse for your top also makes for a good choice.

Other ways to pull off a stylish casual outfit include a classic summer dress with flats, wedges, or sandals. Large floral prints and bright colours are also perfect for warmer months. When the fall months roll around, bring out those boots.

The casual wear arena in fashion has the greatest number of style combinations. Get curious about the types of outfits your friends are wearing and borrow style cues from them. Experiment and develop your own personal sense of style and self-expression. Keep it fun.

FIGURE 6.20: EXPRESS YOURSELF WITH YOUR OWN PERSONAL STYLE

The most important element of any style is for you to own the way you look. No matter the situation or your chosen attire for the day, you want to be confident in what you are wearing. A woman who projects satisfaction with the outfit she has chosen for the day, no matter how casual, will also feel energetic and confident. Own the way you look in the same way that you own being proud of your goals and where you are heading in life. The way you carry yourself is all part of that journey.

STYLE MAINTENANCE

With your newly minted wardrobe possibly in your closet, it's time to become accustomed to the practice of caring for your clothing. To prevent chores from accumulating and causing undue stress, it's best to wash your clothes at least once a week; that way you don't accumulate a large pile of dirty clothes. To minimize shrinkage, dry and wash clothing on low temperatures. Pay attention to the tags on the clothing for specific washing instructions, and be sure to dry clean suits or dresses. In addition, some clothes are best hang-dried as opposed to being dried in a machine. Again, always consult the labels, or ask the sales associates for advice about caring for the clothing items at the time of purchasing the clothes.

The importance of personal appearance and grooming cannot be overstated. Everything—from job opportunities to opportunities for romance—is greatly influenced by how well we present ourselves. In professional settings, for instance, it is common practice to dress one level above that of your clients. If your client is dressing in business casual attire, you should dress in traditional business attire. If you are on a date, dressing smart casual will impress your partner.

DIGITAL LIFESTYLE

ONLINE SECURITY AND PRIVACY

We will now change gears and discuss personal habits of an entirely different nature. In particular, we will meditate on the wonders, conveniences, and potential dangers of today's always online and always connected world. In today's era of smartphones and ubiquitous connectivity, maintaining and securing an online presence is just as important as your in-person encounters. The balance of people reading this book will likely have multiple social networking accounts.

Prospective employers, data miners, advertising agencies, and identity thieves all want a piece of your personal information that is available online. A guiding rule that cannot be overemphasized is as follows: assume that anything you post online will be there *forever* and be seen by *everyone*. When posting any personal content online, ask yourself whether you are comfortable with this fact before posting it.

The public nature of this information is a particular danger for members of the younger generation who will undoubtedly grow up with social networking practically from the cradle but are at an age where they are too young to realize the consequences of sharing personal information online. In order to ensure the safety of your personal information, I recommend setting all social media privacy settings to prevent public viewing. However, even with this measure, the dangers of the online world extend beyond the ill-advised sharing of information. Passwords—a veritable cornucopia of alphanumeric jumbles that nearly every person has more or less memorized—constitute a potential threat to your security as well.

Prudence suggests that readers use long passwords with reasonably unique alphanumeric combinations. In addition, passwords for banking, email, social media, and the like should be changed every six months. Such a practice may seem like a chore, but my observation is that this is very much preferable to having personal information stolen or accounts compromised.

USING SOCIAL MEDIA AND ONLINE CONNECTIONS FOR NETWORKING AND CAREER OPPORTUNITIES

With a mindset emphasizing security firmly in place, let us now turn our attention to the use of social media and web communications as a means to improve career aspirations and personal networking. As mentioned previously, it is likely that you, the reader, already have some social networking accounts (of which there are many) such as Facebook, Twitter, Linkedin, Instagram, Pinterest, and so on. Use these platforms as tools. Communicate with old friends that you may feel are good potential connections for career opportunities. Create a fan page displaying your creative works. Use Twitter to share your thoughts on the latest developments in your field.

As powerful as Facebook and Twitter and other tools may be, the undisputed leader of professional social networks is LinkedIn. LinkedIn is similar to Facebook, but instead of being saturated with party and holiday photos of your friends, the platform is used to post the equivalent of online resumes on profile pages. Many LinkedIn users have received lucrative job offers with virtually no effort on their part other than having a personal presence on the site.[3]

As a final consideration, the reader may want to look into the possibility of starting their own website. It is not nearly as expensive or time consuming as the endeavour may seem at first glance. Many high quality, free user guides on website construction can be found with a quick Internet search online. However, should the process prove to be uninteresting (or too daunting), you can hire a web designer for a small fee. You can register a domain name for as little as $10, and web hosting services can be purchased for as little as $3 to $5 per month.

READING

Beyond the online component of the one's life, the virtues of intense reading should also be discussed. I do not hesitate to say that for anyone who wants to get ahead in life, reading should constitute a significant portion of their spare time. In the same way that food is nourishment for one's body, reading is nourishment for one's mind. To this end, I have included a list of suggested books at the end of every chapter.

Regardless of the personal aspirations you may have, reading will unquestionably help your efforts. I recommend reading nonfiction books on a wide variety of subjects in order to gain broad exposure to society's knowledge; read everything from physics, to biology, to biographies. Drawing on this information, the mind is free to begin drawing inferences, parallels, and new insights between seemingly unrelated concepts. In this way, you might devise new and novel solutions to complex problems.

In addition to books, reading a newspaper, either online or in hardcopy, in order to keep up with current events is highly recommended. Individuals who stay up-to-date on local and global issues are better able to put their daily lives into a larger context. A newspaper is like a societal map, telling the reader what is going on around them. Refusing to step out into the world every morning without a newspaper is analogous to a general refusing to engage in war without a map of the battlefield. While this may seem heavy handed, I have no regrets promoting the innumerable benefits of a simple newspaper. For those in Canada, there are a handful of highly respected magazines and newspaper publications, some read nationwide.

CLOSING THOUGHTS

With this chapter, I hope to have armed readers with a set of personal habits and a mental framework for intelligently navigating their day-to-day lives. It is my position that whether in romantic, professional, or social endeavours, there is always an optimal way to navigate a given activity. In particular, a lifestyle that is centred around diligent planning can absolutely change your life for the better. When you are done reading this book, ask yourself, "What activity do I engage in that will give me the highest possible benefit for the time and cost incurred?" What will you do in the next hour that will benefit you the most? Your life will immediately begin to take on a certain kind of order and tidiness, and chaos will be reined in.

Personal habits constitute a *platform* by which your life success can grow. Without this foundation, your life's endeavours will be vulnerable to even the most common hardships of life. Consider the prospect of having an unclean house and a perpetual pile of laundry that needs washing while trying to pursue a love interest or a new career move. These negative factors, which are small individually, can accumulate into major stressors in life. Prevention is the best medicine. I urge the reader pay attention to detail, and never let the corroding influence of lethargy enter their lives.

ACTION STEPS BEFORE READING THE NEXT CHAPTER

TO-DO: PERSONAL HABITS
- Set up your own to-do list and calendar, either on paper or digitally.
- Clean and organize your home, especially the area where you tend to get work done, such as a home office.
- Look in your closet see whether you have an appropriate wardrobe for business, formal, business casual, semi-formal, and casual occasions. Attire for formal occasions, can usually be rented, however.

RECOMMENDED FURTHER READING ON PERSONAL HABITS

- *The 7 Habits of Highly Effective People*, Stephen R. Covey
- *Getting Things Done: The Art of Stress Free Productivity*, David Allen
- *Think and Grow Rich*, Napoleon Hill
- *Unlimited Power*, Tony Robbins

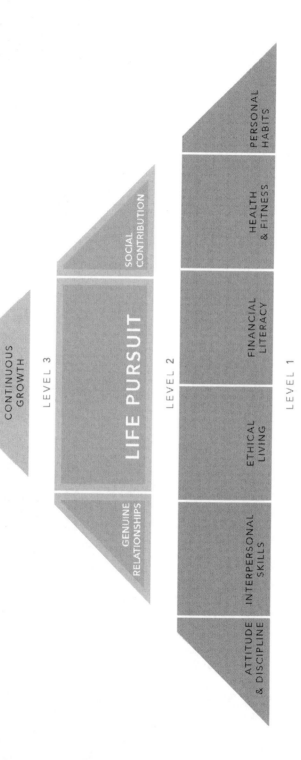

THE PARADIGM OF HAPPINESS

LEVEL 2

CONTINUOUS GROWTH

LEVEL 3

GENUINE RELATIONSHIPS

LIFE PURSUIT

SOCIAL CONTRIBUTION

LEVEL 2

ATTITUDE & DISCIPLINE

INTERPERSONAL SKILLS

ETHICAL LIVING

FINANCIAL LITERACY

HEALTH & FITNESS

PERSONAL HABITS

LEVEL 1

CHAPTER 7
GENUINE RELATIONSHIPS

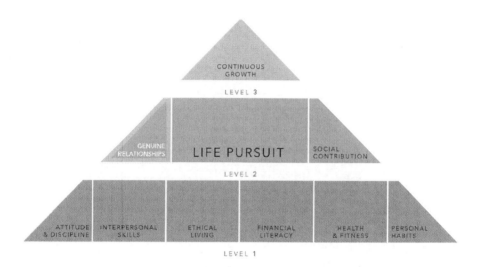

THE PARADIGM OF HAPPINESS

We have now progressed to Level 2 of The Paradigm of Happiness. The first component of this level is the cultivation of relationships with friends and family. It is the author's opinion, unequivocally, that the "human" factor in life, consisting of our relationships with our loved ones and friends, represents an absolute cornerstone to happy living. Happiness is not to be found in loving and coveting our material possessions. Rather, it is found by loving and caring for the people around us. I will repeat what I said at the outset of this book: that one of the reasons why the world is in chaos is because possessions are being loved and people are being used.

Our relationships—and particularly our life *experiences* with those closest to us—are what constitute our most personally fulfilling moments in life. More empirical evidence is mounting in favour of happiness being found in this experiential philosophy. All other things being equal, you are likely to experience much greater satisfaction and enrichment from, say, a trip to Europe with your significant other than from an equivalent amount of money spent on a new big-screen TV and entertainment system. The memories of shared experiences, enjoying new foods together, trying something you've never done before, and even sharing burdens are priceless. Many empirical studies from researchers such as Thomas Gilovich of Cornell University and Leaf Van Boven of the University of Colorado Boulder have affirmed the superior happiness derived from experiences.[1]

Spend as much time as you possibly can with those close to you, because the time you have available to do so is *extremely* limited. This may not seem so if you are young, but the older generation that precedes you will certainly tell you otherwise. Seemingly long durations of time such as decades will seem to slip past like a blink of the eye, in retrospect. Missed opportunities to simply sit down and enjoy the company of parents, grandparents, and friends can become sources of painful regrets in the future. There are far too many people in this world who wish they had received this advice earlier in life. I highly recommend not being one of them.

While I may be emphasizing this point as if it contains some great wisdom, it is, in fact, counsel that does not require particularly brilliant insights. The sense of emotional fulfillment and completeness that comes from fostering relationships should go without saying. I would speculate that it is simply human nature that causes people to take others for granted and sometimes neglect those closest to them. In some cases, this may even evolve into a sort of casual exploitation. A kind of mental check must be put in place to prevent one's behaviour from degenerating in this way. (Recall our relevant discussions on interpersonal skills in Chapter 2 and ethical behavior in Chapter 3.) Casual exploitation of friends and loved ones does not accrue personal benefit to you in the long run.

Perhaps the point can be stated most succinctly by simply saying, *love those who are around you.* The acts of holding grudges, fixating on the smallest quarrels, and always assuming that you will have tomorrow to spend time with someone are mistakes of the highest magnitude. The philosophy of *carpe diem*, or seize the day, rings loudly here. Do not delay in asking out your long-time crush for a date, reconciling with an estranged sibling, reconnecting with a friend, or sitting down and absorbing the sage advice of a grandparent.

FIGURE 7.1: DON'T TAKE LOVED ONES FOR GRANTED

LOVE AND ROMANCE

The one type of relationship in life that requires genuineness and authenticity more than any other is the romantic relationship. I touched on romantic relationships earlier in our discussion on interpersonal skills, and I concluded with some fundamental tenets on how to behave in a thoughtful manner. In this chapter, I would like to delve further into this topic and discuss how to make those romantic relationships deep, sincere, and lasting.

The current cultural attitude in North America toward dating is very casual. With a culture that seems to be obsessed with instant gratification of our wants, we can now find someone to go on a date with or have sex with faster than it takes to order this book from Amazon. This author's observation is that easy access to pornography has often further cheapened intimacy between people.

It seems as though increasingly easy access to abundant opportunities for sexual interaction has not given us the increased happiness we seek out of life. According to researchers such as Barry Schwartz, author of *The Paradox of Choice: Why More is Less*, and Mark Regnerus and Jeremy Uecker, authors of *Premarital Sex in America*, there is a distinct positive correlation between carnal conservatism and overall happiness.[2,3] Being in fewer relationships that are genuine and deep makes us happier than simply trying to sleep with as many people as possible. In this regard, the hook-up culture has encouraged some of the worst tendencies in human nature. Our biological impulses often impel us to mate with as great a variety of attractive people as we can, but our biology doesn't always know what's good for our happiness and well-being—much like how our bodies compel us to eat sugar and fat-laden foods that are bad for our health.

I'm certainly not saying that everyone should wait until marriage to have sex. More pragmatically, what I *am* saying is that it pays to invest time and energy into fewer but deeper relationships with those with whom you appear to connect with on a fundamental level, beyond mere sex. Love brings happiness, and sex does not *necessarily* mean love.

A discussion on romance and intimate relationships inevitably leads us to the topic of marriage. How do we choose our partner for life? The truth is that there is no foolproof way of choosing who to marry. No marriage is absolutely guaranteed to last until death parts us from our spouses. However, there are certainly things we can do to maximize the *probability* of having a happy and lasting marriage. We can start by building on our previous discussions about relationship dynamics; namely, focusing on fewer but deeper connections that go beyond mere passion and into companionship, emotional connection, and shared values. We can take these principles and combine them with our discussion on romantic relationship principles discussed in our *Interpersonal Skills* chapter. These include tenets such as the following: loving the other person as they are, not as you want them to be; ensuring that both you and your partner have your own lives outside of the relationship; always trying to see things from their perspective; and always following through with your word.

To this platform above, we can add one final ingredient, which is a bit of an acid test for your potential partner. Empirical studies suggest that through a mechanism known as hedonic adaptation, the initial, fiery passion in a relationship lasts for a maximum of about two years. Once that sexual passion begins to subside, you start to see that person with *companionate* love rather than *passionate* love.[4] It is this companionate love that contributes to the long-term equilibrium of a relationship.

It is generally at this stage that you can really feel whether or not the person you are with can be your life partner. If you have spent a great deal of time with someone as friends before becoming romantically linked, it may take considerably less time to reach this stage. Remember that marriage is a promise—the ultimate promise—that could last a lifetime. Don't make that promise, or any promise for that matter, if you don't intend on keeping it.

THE ACCEPTANCE OF LOSS

A discussion on building relationships would not be considered complete without mentioning the mental anguish of loss. No relationship, at least in physical terms, can last forever. Despite our best efforts, it is an unavoidable fact of life that people leave and people die. This is something that we must all grow to accept. If you have lost someone, do not focus on your loss. Focus on fond memories, and continue to hold them dearly in your heart. Focus on whom you have left and on forging new relationships. Sometimes relationships are simply not meant to be. Sometimes people pass away before we get to spend our fair share of time with them.

Consider what happens when a romantic relationship fails. Perhaps you made a mistake that you regret and because of it you lost the person you hold dear. It is both natural and healthy to have some measure of grief and remorse over what happened. The biggest potential pitfall here is an *unwillingness to forgive yourself*. This is generally the biggest obstacle in the healing process. You may often think, "Why did I not see this at the time? Why did I not put more effort into our relationship while I had the chance? Why did I act so foolishly? How could I not have seen this coming?" There may be an unbearable feeling that you did not "perform your best," and that things may have been different if you had.

Such a rationale is not justified. Whatever happened, even if you did not act with full conviction and effort when you knew you should have, *it was the best* you could do at the time. Your actions, at any given moment are *the best* you have to offer. Your regret is simply a sign of your growth and increased wisdom since the time of the events in question. A person with no regrets has no growth.

In a similar vein, the loss of a friend or loved one as a result of their death should not be endured from the perspective that such events are in any way abnormal, or that you are to blame. You may feel that the universe at large has served you a great injustice because of your loss. Perhaps you regret not spending more time with this person, or not reconciling your differences before it was too late. A similar wisdom to what was discussed above can be applied with equal force here. Whatever you did was the best you could do given the knowledge, experience, and values you had. There is no reason to regret what your very best was. By the same token, the loss you have suffered is not the result of a planned villainy by the universe or the world around you. These things simply happen. To hold a long and protracted bitterness towards the world around you because of your loss is both counterproductive and against the very nature of living itself: death is a natural part of life.

CULTIVATING DEEP RELATIONSHIPS

AUTHENTICITY: THE KEY TO COMMUNICATION

A large part of fostering truly deep relationships comes from being authentic with one another. What do I mean by this? Well, consider your day-to-day interactions with people. How often do you not share how you truly feel about someone or their actions because of fear of criticism, rejection, anger, or some other unpleasant result? Or, how often do we not take action or speak out so that we can feel justified in our righteous indignance?

These actions lead us to a certain degree of inauthenticity, which fundamentally leads to a divide between how we feel and what we end up communicating to others in both our words and our actions. This divide puts an emotional chasm between the people in our lives and us. Moreover, this inauthenticity inevitably erodes our happiness over time.

We must be genuine and authentic in our communications with others as this is how a deep connection with others is formed. Shallow connections come about when we chat about the weather and our weekend plans, but we do not share how we feel. We tend to make up stories about how it isn't the right time to share a certain thought or feeling. We tell ourselves that doing so is dangerous because we don't know how other people may react.

This is nothing but a plethora of reasons, reasons, reasons. Reasons why it's always the other person's fault the relationship isn't working. Reasons why the hand we've been dealt in a certain situation just isn't good enough. However, we must realize that we can only have one of two things in life: reasons or results. We cannot have both.

It is our own reasons that prevent us from being authentic with other people.

Our authenticity allows us to penetrate the protective barrier that *we all* surround ourselves with, and make deep connections. This barrier, this suit of armour, is something we all don because we are afraid of looking bad. We say things in conversation that we think will be socially acceptable, rather than stating how we are really feeling. This is a form of social sleep walking. We're not really communicating; we're just going through the motions. Be authentic and you can begin to cultivate deeper (more genuine) relationships with your friends and family.

PRESENCE

A related principle to the above discussion concerns presence of mind. Investing time into relationships is, of course, a requirement in strengthening them. No two people ever developed a deep bond without spending significant time with one another. However, the *quality* of time spent matters just as much as the quantity—in some cases, maybe more. Have you ever seen two people in a restaurant sitting across from each other having dinner "together," but instead of connecting they are simply staring at their smartphones? They're together, but they're not really *together*.

This kind of time spent with one another does not constitute a true investment in the relationship. You must be mindful and present with the other person in order for the connection to deepen; otherwise, you may wonder why, despite all the time you are spending with others, your relationships don't seem to go anywhere. Smartphone culture, it seems, has been a big culprit in exacerbating this problem in recent years. People are both more connected and less connected at the same time. (Recall our related discussion on technology's impact on your social connections in Chapter 2.)

This device distraction is something you have to guard against. Put the technology away. Don't let a lack of presence creep into your quality time with your loved ones. Be in the here and now and really engage with the other person. This not only improves the quality of your social connection, but it also shows that you respect the other person on a fundamental level. I'm sure all of us have seen the picture in Figure 7.2. at one point or another in our lives.

FIGURE 7.2: A COUPLE BEING TOGETHER WITHOUT ACTUALLY BEING TOGETHER

SPEAKING THE SAME LANGUAGE AS YOUR LOVED ONES

Deepening your relationships with your loved ones—whether they are your spouse, your friends, or your family—also necessitates speaking the same emotional language as them. Gary Chapman, author of the influential book, *The 5 Love Languages*, tells us that everyone gives and receives love in different ways.[5] Additionally, most people demonstrate love in the way that they prefer to receive it. So, knowing how to effectively communicate love to someone in your life is best accomplished by first observing how *they* demonstrate love and then responding in a similar fashion.

Chapman also introduces the concept of a "love tank" in his work, where demonstrating love to someone in their preferred language fills up their emotional tank, and protracted periods without receiving love in their preferred language drains this tank. This is fair warning to never allow the love tank of the ones you care about to run dry!

One of Chapman's five love languages is words of affirmation. This would mean expressing love and appreciation through verbal communication. This type of person will see their love tank being filled up effectively by being told they are cared for and appreciated. Another language that Chapman posits is that of quality time. This means being present and in the moment with your loved one. For such people, neglecting to regularly engage in activities with them or hang out with them will leave them feeling emotionally unfulfilled.[6] Chapman's theories are simple but insightful. Take them to heart and learn the love languages of those around you.

LEVEL 1 OF THE PARADIGM OF HAPPINESS AS THE FOUNDATION FOR RELATIONSHIP CULTIVATION

It can be seen now that a certain degree of competence in Level 1 of The Paradigm is necessary as a foundation or "platform" in order to progress to Level 2, the cultivation of deep and long lasting relationships. In stating my case, I do not in any way mean to imply that a love for others must be prefaced by anything other than being human. Rather, I wish to suggest that strong relationships with others, and the caring and helping of others can only be facilitated when *we as individuals* are both stable and independent. A person with self-destructive, unstable, or unethical tendencies is hardly in a practical position to build strong relationships.

Only with a sensible structure of personal values and a well-developed competency in core life skills in place can we pursue self-actualization. As I have argued throughout this book, a productive mental attitude, interpersonal skills, an ethical framework, financial literacy, and constructive personal habits are the building blocks to a robust personage. These things are a base upon which you can build your relationships. The disappearance of any one of these components can destabilize your efforts.

UNCONDITIONAL CARING

The core value behind the idea of relationship cultivation is an *unconditional caring for others*. This basic human trait forms the backbone of our relationships. Caring for a fellow person, regardless of our affinity with them, will not only earn the trust and caring of others in return, but more profoundly, a sense of experiencing the very best of being human. Our intellect allows us to rise above our "selfish genes,"[7] and to feel empathy and compassion for other people, even if there is no possible chance of any future reciprocity. It is this idea that leads us to the second component of Level 2 in The Paradigm: social contribution.

ACTION STEPS BEFORE READING THE NEXT CHAPTER

TO-DO: GENUINE RELATIONSHIPS
- Call a loved one or friend that you have not spoken to in a while, and tell them that you care about them and want to reconnect with them.
- Write down the names of five loved ones in your life. After reading Gary Chapman's book, mentioned above, write down the love language you think they primarily use to communicate with you. Is it the same way you communicate love to them in return? Why, or why not? How might changing the language make the relationship stronger?

RECOMMENDED FURTHER READING ON RELATIONSHIP CULTIVATION
- *The 5 Love Languages: The Secret to Love that Lasts*, Gary Chapman
- *The Secrets of Happy Families: Improve Your Mornings, Rethink Your Family Dinner, Fight Smarter, Go Out and Play, and Much More*, Bruce Feiler
- *How to Be an Adult in Relationships: The Five Keys to Mindful Loving*, David Richo

CHAPTER 8
SOCIAL CONTRIBUTION

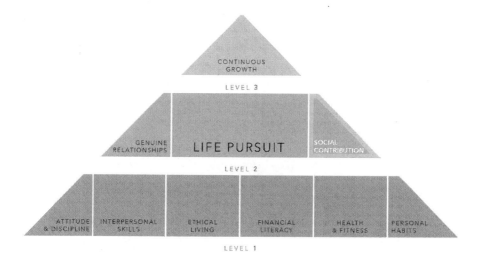

THE PARADIGM OF HAPPINESS

In this book, I have already described the emptiness of a life based on materialism. Beyond that claim, I have also considered the idea that behaving in an altruistic way is both advantageous to the self and desirable from an ethical standpoint. In this chapter I will fully develop this idea into a core tenet of happiness. Striving to contribute positively to society provides gratification that few other endeavours can.

Throughout the process of writing this book, I have held the goal of helping others steadfastly in my mind. The prospect of helping others live their lives and navigate through its ups and downs more intelligently—to make others happy—makes me happy. Happiness breeds happiness. It is also worth noting that the quality of work coming from someone who is happy with what they are doing is going to be noticeably higher than someone who is unhappy with their work.

Human beings have an intrinsic desire to help others. There is a biological basis for this. The phrase "nice guys finish first" is often uttered by evolutionary biologists.[1] Richard Dawkins states in his book *The Selfish Gene* that animals in the wild that behave altruistically often have higher survival rates because the probability of future reciprocity for such behaviour is very high.[2] Many observers have lamented that this assumption of reciprocity could potentially imply that the only reason why people behave ethically and kindly toward others is ultimately due to self-interest. I disagree. While there may always be a vague element of self-interest in altruistic acts, it is the crown jewel of the human condition that we have the ability to reject the blind and callous instincts of our genes. As humans, we can take *intellectual* pleasure (not just instinctual pleasure) in knowing that we can serve a greater good by helping others.

Martin Luther King Jr. revolutionized African-American civil rights in the USA in the mid-twentieth century. Upon doing so, he made an outstanding contribution to humanity's progress in building a better society. This would likely have made King highly satisfied with his life's work, if he'd only had the opportunity to complete it. His work will become no less relevant to society a thousand years from now than it is today. It is in adding to the relentless pursuit of improving society, as Martin Luther King Jr. did, that gives humans the ultimate feeling of personal satisfaction, accomplishment, and gratitude in life.

Let me state with no ambiguity that true happiness is found in giving back to society. Happiness is to be found in accomplishing things for a greater good, as opposed to acting purely for selfish purposes. We can go above and beyond satisfying our petty personal desires and have a vision for improving the society we live in. This vision is what truly separates us from the animal kingdom and makes us human.

Do not confuse the act of striving to be a positive force for change with the mere status of celebrity. All too often, perhaps subconsciously, people act as if the two are synonymous. There are many people in the world who are rich and famous. We see the popular image of a famous musician or singer who has the adoration of all the developed world. Mental images of giant mansions, fast cars, and beautiful companions abound. While there is nothing inherently wrong with being a celebrity, it is not necessarily a status to be held as an ideal. The mere fact that someone is famous does not automatically mean that they have contributed much to the world. It does not mean they will be remembered a generation from now. It does not mean they will be happy. Why is the contribution a movie star makes to society considered to be greater than that of a teacher or firefighter? Money isn't everything. More than this, mere fame will not make you feel happy or fulfilled.

Capitalism is an economic system in which the great bounty of time, energy, and resources are supposed to be invested toward their best and most productive uses. While this system works as intended *most* of the time, this is far from saying it works all of the time. Take the case of day traders in the stock market. Day traders are individuals who attempt to make money by standing at a stock exchange or sitting at their computer all day, trading virtual pieces of paper back and forth. Whether or not this can be done successfully is a point of contention, but that is not relevant to our discussion here. Even *if* it can be done successfully, what good would that person be to the world? What contributions would they be making to society? What goods, services, or knowledge are they offering the world? An entry-level employee working in a fast food restaurant may offer more to society than any day trader, despite the glamorous nature of the latter over the former.

MAKING A POSITIVE CONTRIBUTION TO SOCIETY

Every human being who has a reasonable level of personal stability (which the reader will gain after traversing Level 1 of The Paradigm) should feel a moral obligation to contribute positively to society. What higher good is there? What greater purpose in life can there be? I encourage the reader to reflect, think, read about the world around them, and talk to loved ones about the biggest issues and problems of society. Find a problem or a project that you feel personally connected to. It can be civil rights, the environment, gender equality, or strengthening the lesbian, gay, bisexual and transgender (LGBT) community, or any other cause. At any rate, you will find great satisfaction in working for your cause, and you will be assisting humanity in its relentless march forward. It is a win-win proposition.

MOTIVES MATTER

Readers should strive to engage in community involvement and social change activities based on a genuine passion for the cause rather than simply because it makes them look good or adds substance to their resume. Both prudence and life experience show that motive matters. Having a true passion for a cause is what gives people the drive to work the late nights, extra weekends, and go the extra mile. Those who contribute to the community or society for the vain reasons of attention and popularity will inevitably quit. Generally, the quality of their work will be subpar as well. Ultimately, such endeavours will amount to nothing but a waste of time.

Exposing ourselves to different people, activities, social groups, and reading many different kinds of books is the key to finding a cause. A person who does nothing but sit at home and constantly play video games will not be in a position to discover a fulfilling social or community endeavour to get involved in. Therein lies the importance of actively striving to widen one's perspective on the different ideologies and perspectives that exist in the world. Even the simple act of spending 20 minutes a day reading the newspaper can do wonders for one's cultural exposure. For readers in Canada, I recommend checking out *The Globe and Mail* newspaper. This publication is often referred to as Canada's paper of record. The *New York Times* is generally held in the same regard in the U.S. Copies of these publications can typically be accessed for free at your local library. (As an aside: while there are many other reputable news publications in North America, be on your guard for fake news outlets. The problem of fake news, particularly on the Internet, has been of growing concern amongst the public.)

RESEARCH FINDINGS ON VOLUNTEERING AND COMMUNITY ENGAGEMENT

The benefits of genuinely giving back to society and contributing to one's community have been substantiated by academic research. We have already discussed the concrete benefits of altruism in the chapter on ethical behaviour, but the impact on our own mental well-being is just as significant. A paper published by Gillian Brunier in the *Journal of Advanced Nursing*, titled "The Psychological Well-Being of Renal Peer Support Volunteers," demonstrated that individuals who became support volunteers for those suffering from chronic renal problems (even fellow patients) experienced remarkable improvements in their quality of life. The results suggest that significant personal growth and enhancements to well-being can stem from an act that, at first blush, doesn't seem to benefit you in any way.[3]

In the same vein, another study published by Carolyn Schwartz in *Social Science and Medicine* entitled "Helping Others Helps Oneself: Response Shift Effects in Peer Support" found that the act of listening compassionately and offering volunteer support to those ailing from disease tangibly improved mental well-being. This included improvements in confidence, self-esteem, and quality of life. The impact was so pronounced that it turned out that those who were giving the volunteer support derived greater mental benefits than those receiving the support. This is the meditative and regenerative power that comes with helping others.[4]

Finally, a 2007 paper on taxing and charitable donations published by *Science* describes the impact of charitable giving on the mind. The paper found that "even mandatory, tax-like transfers to a charity elicit neural activity in areas linked to reward processing." People overeat, drink, and do drugs to chase pleasurable feelings. How much further could we go if people chased that same feeling through altruism? This is a question that is truly worth pondering.[5]

THE RIPPLE EFFECT

The causality we all experience in life is strange to say the least. The mechanics of cause and effect are often elusive, and sometimes we get great results in life without knowing how they came about.

Perhaps we sometimes just get lucky? Well, luck certainly plays a part. We don't choose what country we are born in, our parents, or whether we are male or female, etc.

Despite this, I would contend that there are certain key actions and habits that we take in our lives that allow positive outcomes to *gravitate* toward us. The connection isn't always explicit, and sometimes it's even mysterious; however, there is definitely a kind of connection that brings together positive people and positive results.

When we put our passions on the line and put weight behind them, we become truly self-expressed and this attracts others to our cause. Like-minded individuals can see someone that they may admire, so interesting and accomplished people become enchanted by you. Widening your social circle will have an impact not only on your professional life, but also on your social life and romantic life. There will be a *ripple effect*, and your positive contributions to society are like the stone that is thrown into the lake and causes those ripples.

In the end, the ripple effect will extend so far out that your life will begin to become enriched in ways that you could never have even foreseen. The world is a small place, and the ripple effect can work wonders in your life. All you have to do is throw that stone!

EXPERIENCES OF THE AUTHOR

I, myself, am Buddhist, and have volunteered at my local Buddhist temple's youth camps several times in the past. Doing so has not only been fulfilling but has given me the opportunity to meet many wonderful people as well. The context of meeting people within a volunteer environment is fundamentally different from meeting people in the workplace or at a party. The shared sense of purpose and the fact that everyone there is voluntarily spending their valuable time on something they believe in makes for fertile soil in which friendships can grow. Note that we made a similar observation of how "birds of a feather flock together" in Chapter 2. Making a positive difference in your community and making friends at the same time provides one with an emotional fulfillment that few other endeavours in the world can match.

Additionally, remember that potential employers tend to find volunteer experience on your resume as being a favourable indicator of your character. This can help with career progression, and has certainly been my experience. Recall our discussion on this topic in Chapter 3 on how behaving ethically and even altruistically can be incredibly beneficial to one's own self-interest. Truly, the different components of The Paradigm create a certain kind of synergy, where each element will reinforce and strengthen the others.

FIGURE 8.1: SHARED SOCIAL CONTRIBUTION CAN HELP TO BUILD DEEP RELATIONSHIPS

THERE ARE MANY WAYS TO MAKE A POSITIVE SOCIAL IMPACT

Keep in mind that there are many different ways you can make incredibly impactful social contributions in the world. The method you choose will depend highly on your own personal circumstances and inclinations. As an example, many retirees who are no longer working may find themselves with an abundance of time, so they may be willing to contribute to helping out at food drives or helping to serve food to the homeless at soup kitchens. Those who are very wealthy of course will tend to donate money to philanthropic causes. An example would be the famous Li Ka-shing—a Hong Kong business magnate—who has pledged to donate a third of his fortune to improving education and health.[6]

Still, there are other ways to make a social impact. For instance, American entrepreneur Elon Musk has used his business acumen and entrepreneurial drive to accelerate the use of renewable energy and electric cars via ventures such as SolarCity and Tesla. His chosen social mission dovetails perfectly with his core competencies and skills.[7] Playing to your strengths can significantly enhance the effect your efforts have on the world.

Apply these lessons to your own life and think about how you too can play to your strengths. In what way can you be most impactful? Whether it is through contributing ideas, time, or money, leading people, or building things, there are myriad ways to go about engaging in any cause.

TAKING THE FIRST STEP

In talking about social contribution, I'm not trying to suggest that the reader needs to take the extreme action of dropping everything right now, and boarding a flight to a less developed country to start participating in building shelters. Nothing of the sort. It's more about keeping positive social contributions in mind as part of your decision-making process when deciding what to do with the time that has been given to you in your life. It's about shaping your own mindset, taking a first step, and developing a "taste" for giving back to society if you do not have it already.

Small acts, such as doing a couple hours of tree planting on the weekend, can change the horizon of your thinking and help to start integrating considerations of social contribution into other areas of your life. This contribution might include how to make your own line of work more socially conscious.

The following are just a few examples of some broad-based social causes that this author thinks may be worthy of your attention and talents:

- Feminism—advocacy for women's rights, freedoms, and social equality.
- Environmentalism—protection of the health of the environment and climate.
- Renewable Energy—research and advocacy for energy sources that are replenished faster than they are consumed.
- Education—improvements in the quality of public education, access to education, or reductions in cost.
- Economic Inequality—reducing extreme stratification in the standard of living experienced by people in society.

In addition, the following are just a few examples of great community hubs for the above mentioned social causes:

- *Feminist Majority Foundation* — www.feminist.org
- *The Nature Conservancy* — www.nature.org
- *David Suzuki Foundation* — www.davidsuzuki.org
- *No-Pay MBA* — www.nopaymba.com
- *Center for Community Change* - www.communitychange.org

If you're not too keen on getting involved with larger organizations such as the ones above, you can also elect to start your own Action Circle. Action Circles are groups of, say, five to eight people that get together regularly to discuss and engage in positive community involvement. They are informal and highly suitable for grassroots movements. Be The Change Earth Alliance (BTCEA), a Canadian charitable organization, has instructional guides on how to effectively go about starting and maintaining an Action Circle at www.bethechangeearthalliance.org/action_circles.

WHAT THIS MEANS FOR YOUR FUTURE

Ideally, we would like the social cause about which we are passionate to be the same theme that we pursue on a daily basis for work. Unfortunately, in life, sometimes they aren't the same thing. Sometimes the social cause we are passionate about doesn't put food on the table.

It just doesn't pay the bills. Often however, it does. And that's a very exciting prospect indeed. In our next chapter we'll be exploring your life purpose, how to find it, and how to integrate it into your life.

ACTION STEPS BEFORE READING THE NEXT CHAPTER

TO-DO: SOCIAL CONTRIBUTION

- From the list above, pick the social cause that you are least familiar with. Explore it by joining a discussion forum or talking with a friend who is involved in that cause about why the cause matters to them.
- If there is a social cause you already care about, find at least one way to get more involved and write down when you will follow through on your to-do list or calendar (Chapter 6 contains our discussion on time management tools).

FURTHER RECOMMENDED READINGS ON SOCIAL CONTRIBUTION:

- *Giving Back: Discover Your Values and Put Them Into Action Through Volunteering and Donating*, Steven P. Ketchpel
- *Start Something That Matters*, Blake Mycoskie
- *Social Entrepreneurship: What Everyone Needs to Know*, David Bornstein, Susan Davis
- *The Promise of a Pencil: How an Ordinary Person Can Create Extraordinary Change*, Adam Braun

CHAPTER 9
YOUR LIFE PURSUIT

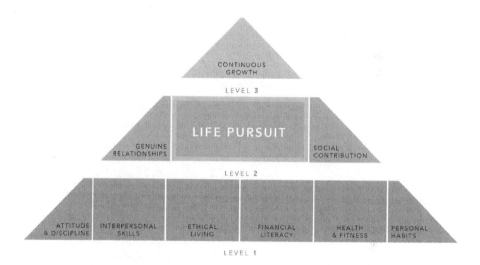

THE PARADIGM OF HAPPINESS

We now enter the third and final component of the second level of The Paradigm. This chapter is arguably the most important in this entire book. Let us begin with some propositions and logical deductions. I have already stated that the goal for humans is to create satisfaction, happiness, and contentment with life. The means of achieving these goals is through *self-actualization*, a never-ending process of personal fulfillment and growth. Knowing what path to take in life necessitates knowing where exactly it is you intend to go. Once this is decided upon, you make a concerted effort to lay out a plan and follow through with it.

So that there is no ambiguity, I will state plainly that self-actualization is achieved primarily by *realizing your full potential in your life's passion.* Self-actualization is becoming everything you are capable of becoming. It is your reason for existing. It is your purpose in life. It is the quest that gives you the enthusiasm to jump out of bed every morning. You and your passion are one and the same. The same being. The same entity.

> *Your passion in life is the cornerstone of your happiness. You will know you have found your passion in life when your work and your pleasure become indistinguishable.*

FINDING YOUR PASSION IN LIFE

Finding your passion in life is simply finding your home. If you do not know what you want to do in life, your *immediate* task is to find it. The longer you wait, the more you will regret not starting sooner. The earlier you start, the more doors in life will be open to you. At the age of 10, the sky is the limit in terms of what you can accomplish. By the time you are 50, the question of becoming, say, a professional athlete has already answered itself. There are still many things you can set out to accomplish regardless of your age, but endeavours such as sports may not be one of them. Realizing that you've missed the opportunity to achieve such a life goal can become a source of great regret.

Life is the ultimate thrilling adventure. It has unbelievable highs and equally incredible lows. There are an unlimited number of life pursuits in which you can engage. You may think you are already aware of all the things you might want to do in life, but that is likely not the case. More often than not, the human psyche cannot judge the enjoyment of an activity or pursuit without actually having ever tried it. Furthermore, the number of life pursuits that you could fall in love with will be myriad.

Passions differ, and there appears to be no semblance of logic as to why certain people "click" with certain professions while others do not. Some people may pursue the performing arts, literature, or humanities. Others decide on engineering, sciences, or finance. It is important to realize that it is nearly impossible to rationalize why something may be your passion. It just is. It is never a (completely) intellectual process with a conscious decision. Finding what you love to do in life is like falling in love with a person. You can't explain why you love person A instead of person B. You just *do*.

Finding what you want to do with your life will give you a level of satisfaction and contentment with life that no other endeavour, possession, or state of being can offer. I will not hesitate to repeat that if you do not know what your life's passion is, it is your top priority to find it. Without knowing what it is you want to do in life, you will have no direction. Knowing that you are accomplishing something that is meaningful to you and has a positive impact on society will make you truly happy.

Having said this, no one is born with only having one passion in life that is compatible with their interests. There will be many different fields, professions, and hobbies that you can and will fall in love with. Some of them may not even be practical or realistic. One of the most important skills you will have to develop in life is the ability to adapt to changing circumstances. Sometimes, the simple fact is that you don't always get what you want. Do not let such a notion undermine the importance of perseverance—one of the most important qualities a self-actualized person must possess. Not giving up, even when all odds seem to be against you, is a virtue. However, there is something to be said about being realistic.

What I mean by adaptation is realizing that if you cannot be successful one way, you must accept this and strive to be successful another way. Growing up, I wanted to become a professional athlete, but a head and neck injury I sustained from a car accident prevented me from passing the physical examination. I became depressed for quite some time. In my situation, no amount of perseverance was going to do me any good. I spent a few years moping without any real direction. It took me a long time to realize that conceding to this kind of personal misfortune was neither useful nor healthy. I had to find a way to maximize my time and opportunities in life in some new way.

I began to branch out from athletics to explore other possible interests. I began to read voraciously on everything from physics to environmentalism and business. I started trying out new hobbies in music and arts. In the end, I discovered that the areas of business, finance, economics, and entrepreneurship were my passion—a passion that was even stronger than I had for athletics. I started to realize that one of the most gratifying and productive things a person could do with their time was to help others. One of the products of that realization is the book you now hold in your hands. Remember, just as there are many different people out there who are compatible with you romantically, there are many careers and potential passions out there that you will be compatible with as well.

MONETIZATION

One of the most difficult areas of discussion regarding life pursuits is that of monetization. Some lucky people, when they find a life pursuit that genuinely resonates with them, are able to turn it into a career and generate income. It is fashionable to dismiss the question of money when it comes to career choices and simply "follow your dreams," but such notions are misguided. Make no mistake: if a passion cannot be monetized, then it is not a career, it is strictly a hobby. Should this passion be abandoned in favour of something else just because it cannot generate satisfactory personal income? It would be impossible, and nothing short of presumptuous, for me to try and answer this question for you. Your individual circumstances will obviously have the strongest bearing on the answer.

It might be possible to pursue your passion as a hobby alongside another interest that serves as a career, but this may entail a lifestyle compromised by lots of stress and time shortages. You could abandon the passion entirely in favour of something more lucrative, but you might not consider this to be emotionally palatable. Or, you may try your best to make your hobby profitable. I encourage you to weigh your options very carefully before deciding on one path over another. No matter how much love you may feel for a particular life pursuit, you must still find some way to put food on the table! Remember to use tools such as your Personal Constitution when making these all-important life decisions.

EDUCATION

The question of education in our discussion is a pertinent one. Every generation, an ever-growing number of young adults ask a question that is becoming increasingly difficult to answer: Should they obtain a university degree? In general terms, the answer is still yes. There are many fields such as medicine in which obtaining formal education is an absolute must. However, that doesn't mean that you should copy the behaviour of friends and family and decide to attend college just because "everyone else is doing it." Such an action would be foolish. Rather, the decision should be made based on *what you want to do with your life*. You should only enroll in college or university when you have made an honest decision with yourself that doing so will help you accomplish what you want in life. If you haven't laid out a clear rationale and plan, don't go. Talk with your parents, friends, and academic advisors about the matter. Look at the personal consequences of going versus not going.

One of the worst mistakes that countless high school graduates make every year is to attend college, spending thousands of dollars in the process, in the hopes that they will find what they want to do in life when they are *already attending classes*. They spend less time deciding on their major and program than they do choosing what to have for their afternoon lunch. (I am being hyperbolic, but I think you get my point.) College education is an investment in the truest sense of the word, so this type of attitude is nothing short of ludicrous.

If you are unsure of what you want to do with your life, or what type of education will serve you best, consider taking a year off from school to work at a job while you collect your thoughts and figure it out. Do you want a college education in order to learn a trade? To start a business? To become an academic? It is absolutely critical that you figure this out to the best of your ability before spending money on classes. It is perfectly normal to change goals and aspirations multiple times—even in later life. However, this is not an excuse for going in without a solid plan to begin with.

CHOOSING A DEGREE PROGRAM

A very useful criterion to consider when deciding on a college education is the amount of income a degree will generate over and above a high school education versus the cost of acquiring the degree itself.[1] This type of decision making process first requires a close examination of all the different possible professional fields that one could study in university. Start by compiling a list of all the fields of study that you find interesting. For each of the acceptable degrees, list all of the direct and indirect costs of obtaining the degree, including tuition, books, and wages that were not earned as a result of studying instead of working. The next task is to obtain an estimate of the extra income the degree would generate annually, over and above that of a high school education, and multiply that by the number of prospective working years.

As an example, you might conclude that a degree in the natural sciences could potentially earn you an average of $30,000 a year over a high school education. This $30,000 multiplied by 40 years of your working life would equal $1,200,000. Take this $1,200,000 figure, subtract the initial cost of getting the degree (say $50,000) and you can value the degree at $1,150,000. Repeat this procedure for all the prospective degrees, and the degree with the highest value would become the logical choice. While this is not a silver bullet solution for choosing a university degree, it offers a useful way of thinking about the problem. Figure 9.1 is an example of such an exercise.

---

[1]   Technically, we would also have to consider something called the 'time value of money' in such an analysis, but we will ignore it in this book for simplicity. Additionally, since all educations would be discounted at the same rate for approximately the same length of time, they would roughly "cancel" each other out.

FIGURE 9.1: AN EXAMPLE OF USING A TABLE TO EVALUATE DEGREE PROGRAMS BY FUTURE EARNINGS

—————— ADAM'S UNIVERSITY CHOICE ——————

Subject Area	Cost (Normalized for this exercise)	Total Increase in Future Income	What Intrigues Me About this Field?
Biology	$50,000	$600,000	
Astrophysics	$50,000	$760,000	
Chemistry	$50,000	$690,000	
Economics	$50,000	$1,080,000	

We can see that Adam, a hypothetical prospective student, is interested in the sciences generally. So, narrowing down his academic choices to this point was likely fairly easy for him. He is now at an impasse. What area of the sciences should he focus on? He has determined that a degree in Economics is likely to give him the largest possible boost in earning power, so that is an important consideration, but it is not enough. Let's see what happens when he fills out the qualitative boxes regarding his inclinations and future prospects in Figure 9.2.

FIGURE 9.2: AN EXAMPLE OF USING A TABLE TO EVALUATE DEGREE PROGRAMS BY FUTURE EARNINGS AND INTEREST IN THE AREA

——————— ADAM'S UNIVERSITY CHOICE ———————

Criteria	Biology	Astrophysics	Chemistry	Economics
Cost (Normalized for this exercise)	$50,000	$50,000	$50,000	$50,000
Total Increase in Future Income	$600,000	$760,000	$690,000	$1,080,000
What Intrigues Me About This Field?	I was inspired to pursue the origins of life by the work of Richard Dawkins. Biology is fascinating to me because it speaks to my deep sense of wonder regarding the nature of life. I would love to pursue laboratory work in this area.	The study of the physical workings of the entire universe is an extremely gratifying field of pursuit. I feel like I would be involved in the most central of all sciences in this field. Physics also involves learning mathematical skills than can be applied to other fields.	Chemistry, to me, seems to be a field of science that provides a kind of "missing link" between physics and biology. It is a mix of both worlds, and I think I would find work in this field to be invigorating. I am inspired by the work of Emil Fischer.	Economics differs greatly from the other fields on this list in that it is a social science rather than a hard science. Even still, I think that economists contribute useful output to the well-being of society. I would be interested in studying and researching the economics of black markets.

After some deep introspection on the qualitative aspects of his different choices, Adam now decides that he would like to pursue Astrophysics. He feels that studying the mechanics of the basic physical systems of the universe will be enriching. He will also learn valuable mathematical skills that can be applied to many different industries. Additionally, the future-income estimate for this educational path is second only to Economics in his list of choices.

Make use of as many informational sources as you can when filling out the qualitative aspects of this matrix. Talk to graduates of the programs you are considering. Talk to parents, teachers, and friends. Consult your federal government's website for employment statistics for median income and future job growth in the field. As with any research, having more sources of data is generally better than having less.

Although I shall repeat that choosing your educational path is not something to be taken lightly (research into career outcomes is a must!), remember that what you are doing in school is not set in stone. You *can* change your educational direction if you discover you have a passion for something else, but make sure you put serious thought into doing so.

CHOOSING YOUR POST-SECONDARY INSTITUTION

Now that you have determined the field of study you want to enter, the next question is: which university should you choose. The way this author sees it, the choice boils down to a handful of key criteria:

- Location
- Strength of the program you are interested in (uniqueness, class sizes, availability of your professors)
- Cost/budget/availability of financial aid
- School reputation
- Culture
- Academic schedule
- Extracurricular factors (research opportunities, varsity sports, etc.)

Location   The first thing to consider is the location of the educational institution you are thinking of attending. For example, if you are fresh out of high school, you may be leaning toward universities that are within a 50 kilometre (31 miles) radius of your home. By living with your parents during your studies, you can keep your costs contained. However, the flip side of this is that you will not experience the lifestyle of living on campus. College life in dormitories is an experience that you will not get anywhere else, so this needs to be factored in as a valuable life experience, considered in juxtaposition with the increased costs. If you decide that dorm life is the way to go, this means that you will not be constrained to studying within a certain distance of home. Schools across the country (and even other countries) become viable options. Living off campus (but not with your parents) is also an option, but remember that the proximity and frequent contact with potential new friends will not occur as easily when living off campus as opposed to on campus.

If off-campus living sounds more compelling to you, carefully consider how you will get to school on a daily basis, and factor in the cost of this transportation in your decision. Will you take the bus, or will you drive? Or is the school within walking distance? Long commute times can make your school years a nightmare, and the high cost of owning a car may be prohibitive. Taking the bus is often a good compromise: just be sure that the bus schedule from your home will accommodate your class schedule.

Strength of Program   Various schools around the world are especially famous for one or two particular fields of study. Cambridge is famous for its work and history in the field of physics. The University of Chicago is a great intellectual hub for economists around the world. Clearly, universities around the world have different strengths and weaknesses, just as different people have various strengths and weaknesses. If a school that is local to your city has a strong reputation for the subject you are looking to pursue, consider yourself fortunate. Having a strong reputation in a particular field attracts the best and brightest minds to that university; in turn, this creates a self-reinforcing loop, where those brilliant minds further the strong reputation of the school. Do not underestimate the value of being in close proximity to great intellectuals in your area of interest.

Cost/Budget/Availability of Financial Aid   The cost of education is a funny thing. Despite the fact that education is intangible, you usually get what you pay for. The top ten Ivy League schools in the U.S. command the highest tuitions, but that's because they usually lead to the very best jobs. Ivy League schools aside, the other type of institution that commands high costs are religious schools. Because of the specialized nature of the curriculum, there is a premium cost for attending school in that type of environment.[1,2]

Aside from top 10 schools, the price of education at most mainstream universities is pretty similar. In Canada, you will likely be paying between $3,000 and $5,000 for each full-time semester of school.[3] This includes institutions such as the University of Toronto and Simon Fraser University, both of which are popular schools in their respective regions.

Student loans are ubiquitous amongst students, particularly because the cost of education has risen dramatically over the past few decades. This means that fewer and fewer students will be able to get their degrees without incurring some level of debt. Many students today graduate with student loan debts that are tens or hundreds of thousands of dollars. This level of personal debt should not be taken lightly, and it is vitally important that a university degree is chosen that will offer reasonably high-paying job prospects so that debt can be paid off. That is why the above exercise we performed was so important.

If you decide that student loans are the way to go, a financial-aid department will be available at your university. Call them or pay them a visit. They will be more than happy to answer all of your questions or concerns that you may have. It is almost *always* preferable to have student loans from the government than from private organizations. Government student loans have more lenient payment terms and lower interest rates. In fact, most student loans do not require payment until you have stopped taking classes for six months to a year.

School Reputation   It might seem shallow at face value, but a school's reputation is an important consideration when looking at your university options. It might cost two or three times more to get a degree at Stanford University in the U.S. than your local post-secondary institution, but the results in terms of future earning power typically justify the increased cost. News magazines such as *Maclean's* and *Forbes* publish an annual list of the top ten universities in Canada and the USA, respectively, based on a series of ranking criteria. *Maclean's* identified Simon Fraser University, the University of Waterloo, and the University of Victoria as the top three Canadian universities in 2016.[4] *Forbes* identified Ponoma College, Williams College, and Stanford University as the top three U.S. universities in 2016.[5]

Culture   Culture, because it is so nebulous, is difficult to evaluate, but the exercise has value, nonetheless. As a concrete example, the University of Victoria here in Canada seems to have a very sleepy and laid-back culture. On the other hand, according to some alumni, the culture of Simon Fraser University tends to be one of institutionalization. Investigate whether the culture or the "feel" of the university is in keeping with your personality and your expectations as to what you imagine a university should be like. Do you like a highly competitive environment? Or would you prefer something more laid back? Talk with current and former students and listen to what they have to say.

FIGURE 9.3: CAMPUS CULTURE, AS INTANGIBLE AS IT IS, IS AN IMPORTANT PART OF DECIDING WHICH UNIVERSITY TO ATTEND

Academic Schedule   This is an often overlooked area of education. Universities are not like high schools where the daily class schedules are standardized for everyone. Rather, each university creates its own class schedule in keeping with how they think students and faculty will be best served. If you are a working adult already in the work force, then chances are a university with many evening classes will appeal to you most. On the other hand, if you are fresh out of high school, having a daytime class schedule would probably work fine for you. Check out your prospective university's class schedule first, before paying your deposit, to ensure that it works with your personal schedule.

Extracurricular Activities   Extracurricular activities include varsity sports, clubs, and research opportunities. Think about what you want beyond your classes and traditional education. What kind of people would you like to associate yourself with during your downtime? What kind of side interests would you be interested in pursuing? If, for instance, you were highly interested in joining a kick-boxing group, knowing that such a group already existed at the university you are considering would be valuable knowledge. (See more about exercise and sports teams in Chapter 5.)

Wrapping it up. Now that you have a set of criteria to help you choose your educational institution, the remaining piece of the puzzle is to maintain the discipline to actually use those criteria. Your choice of university will have a powerful impact on your future. Choose wisely!

CAREER DISSATISFACTION

No matter what your career goal, and regardless of how well educated you may be, there will likely be periods of your life, especially early on in your work life, when you may be working in a role that does not give you much satisfaction. Many people refer to this as "paying your dues." This is a natural part of most people's lives and should be viewed as a learning opportunity. Observe how the business you work for is run and what strategies they employ to gain and retain customers. Watch how your coworkers behave and how management responds to different types of behavioural patterns. These insights can be invaluable to your future career endeavours.

If you find the work truly dissatisfying, use it as motivation to achieve something more. Our globalized economy has made social mobility and the pursuit of prosperity available to more people than ever before. An unpleasant situation is not something to be lamented; rather, see it as a challenge to be met and overcome. That is a truly constructive perspective on the problem. Work hard, make a focused effort to get ahead, and the unpleasantness will not last.

READING AND RESEARCH

To really know what you want to do in life, and to improve your chances of finding it early on, reading and research are imperative. Reading is like furnishing your mind. Without it, your mind is like an empty house. With it, your mind becomes your home. I recommend starting with the great works of the intellectual "giants" in history. This list includes *The Wealth of Nations*[6] by Adam Smith; *On the Origin of Species*[7] by Charles Darwin; *Principia*[8] by Isaac Newton; and other philosophers and thinkers from around the world and throughout history.

The point is to give yourself the broadest possible exposure to the intellectual best that humanity has to offer. This will give you a guiding influence in life and bring clarity to how you see society around you. Problems in the world that need solving, which may not have been obvious at first, will become more and more apparent. As you grow, the possible solutions to those problems will similarly present themselves. Reading will make you rich in more ways than one.

Research the career paths that are relevant to your interests. Do not simply acquire an education and hope for the best. This kind of approach is nonsense. Let us say that you are interested in biology. Use the Internet to research the possible degree programs and career paths available in this field. Also, talk with anyone you can find who has pursued this career path and ask them about the job opportunities, the difficulties of the work, and the expected salary. Many of the faculty members at your college or university would be happy to speak with you. If you can't find anyone to speak with, do an Internet search for a forum and post your questions there. The bottom line is to do your research. Become informed!

It is also worth noting that acquainting yourself with, and developing positive, professional relationships with established figures in any field of work will make it that much easier to gain employment and start a career in that field. While I am a firm believer in a system of meritocracy, networking and getting to know influential people is nonetheless a valuable asset. Consider getting a set of business cards made that you can leave with people upon meeting them. Most of the business cards you give people will be placed in a desk drawer and forgotten, but when playing the odds, the one in every hundred people who call you may be your ticket to the next level in your career.

LAUNCHING YOUR CAREER

Before we even approach the topic of job hunting techniques and the labour market, consider whether or not a traditional career path is even right for you. By following a traditional career path I mean applying for jobs and starting a career in an established company, working your way up through the ranks. Whether or not this is a good idea for you depends on your personal inclination towards entrepreneurship and whether or not your chosen calling in life demands striking out on your own or going with an established company or organization. There are many professions and lines of work that could go either way. Let's say you wanted to become a software programmer. Skilled programmers could either find work at an established company such as Microsoft or could start their own software company.

Continuing with our software programming example, let's say you decided that striking it out on your own and working for an established company are equally feasible options. This means that your decision will hinge on your own personal desires and inclinations. There are certainly many psychological gratifications that come from starting your own business, and obviously there are certain financial rewards to be had if you are successful. However, the trade-off is a lot of work and potential risk if not managed properly.

Working at an established company is often seen as being the "safer," of the two options. This is generally true as far as financial risk and overall security is concerned. Your risk tolerance needs to be tempered, and weighed overall against the potential benefits of being an entrepreneur. The question of whether or not entrepreneurship or a traditional career is right for you is largely a question that only you can answer. Take a walk and do some soul searching. Talk with your closest confidants to bounce ideas off of them. Make your decision after careful reflection.

If you become an entrepreneur, it is rather axiomatic that you are your own boss. However, the situation is not really any different even if you are working at an established company. Remember that you and the employer are partners in a transaction. You do not work for the company. You work for yourself. You are working for yourself, and you are trading your labour for a company's dollars. Keep this distinction strong in your mind. You don't work for a company; you work *with* a company in an equal partnership. Many people, when searching for a job have a tendency to behave as if the employer has all the power. They submit themselves and automatically concede to the supposedly greater power of a company's management. This is nonsense. Do not treat a company and its management with unquestioning deference. While it is important to respect a certain chain of command within an organization, never lose sight of the fact that we are all fundamentally equal as people in this world.

LET'S GO JOB HUNTING

So, let's say you found your passion in your early twenties. You want to be a journalist. You love the news and what a free, healthy press does for society. It's meaningful. It's huge. You've wanted to be part of the scene for years. You've received your journalism degree, and now you're ready to go out job hunting. Where do you start? What do you do? Let's start off with some principles. Getting a job is about two things:

1. What you know (your skills)
2. Who you know (your connections)

This is what it boils down to in a nutshell. Your skills determine what you can contribute to society. That's why education is so important. After that, your connections determine what type of job you can get. That's why business professionals network so much. It's that simple. So, it makes sense that your efforts in your career be focused on these areas of skill building and connection building.

Remember that your education does not end just because you have finished school. Take the opportunity to continue building your skills through classes, online courses, books, and any other skill-building resources you can get your hands on. This will not only give you a more fulfilling life, but will also prevent your current skill set from becoming obsolete as society and the economy inevitably change through time.

When I say build connections, I'm not just referring to your friends or the connections you already have. Have you ever had an interview with a hiring manager and it didn't go your way? That manager is now an industry connection, even if they didn't offer you the job. A connection, even post-interview, can be established by simply sending a thank you email to them after your interview. In the future, should you ever need advice on a topic on which they are experts, it does not hurt to simply ask them. Ninety-nine percent of people out there will be more than happy to help you if you simply ask. That's what a network is for. And what about the remaining one percent, you ask? The worst thing that can happen is they simply say no!

Job Hunting Specifics   Now that we are done with general principles, let's advance to the specifics. The job market is literally that—a market where there are buyers and sellers for people's labour. So, you've got to treat your job hunt exactly that way: you are selling your services. To a certain extent, you are trying to get the highest possible price for the service (your labour) that you are selling. On the flip side, the buyers of your labour are companies that are looking to get the highest quality product for the lowest possible price.

This sounds a bit like the task of purchasing groceries doesn't it? The various grocery stores want to make a sale, and you, the buyer, want to purchase the highest quality product at the lowest possible price. When you go shopping, you have to walk out to the various markets to find the milk, eggs, vegetables, fruits you want, and you shop for the best price. Sometimes, there are certain not so well-known shops that have prices lower than the big chains. There are great deals to be had if you are willing to look for them. Sometimes these searches yield results, sometimes they don't. It's usually worth the try, though.

The truth is, the labour market is a lot like shopping at the grocery store. You want to sell your labour? You have to go to the market, where the action is. So, what is the labour market equivalent of the grocery store? Let's think of some markets.

- *Popular Internet job sites*
    - www.indeed.com
    - www.simplyhired.com
    - www.monster.com
- *Job fairs*
    - Visit local universities
    - Public libraries and recreation centres often hold these types of events
    - Sometimes job fairs are hosted in hotels
- *Your network*
    - Tap a personal connection
    - Ask for a referral for a position you are interested in
    - Attend networking events to broaden your connections
    - Look for career postings by connections and companies on your LinkedIn profile (www.linkedin.com)
- *Direct to company*
    - Go to the careers section of the company website
    - Call the company directly

If the company has a public presence, such as retail branches, pop in and start asking the manager questions about the nature of the business. This kind of interest and passion can frequently lead to a job.

These are the areas in which buyers and sellers in the labour market can come together. Tap all of the above possibilities to make contact with an organization where you want to work. Your goal once you make contact with an organization you want to work with is to get an interview so the company and its hiring managers can see your enthusiasm and your passion for the work. This kind of energy, more than anything else, is what can translate into a job offer. Companies know that they can train you if you lack certain skills, but if you don't have a great attitude and energy, that's not something they want to help you correct.

Your Resume   Before calling you in for an interview, most companies will want to see your resume or a portfolio of your work. This is the first step for them to screen out potential candidates that simply aren't appropriate. (For example, it may not be appropriate for someone with no skills or experience as a computer technician to apply for such a job, no matter how skilled they might be in some other field.) So, your education and experience are very important, and your resume communicates this to potential employers very quickly. Figure 9.4 shows an excerpt of a good, clean resume and cover letter format. Feel free to follow this format for your own resume.

FIGURE 9.4: AN EXAMPLE OF A CLEAN COVER LETTER AND RESUME LAYOUT

Adam Friedman

July 21st, 2016

XYZ Manufacturing Co.
Human Resources
Suite 1000, 12345 Smith Avenue
Anytown, Province A1B 2C3

XYZ Manufacturing Co.,

Lorem ipsum dolor sit amet, consectetur adipiscing elit, sed do eiusmod tempor incididunt ut labore et dolore magna aliqua. Ut enim ad minim veniam, quis nostrud exercitation ullamco laboris nisi ut aliquip ex ea commodo consequat. Excepteur sint occaecat cupidatat non proident, sunt in culpa qui officia deserunt mollit anim id est laborum.

In aliquam sem fringilla ut morbi tincidunt. Auctor elit sed vulputate mi sit amet mauris. Vitae congue mauris rhoncus aenean vel elit scelerisque mauris pellentesque. Convallis a cras semper auctor. Justo laoreet sit amet cursus. Aliquet lectus proin nibh nisl condimentum id venenatis a condimentum.

Ipsum suspendisse ultrices gravida dictum fusce ut placerat orci. Eget nunc lobortis mattis aliquam faucibus purus in massa. Diam sollicitudin tempor id eu nisl nunc mi. Pulvinar mattis nunc sed blandit libero volutpat. Diam quam nulla porttitor massa id. Facilisis sed odio morbi quis. Faucibus a pellentesque sit amet porttitor eget dolor.

Excepteur sint ut enim ad minim veniam, quis nostrud exercitation ullamco laboris nisi ut aliquip ex ea commodo consequat a cras semper auctor.

Adam Friedman
Adam Friedman

**12345 Smithfield Street, Anytown, Province S1C 2B9
Tel: 555-123-4567 | Email: friedman.adam@myemail.com**

FIGURE 9.4 CONTINUED:
AN EXAMPLE OF A CLEAN COVER LETTER
AND RESUME LAYOUT

Adam Friedman

Tel: 555-123-4567 | Email: friedman.adam@myemail.com

Skills

Lorem ipsum dolor sit amet, consectetur adipiscing elit, sed do eiusmod tempor incididunt ut labore et dolore magna aliqua. Ut enim ad minim veniam, quis nostrud exercitation ullamco laboris nisi ut aliquip ex ea commodo consequat. Excepteur sint occaecat cupidatat non proident, sunt in culpa qui officia deserunt mollit anim id est laborum.

- Supply chain analysis
- Shipping logistics
- Online marketing
- Upstream marketing relations
- Inventory management
- Technical writing
- Data mining
- Data analysis
- Wesbite monetization

Education

Bachelor of Commerce - Marketing Management | University of British Columbia | 2001 - 2004

▶ **Lorem ipsum dolor:** Lorem ipsum dolor sit amet, consectetur adipiscing elit, sed do eiusmod tempor incididunt ut labore et dolore magna aliqua.

▶ **Ut enim ad:** Lorem ipsum dolor sit amet, consectetur adipiscing elit, sed do eiusmod tempor incididunt ut labore et dolore magna aliqua.

▶ **Excepteur sint occaecat:** Lorem ipsum dolor sit amet, consectetur adipiscing elit, sed do eiusmod tempor incididunt ut labore et dolore magna aliqua.

Work Experience

Assistant Marketing Manager | DEF Company | July 2009 - Current
456 Davidson Street, Anytown, Province B95 4L2 | 555-123-4567

▶ Lorem ipsum dolor sit amet, consectetur adipiscing elit, sed do eiusmod tempor incididunt ut labore et dolore magna aliqua. Excepteur sint occaecat cupidatat non proident, sunt in culpa qui officia deserunt mollit anim id est laborum. Excepteur sint occaecat cupidatat non proident.

Upstream Market Analyst | GHI Company | Jan. 2005 - June 2009
789 Smith Street, Anytown, Province V5M 9E4 | 555-123-4567

▶ Lorem ipsum dolor sit amet, consectetur adipiscing elit, sed do eiusmod tempor incididunt ut labore et dolore magna aliqua. Excepteur sint occaecat cupidatat non proident, sunt in culpa qui officia deserunt mollit anim id est laborum. Excepteur sint occaecat cupidatat non proident.

Certifications

Lifesaving Society of Canada and Canadian Red Cross
- Bronze Star lifeguarding certification
- Bronze Cross lifeguarding certification
- First Aid and CPR

Community Involvement

I have 4 years of volunteer experience as an Impact Speaker for The United Way (November 2012 - present). The duty of the Impact Speaker is to engage audiences at over 150 program events per year in order to drive community involvement.

First, let's start with some general observations. Notice how the resume is laid out on the page. All the spacing between sections of the document is equal. There is a sufficient amount of white space around the margins. Be sure that you have no spelling mistakes. (Spelling mistakes are a big red flag to employers.) Beyond this, notice that the resume is a single page. There are a couple of schools of thought surrounding this topic. Some say that a resume should never be more than one page. Others say that two pages should be the limit. Neither is right or wrong, but most would agree that shorter and more concise is generally better. This author's view on the subject is that two pages is a comfortable limit; as you gain more experience, one page may not be sufficient to encapsulate all of your qualifications.

Notice the order of the content in this resume. Because this person has spent some years in the work force, they have accumulated valuable skills. This is the reason why skills are emphasized at the top of the resume. Next is education, as this person's academic accomplishments are still somewhat recent. As you progress further and further in your career, you can move your education credentials down in your resume, and your work experience can supersede your academic credentials. This brings us to a general principle: your greatest strengths and your proudest accomplishments should generally be at the top of your resume so that your potential employer can see them immediately.

Your resume details your work history and education. As such, you generally shouldn't be changing it as you submit it from one employer to another. However, your cover letter should be individually tailored to each potential employer. Changing the receiver's name is an obvious start, but also mentioning specific things you have learned about that company through your research such as core values, the company's mission, and recently developed products and services is a good strategy. Get those resumes and cover letters out!

The Interview   So, you've got your resume and cover letter out there and you've received a few callbacks. Now you have to prepare for your interview. Now, exactly what kind of preparation should be done is highly dependent on what position you're applying for, and in which industry. However, there are seven universally accepted rules that all job applicants should follow when interviewing.

First, be on time for the appointment. Better yet, arrive 15 minutes early.

Second, be well groomed. Shower, and style your hair. A groomed and polished appearance will add to your overall professionalism.

Third, dress at *least* one level above the people in the work environment you are entering. It might be easy to simply recommend that you dress in a business suit for all interviews, and 80 percent of the time, this advice would probably be sound. However, there are cases in which this might be off-putting. For instance, if you were interviewing for a factory position or certain jobs in the service sector, arriving at the employer's office in a business suit would probably be incongruous. So, while it's still better to be overdressed than underdressed, it is also possible to overdo it. A better policy is to dress at least one level above everyone else in the work environment. So, in our examples above, the workers will probably be all dressed casually or in coveralls. As such, opting for business casual wear would likely be sufficient. Use your best judgment for the situation!

Fourth, make sure you bring at least three hard copies of your resume and cover letter: one copy for you, one copy for the interviewer, and an additional copy as a backup. Never assume that your interviewer will have printed a copy for themselves. Also, bring hard copies of any past work of which you are particularly proud (assuming you have permission to do so from previous employers). These portfolio pieces can really help you hit a home run.

Fifth, make sure you research the company before your interview. Research the company's history, its products or services, and its core values. It is not enough to simply know superficial things about what a company does. If the interviewer asks what you think about the company's core values or mission and you don't have an answer, it will reflect badly on your diligence as a job candidate. Finally, perform an Internet search to find and talk to current or former employees about the *types* of questions that will be asked. Some companies such as Google and Microsoft ask vexing questions to candidates as a way of gauging how well applicants can think on their feet. Be prepared.

Sixth, bring confidence to the interview and remember that it is a two-way conversation. The biggest mistake I see interviewees make is that they view the interview as being one directional. They think that interviewers are there to simply ask questions, and that the candidate is just there to answer the questions. This is the wrong approach. Interviews should be *conversational*. The interviewees who achieve the best results are typically those who have established a rapport during the interview. Genuinely open up. Talk with the interviewer. Share your thoughts about where you think the industry is headed. Share your philosophy about what makes a great contributor in this field. Furthermore, share your passion. Pretend you are talking with a friend about why you love this field. Being open and enthusiastic is a powerful combination. In addition, consider asking the interviewer whether you may add him or her to your LinkedIn profile at the interview's end.

Seventh, send a thank-you email to your interviewer afterwards, thanking them for both their time and consideration. This small gesture not only makes the interviewer an ally, but also improves your chances of landing the job. I emphasize small gestures like this because it's usually these small considerations that accrue over time and make great positive impressions on people. I have heard of a job candidate who was given the job over another candidate, who was equally as good, because the other person did not write a thank-you email after the interview. This small differentiator was all it took to tip the scales. Don't underestimate the little things!

LET'S START A BUSINESS

Let's move on now to the prospect of starting your own business. This is not a simple matter. However, some things in life are hard, and some things in life are right. For some people, starting a business is both. It is a necessary path for achieving certain dreams and goals. When you reflected on your life pursuit earlier in this chapter, you may have decided that starting your own business was the right path to take. However, sometimes it's not an obvious conclusion. It takes much introspection before coming to the conclusion that entrepreneurship is the right path to take. Consider a hypothetical scenario in which you decide to become a financial planner or advisor. There are many ways to become a financial planner working with an established company, but there are also many ways to start your own practice. With some thought, you may come to the conclusion that starting your own practice and having a certain kind of entrepreneurial freedom is exactly what you want from your work.

There are many ways to go about starting your own business, and the exact way in which you should go about doing so will depend on a variety of factors. These factors include the laws governing startup businesses in your country, what type of industry you are entering, whether you need outside investment, whether you're selling a product or a service, whether you are incorporating or not, and many other things. The space and detail required to put together a seriously comprehensive guide on starting your own business is well beyond the scope of this book. However, like all of the other topics discussed in this book, there are some fundamental principles that should be followed when starting your own business, regardless of the industry or context.

Beyond principles, it's important to realize that there is no "typical" flow of how entrepreneurs who start businesses become successful. It's not a linear path that goes from step one to step two and so on. Rather, the path of entrepreneurship is a cyclical one that often goes from victory to defeat and back again in the blink of an eye. Having said that, let's get on to our principles, outlined in each of the subsections below.

Know your Objective   This means that you need to know where you are going. What's the goal? What is the outcome you are trying to achieve? Once you know the outcome, you can begin to plan backwards from there to the present. You can have the best ship in the world, but if the captain doesn't know where to go, the ship will simply drift aimlessly around. So, it's important to know where you are going. What is your business going to look like five years from now? Twenty years from now? Be specific. Simply saying you want your business to be successful is not enough. However, saying that you want to start a biotech company that will completely rid the world of congenital diseases within three decades *is* specific. Saying you want to start a consulting company that operates all across the country, and will generate at least a billion dollars' worth of annual revenue within 15 years *is* specific. Bill Gates' goal when he founded Microsoft was "to put a computer on every desk and in every home."[9] He started with his objective in mind.

Protect yourself at All Times   This principle is borrowed from the sport of boxing where contestants are told to never let their guard down. In the world of business, this means doing everything you can to prevent yourself from being taken advantage of or being put into any position in which people other than yourself can determine your fate. As a concrete example, as part of your advertising campaign you may decide to film an advertisement to be broadcast online. However, in your haste you forgot to get one of the cinematographers to sign a release form that specifies you are allowed to use the material they have filmed. A couple months later, the cinematographer takes advantage of this situation and decides to sue you for copyright infringement. The ensuing legal battle could have been easily avoided by always remembering to protect yourself at all times.

Stay Disciplined   Don't let yourself get distracted when you know you should be working on your business. Focusing and working on the task at hand when other things are vying for your attention is an incredible virtue. When Arnold Schwarzenegger was training for Mr. Olympia, his father passed away. Despite the tragedy, Schwarzenegger did not travel back home to attend the funeral or comfort his grieving mother.[10] He remained 100 percent focused on his training and the competition. While I am not necessarily advocating skipping the funeral of a loved one, it is important to note that this is the type of focus and discipline it takes to be successful as an entrepreneur.

Surround yourself with Only Those you Trust   When it comes to business, you must be able to trust your partners. (Recall our discussions on genuine relationships in Chapter 7.) Business is about dealing with things that are valuable. This includes cash, intellectual property, computers, equipment, and your reputation. If you do not feel that you can trust the people you are working with, don't work with them.

Have a Plan, but Always be Willing to Change It   The future is always uncertain; nonetheless, we must always have a plan for our life goals if we expect to have a reasonable chance of achieving them. What I have found useful is to plan future goals based on laddered time horizons. As we discussed earlier, it helps to start with the objective in mind. This doesn't just apply to business but to any goal you want to achieve in life. As a case in point, let's say you want to become a physicist. If this is so, talk to others who have already achieved this goal, and then map out their career path as a template that you can follow. Not only does this give you an approximate time horizon, but by analyzing the paths taken by those who have come before you, you can also find shortcuts. Sometimes people achieve certain things in a roundabout way. You could potentially shave years off the process of reaching a goal by simply looking at areas where others have stumbled.

Figure 9.5 shows an example of an individual using laddered time horizon planning—or what I call the TAG (time, activity, goal) model—to map their goals of becoming a physicist. This works for business planning, career planning, and personal planning. As always, you can map this model either with pen and paper or digitally, according to your preference.

FIGURE 9.5: USING THE TAG MODEL TO BECOME A PHYSICIST

Time	Activity	Goal
Today	Research different university options for physics via print and web sources.	Decide which universities I want to visit as part of my research.
1 Week from Today	Do campus visits of the universities I'm interested in.	Evaluate each university in terms of culture, feel, and the availability of amenities.
1 Month from Today	Talk with graduates of each university. See what they have to say, and look at their career paths.	Settle on a university and pay my registration deposit.
3 Months from Today	Buy necessary supplies, sort out transportation, financing and budgeting.	Be ready to start classes
6 Months from Today	Start studying	Begin classes
1 Month from Today	Talk with graduates of each university. See what they have to say, and look at their career paths.	Settle on a university and pay my registration deposit.
2 Years from Today	Talk again with graduates of the university and reflect on what areas of the last 2 years of study have interested me most.	Decide my third year specialization in physics.
5 Years from Today	Graduating	Finish my degree!
10 Years from Today	Working in a career in physics!	Be a physicist!

Learn the Language of your Business   Business has its own language concerning legal terms, financial terms, contracts, and the like. Many of these topics aren't exactly the most exciting in the world, but there is great power to be had in learning them. There are some areas that are more important than others. I would suggest focusing on the following:

- Financial accounting
- Business law
- Business plans

There are many books available that can be used as learning resources for financial accounting. Accounting is important in business because it allows you to understand the health of the business itself; namely, tracking your cash flow, assets, debts, revenue, and expenses. If you do not understand accounting, you will have a difficult time understanding what is happening inside of the business. Pick up any book from your local library on the subject of accounting and absorb its basic principles. You are not required to go as far as becoming an actual accountant, but being familiar with fundamental concepts will pay dividends in the future.

Familiarizing yourself with business law is important because it's like learning the rules of the game. Learning business law will teach you everything from what kinds of organizational structures there are to the types of standard contracts available for the purchase and sale of assets. Knowing about business taxes is of huge benefit. Other topics such as patenting and intellectual property are good to be familiar with as well. As with accounting, you can borrow books on business law and taxes for free from your local library.

Finally, knowing how to write a good business plan is an invaluable skill. Even if you are not planning to pitch your idea to an external investor, it is still beneficial to get your idea formalized on paper so that you can clarify your own thought process. In addition, it may be useful in the future for sharing with your partners or employees. While there may be good books on how to write business plans out there, a better route may be to request some help in this area. This brings us to our next principle.

Get a Mentor   A business mentor is someone who can guide you in the right direction and steer you away from common pitfalls. If you are in college or have recently finished college, consider asking one of your professors, or make acquaintances with someone in the business department. Perhaps a family friend that has experience running a business, or a former boss whom you consider to be competent and trustworthy might be willing to mentor you.

Getting help with your business plan is only the beginning in terms of what a mentor can help you with. As your plans grow into action, a mentor may give you advice that could save you from very expensive and time-consuming mistakes. Don't underestimate the value of this kind of relationship.

Treat Cash as a Precious Commodity, and Avoid Debt Whenever Possible   Cash is the lifeblood of any business. Without cash, no company can survive. Treat your cash as if it was the water in your canteen and you were stuck in the middle of the desert. As a rule, a business should only spend money when it seems likely that the amount of money to be made from an expenditure exceeds the expenditure itself (i.e., the benefits outweigh the costs). For instance, you might spend $5,000 on an industrial-strength machine for your carpet cleaning business, but doing so would be prudent because you plan on making that money back (and then some) from actually using it to clean carpets. Beyond conserving cash, avoid getting into debt as much as possible. While certain business ventures do require going in to debt to some degree, it should always be minimized as a matter of reducing your financial risk. Owing money in business is like owing someone some of your water when you're stranded in the desert! Do so only with caution! (Read more about debt in Chapter 4.)

Starting a business is both risky and exhilarating, but if achieving your dream requires you to go down such a path, don't be frightened at the prospect of doing so. If you do not go for it, you will most certainly regret forgoing your opportunity. Who dares, wins.

THE BOTTOM LINE: DO NOT DELAY

Time flies. This one statement encapsulates the very essence of the fleeting lives we all live on this planet. Do not delay in finding your passion in life. You only have one opportunity to live life to its fullest and experience self-actualization and true happiness by maximizing your personal potential. Do not squander that opportunity. We are all lucky to be alive at this time in history. The number of incredibly improbable events that had to occur in history in order for you to be here right now absolutely boggles the mind. Life is a gift in the truest sense. Your life, like anyone's life, may end at any moment. It is a privilege, rather than a right, to be alive with the opportunity for self-actualization available to us. The longer you wait to take action, the more of this precious opportunity you will be wasting. Find your passion. Start now.

ACTION STEPS BEFORE READING THE NEXT CHAPTER

TO-DO: YOUR LIFE PURSUIT
- Go for a walk outside by yourself and think about your passion in life. Is what you're doing now making you happy? Is your work indistinguishable from your pleasure?
- If you are a youth in high school, use the post-secondary planning tool to figure out what to do after high school.
- Fill out the TAG (time, activity, goal) model with your own specifics to map out how you will pursue your passion in the days, months, and years ahead.

FURTHER RECOMMENDED READING ON YOUR LIFE PURSUIT
- *Think and Grow Rich*, Napoleon Hill
- *The Happiness of Pursuit: Finding the Quest That Will Bring Purpose to Your Life*, Chris Guillebeau
- *Hustle Believe Receive: An 8-Step Plan to Changing Your Life and Living Your Dream*, Sarah Centrella
- *Make Your Own Lunch: How to Live an Epically Epic Life through Work, Travel, Wonder, and (Maybe) College*, Ryan Porter

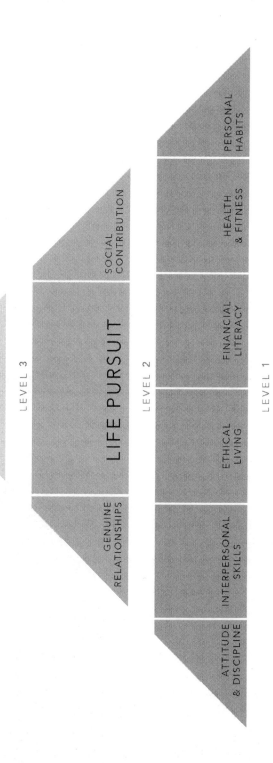

THE PARADIGM OF HAPPINESS

LEVEL 3

CONTINUOUS GROWTH

LEVEL 3

LIFE PURSUIT

GENUINE RELATIONSHIPS

SOCIAL CONTRIBUTION

LEVEL 2

ATTITUDE & DISCIPLINE

INTERPERSONAL SKILLS

ETHICAL LIVING

FINANCIAL LITERACY

HEALTH & FITNESS

PERSONAL HABITS

LEVEL 1

CHAPTER 10
CONTINUOUS GROWTH

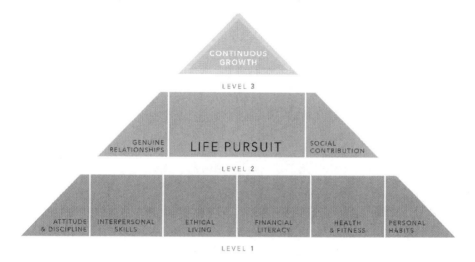

THE PARADIGM OF HAPPINESS

From the outset of this book, I have proposed that the purpose of human endeavour is to maximize happiness. Furthermore, the purpose of this book is to help readers pursue a course of action that will maximize their happiness with whatever resources they may have at their disposal. By now, you will have begun to see how small, incremental, positive changes in your life—starting with your own attitude—compound into wonderful results. Positive changes in one part of your life tend to encourage and reinforce positive changes in all the other aspects of your life.

I have presented a working model for realizing self-actualization and achievement. As we have learned, a positive attitude, a Core Principle, an ethical lifestyle, the effective use of money, genuine relationships, healthy eating and exercise habits form the foundation for the pursuit of life's most fulfilling endeavours. More than anything, I hope I have guided the reader away from a life path that may prove ultimately unfulfilling.

I have tied together all of the facets of **Level 1** of The Paradigm with a framework of constructive personal habits. Using time management tools, such as to-do lists and time trackers, allows for the intelligent coordination of day-to-day activities. Organizing your personal home and work space similarly allows you to be more productive. And when you're ready to go out and conquer the world, I've made sure that the readers have an adequate knowledge of wardrobe and style nuances as well.

Following the basics in **Level 1**, I have introduced the three components of **Level 2** of The Paradigm, which constitute the three sources of happiness for the human condition. The first source is cultivating *real* relationships with friends and loved ones. Being a genuine friend, establishing deep connections, and cherishing the time you have with your loved ones brings substance to your existence in a way that shallow relationships never can. It is a distinct form of joy that is one of the most wonderful parts of being human.

The second source of happiness is contributing positively to society. Many people take for granted what society has given them. There is hardly anything more gratifying than knowing you have given back to the wealth of society as opposed to simply taking from it. This might mean being part of the academic team who establishes the next breakthrough in physics or chemistry. Perhaps for you, giving back may mean helping to eradicate social inequality in the developing world. What you want to create is completely your choice. There are no limits to the possibilities.

Finally, the most important of the three sources of happiness, is finding your passion in life and pursuing it wholeheartedly and honestly. Finding your passion in life is like finding yourself. Like a soulmate, it becomes part of you, and eventually, indistinguishable from you. Without a life pursuit, you will find it difficult to ascertain your direction in life; like an astronaut in deep space, with no way of knowing one direction from another. If you do not know what your life's passion is, your *immediate* task is to find it.

My motto: *pursue your passion!*

THE THIRD AND FINAL LEVEL

There is one final level (**Level 3**) of The Paradigm of Happiness we have not discussed yet. It will be the focus of my discussion for the remainder of this chapter. The final level is the realization, the epiphany, that there is no finish line. Self-actualization, happiness, and achievement are an endless journey in which the journey is the reward. There will certainly be plateaus, but you must resist the temptation to stagnate when you plateau. Your life should never take on a final, crystallized state. Life is movement. Stagnation is death.

There are an unlimited number of things in this world for you to experience, but time is limited. You have infinite experiences available to you and finite time. In other words, you have no time to waste. Many people may despair at the realization that they have not been making the most of the time they have been given so far in life, but such an attitude is misguided. The realization that there are far more constructive and fulfilling ways to use one's time should be considered a victory of consciousness and reasoning, never a reason for despondency.

The key idea I am conveying is that no matter how much success you have achieved in life, and no matter how much you have experienced, it would be both an egregious waste of time and a self-abdication of life's meaning to simply give up on achieving and experiencing more. This is not to say that you should not ever rest, relax, go on vacation, or "stop and smell the flowers," but your work gives your life meaning, and exploring new paths makes it worth living. That the human animal is never satisfied with the status quo has been viewed by many as a negative trait of human nature. It is, however, far from this. Never being satisfied with the current state of things motivates us to strive to achieve more. This pushes the human race forward.

Be honest with yourself about what kind of mark you want to leave on the world when you die. While no person can live forever, maybe our ideas can. For most individuals, at best, few people will remember them 100 years after they die. Is it your desire to leave a positive mark on this world? To be remembered? Will you leave a legacy? Such questions are not meant to scare the reader; rather, they are meant to stir the consciousness. How will you be remembered?

Although not substantiated by historians, a relevant legend alleges that Alexander the Great, in testimony to the impermanence of possessions and the material world, elected to have his hands hanging out of his coffin upon his death. Why? In order to show everyone around him that he would leave the world just as he came in—empty-handed.[1] Mere wealth and material possessions will not fulfill us. Rather, we should focus on enriching experiences, what we can contribute to society, and our loved ones.

Read more. Enjoy the endless journey. Discover the mysteries of the universe with physics and astronomy. Read about history. Learn about politics and the differing views on how nations should be organized and run. Absorb society's past and learn where we came from. Do not be afraid to venture into new and unfamiliar territories. There are amazing experiences to be had in these uncharted realms. Jump into a new line of work or study. After 10 years as a proprietor, become a musician. After seven years as a musician, move to Paris and play in a band. Experience different cultures, different ways of living, and different ways of thinking. Know what it's like to live in the bustling cities of China, near their markets that never sleep, or what it's like to live in New York, the entire city that never sleeps. Experience everything in life that you can. There is no finish line, but your time is limited. That is the essence of our existence.

YOUR CIRCUMSTANCES

No matter who you are, which year you are reading this book in, or where you are reading it, there will be parts of your life that you may rightly feel have been unfair for you. Conversely, you may also feel guilty for having been given privileges and luxuries that are far above the norm. Do not dwell on such matters. You may be born a genius or not so smart. You may be born able-bodied or with disabilities. You may be born rich or poor. You may be born male or female. You may be born into any number of countries or social structures. What you must realize is that nobody has control over the hand that they are dealt in life. The only thing we can decide is how to play the hand that we have been given. Do not focus on your circumstances, unfair as they may be. Never think of yourself as a victim. Focus on the possibilities.

You can be successful in life regardless of what circumstances you have been born into. Bill Gates, one of the richest men in the world, was born into an upper middle-class family. Despite this, he did not let his family's fortunate circumstances ruin his drive to succeed and make something of himself.[2] He refused to be complacent.

Consider a woman born into the opposite circumstances. Rose Blumkin, founder of the famous Nebraska Furniture Mart, was an illiterate immigrant who travelled by boat in 1917 from Russia to the United States, and founded the single most successful furniture store in the country. She started with a $500 initial investment that she managed to scrape together after 17 years of hard work.[3] Your drive, your attitude, and the passion behind your pursuit are what will propel you to achieve your dreams. Your circumstances do not dictate your potential, only you do.

Our thoughts and beliefs truly do create our reality. We impute meaning to the events that occur in our lives. We create a narrative where we implicitly tell ourselves things such as, "I was born into a poor family. I've been told since my youth that I would always be labouring to make a dollar, and that life would be a day-to-day struggle until my dying breath." We may not even realize these thoughts are trailing through our minds, but they are. It's important that we become cognizant of these narratives, *and* realize there is no real substance behind them. Actively work to create your own narrative instead of accepting the one that life has thrust upon you. Allow yourself to be whatever it is you want to be. Do not allow detractors and difficult situations (and there will *always* be one or the other or both) to discourage you from your dreams.

SELF-REFLECTION

Do not forget to reflect on and evaluate the trajectory of your own life on a regular basis. Through the rigours of our daily struggles, we tend to lose ourselves in the matters at hand, as in the depths of a mathematical problem. As a result, we sometimes lose sight of our long-term goals, values, and ambitions. In your room, office, or on public transportation, quietly reflect on yourself, and whether your day-to-day activities are truly adding value to your life and helping you to accomplish your life's vision. This self-evaluation is extremely important. Knowing and mentally reinforcing your path in life will prevent you from "sleep walking" through life.

Revisit your Personal Constitution daily, along with making time for your reflections. Have your plans and activities kept up with the core values you pledged yourself to? Or perhaps your Personal Constitution needs some updating? Amending your Constitution isn't something that should be done willy-nilly on a daily basis, but it may be appropriate when you feel you have experienced fundamental changes in your values. Deep, introspective realizations can emerge from quiet contemplation. Sometimes new facts and information can be realized even from memories that are years old. This gives you the opportunity to grow as a person.

Ten to twenty minutes of quiet self-reflection should suffice on a day-to-day basis. Of course, readers are welcome to do more, should that feel appropriate. During this time, remove all potential sources of distraction from your environment. Don't listen to music or have your computer on during this time. This time is for your mind to be by itself. Silence is preferred. Allow your mind to wander and explore the different facets of your life and feelings. If a silent environment is unavailable, listening to soundtracks of falling rain or other sources of "white noise" are suitable substitutes.

Don't be discouraged if your thoughts wander to seemingly senseless and irrelevant topics at first. The mind, especially with our hyperactive lifestyles, tends to be noisy and easily distracted. However, with time, you will find that your mind *does* quiet down. This can take a while, but results will come with patience. This translates to greater mental focus in other areas of life as well. This kind of reflection has the added benefit of providing practice for learning to *control* one's own mind.

I have spoken with many people, some of whom are well into old age, who have admitted to me that they have never actually done this. They have never quieted their minds. They have never stopped to simply listen to their own minds and their thoughts. This is truly sad. In Western society, the closest we ever come to this state is typically when we are actively focusing our thinking to solve a specific problem, such as how to fix a leaky faucet, or something similar. However, this isn't the same thing. Quiet contemplation, and simply being with your thoughts, is not the same thing as rummaging through one's intellect for the solution to a problem. One is passive and observing, the other is active and noisy. Do not try. Just *be*.

DECISION MAKING

With an improved clarity of mind and deeper level of self-reflection, we are now ready to discuss the next topic, which concerns decision-making habits. Decision making is, in many ways, the most important facet of the human condition with which we concern ourselves. This is clearly the case since personal decision making encapsulates the essence of free will. The critical question is: how do we best decide what to do with the time we have? Certainly a simple, logical, and systematic way of making decisions must exist.

Economists have formulated what I consider to be the very essence of sound decision-making, applicable to all of life's decisions—from the most mundane day-to-day choices, to the most daunting life dilemmas. The concept is called the *margin of benefit*.[4] It is a concept that has been adopted from economic theory, and constitutes a sound, universal method for decision making. Because of its overarching importance, I will treat the subject at length here.

Every decision you make in life has two key variables: price and value. This is sometimes alternatively phrased as cost and benefit, or risk and reward. I prefer price and value. As a concrete example, you are currently reading this book because you have decided—either consciously or subconsciously—that the advice and counsel within it (the value) is greater than the cost of buying it and the time spent reading it (the price). This favourable discrepancy between price and value constitutes the margin of benefit. The larger the margin of benefit is, the greater the amount of benefits accruing in your favour.

Alternatively, imagine you are the manager of a retail store and need to decide which of two recent job applicants to hire. Given an hour to mull things over, by what criteria would you make your decision? Their grades in school? Their work history? Maybe. Ultimately, the most rational decision would come down to a comparison of the price of a person's labour to its value (the price being the wage paid to the prospective employee, and the value being the amount of sales the new hire would generate). Since both applicants are vying for the same job, we can assume their compensation arrangements would be about equal. The only thing left to consider would be an estimate of what sales the employee would actually tally. This estimate would come about from various qualitative and quantitative analyses. The point to be made is that the person with the larger discrepancy between price and value— and therefore larger margin of benefit (to the employer)—would be the logical hire.

As a final example, suppose you are a high school student who has been presented with the opportunity to engage in some dishonest but highly lucrative behavior, such as theft or cheating on an exam. If you give in to temptation, the price paid will be a guilty conscience and a moral self-destruction. However, the payoff may be a higher final exam score that might be the difference between you attending a prestigious university or not. The other option would be to refuse any involvement in the behaviour and remain perfectly honest. The price paid might mean a lower exam score, but the value of the action would be the preservation of personal integrity, dignity, and self-respect. Let us consider the price to value relationship of our two options. Ethical issues are, admittedly, highly subjective, but I think most reasonable individuals would consider the path of honesty to have a higher margin of benefit. The "price" paid by being honest may perhaps be higher than that of cheating, but the value of moral integrity substantially dwarfs the value of a falsely earned exam score.

Readers who are familiar with economic concepts may find that the margin of benefit principle seems to parallel a similar canon known as opportunity cost. While this is true to an extent, they are nonetheless distinct concepts. As the name suggests, the opportunity cost of a given entity or action is defined by the alternative choices the person in question has available to them.[5] The margin of benefit encompasses such decision-making capacities, but also allows for the attractiveness of various choices to be considered individually and in isolation. To give concreteness to the foregoing explanation, consider our above scenario where you have one hour of spare time and are considering using that time to read a book. Should you proceed with reading? Making this decision based on opportunity cost would be impractical, since the available alternative choices you have to spend an hour of your time are, in practice, unlimited. However, by relying on the margin of benefit, only two factors would have to be considered: price and value. The price paid is obviously an hour, while the value in reading would be dependent solely on the utility of the material to be read.

It is my position that a person who exercises the margin of benefit concept in day-to-day decision making as a matter of habit will unquestionably maximize their personal potential. By consistently making decisions based on trying to obtain the maximum possible benefit for the lowest possible price, it is only logical that the greatest gains would accumulate in your favour.

In sum, the margin of benefit concept represents a rational and sensible framework for day-to-day decision making, not just for matters involving money. When faced with any choice in life, monetary or not, it is prudent to ask, "Am I getting at least as much value as I am paying in price?" Such decision making, even when unconsciously executed, has brought countless rewards to many. The value in learning computer programming was very obviously greater than the price paid in time by Bill Gates. The value of Coca-Cola stock was unquestionably greater than the price paid in dollars by Warren Buffett.[6] The applications are limitless. Follow the margin of benefit principle, and you will not get a poor result from your endeavours in life.

FINAL THOUGHTS

I want you, the reader, to never stagnate. Your work, your passion, your achievement, and your own continuous self-improvement will bring true meaning to your life. Self-actualization is a wonderful, endless journey. Never let anything in life limit you. Strive to achieve more and contribute more to society. There is no finish line.

Finally, internalize the fact that your time is limited. The greatest folly of human beings is our belief that we will always have tomorrow. Our lives are extremely short—even if we are so lucky as to be able to live until old age (which is not guaranteed). Years pass by like the blink of an eye. Don't fool yourself into thinking you have an abundance of time. All you have is the now. Go out and create your future.

FIGURE 10.1: YOU CAN DO IT

ACTION STEPS BEFORE READING THE NEXT CHAPTER

TO-DO: CONTINUOUS GROWTH

Stop reading and think about how you want to be remembered a generation after you are gone. What legacy do you want to leave? How does this impact the direction you will go with your life pursuit?

FURTHER RECOMMENDED READINGS ON CONTINUOUS GROWTH

Read anything and everything—from philosophy, business, and politics, to art, literature, and poetry. Read as much as you can about as many things as you can. Your education is also an endless journey.

CHAPTER 11
WARREN BUFFETT:
AN EXEMPLAR OF HAPPINESS

I would like to bring all of the topics in The Paradigm of Happiness together in a case study that depicts a single individual who exemplifies all the principles and qualities that we have discussed— all of the levels having been transcended by a single person: Warren Buffett.

Warren Buffett is one of my personal heroes. For those of you not familiar with him, he is the Chairman and CEO of a company called Berkshire Hathaway, an investment holding company. Buffett is one of the richest men in the world and perhaps the most sought after for advice and counsel regarding life, success, business, and world trends. The most admirable part of his story is that he has made his fortune in a completely honest and ethical way—something that many billionaires cannot claim. He is also a truly happy individual. As such, he is a perfect role model for us to study.

Warren Buffett was born on August 30, 1930, in Omaha, Nebraska, U.S.A.[1] From an early age, he loved doing business and working with numbers. Whether it was selling used golf balls, collecting unused stubs at the race track, or running a chain of pinball machines, his mind was always active. According to a BBC documentary, *The World's Greatest Money Maker*, the young Buffett did have some adolescent turbulence. Around the age of 12 or 13 he got into a habit of shoplifting and fraternizing with a bit of a rough crowd. Aside from this childhood phase, Buffett has lived his life with complete integrity.[2]

He became interested in the stock market at an early age, purchasing shares of a company called Cities Service Preferred at the age of 11. By the time he was in his twenties, Buffett was already an accomplished investor, and began managing money for other people via a partnership.[3] After 13 years of success via this partnership, he took the helm of the ailing textile company Berkshire Hathaway. The textile operation eventually went out of business, but Buffett used the company as a platform to build his business empire. Today, Buffett's success is something that he says is not due to his IQ or anything inherently special about him, but rather qualities of character, temperament, and behaviour—qualities that can be developed by anyone.[4] Let's investigate how Buffett's qualities for happiness and success in life compare with The Paradigm of Happiness.

CHAPTER 1: ATTITUDE AND DISCIPLINE

In the first chapter, we discussed how everything in life begins in your mind. As Zig Ziglar once stated, "Your attitude, not your aptitude, will determine your altitude."[5] One of the key lessons for you is to learn to focus your energies on constructive and positive thoughts, rather than dwelling on the negative. Buffett, during various speaking events and conventions, is often asked what kind of regrets or mistakes he has had in life, and what he has learned from them. "You can only live life forwards," says Buffett.[6] While there is much to be said about learning from your mistakes, it doesn't make any sense to dwell on them. Move on and focus on the future. There is always something to live for. Focus on positive changes and contributions you can make to the world. This is a very constructive and admirable mental attitude.

Another one of our principles from this chapter is that personal confidence comes from repetition, particularly when it comes to potentially nerve-racking activities such as public speaking. Buffett admits that when he was in his teens and early twenties, he could not do public speaking. He took a public speaking course with self-help guru, Dale Carnegie, and started working to develop his confidence in front of crowds.[7] As soon as he finished the course he began teaching an evening course on investing so that he would not lapse back into his old nervousness.[8] Buffett clearly knows that practice is what makes perfect in life. The flip side of that old aphorism is that you lose what you don't use!

Finally, let's talk about role models. "Tell me who your heroes are and I'll tell you how you'll turn out to be", says Buffett.[9] Buffett credits much of his directionality in life to the heroes and teachers he had growing up. Whether it was his college professor Benjamin Graham, his father Howard Buffett, or his first wife Susan Buffett, he was surrounded by people whom he loved and admired. He absorbed the great qualities of these people and integrated them into himself. By the same token, he observed people with qualities he did not like and pledged to reject those qualities. Truly, people tend to gravitate in the direction of the people they associate themselves with.

CHAPTER 2: INTERPERSONAL SKILLS

In this chapter, we discussed the very important concept of focusing on *real* friends. It's great to have lots of friends and people to invite to your cocktail parties, but the people in your life who will truly make you happy are the ones who are with you through thick and thin. These are the kind of friends who feel like family members and will enjoy your company regardless of the activity, the kind that will always be there for you.

Buffett lives a simple lifestyle.[10] You'd think that as a billionaire, he would have spent his life flying off to the world's best parties and celebrity events. This hasn't really been the case. Buffett has close friends such as Charlie Munger, Bill Gates, and Sharon Osberg who are also very down to earth. These are people whom he trusts and admires, and who enrich his world. Buffett hasn't lost sight of these kinds of people in his life. This is a lesson we should all follow.

We can also observe that Buffett treats others in the same way he would like to be treated. "We eat our own cooking," remarks Warren Buffett, in reference to the management of his partners' money.[11] During his tenure as a money manager and as the CEO and Chairman of Berkshire Hathaway, Buffett has never done anything with his partners' money that he would never do with his own money. In Buffett's eyes, his partners are friends and equals to him, and they deserve to be treated that way. He has maintained this philosophy throughout the nearly nine decades of his life.[12]

Finally, according to those close to him, family life has always been important to Buffett. Despite his focus on building his wealth and company, he has always spent time with his family. His three children, Susan, Peter, and Howard all speak fondly of their childhoods and the valuable life lessons their father imparted on them.[13] Buffett also paid special attention to the issue of inherited wealth when raising his children, making sure they did not grow up as spoiled individuals who did not know the value of hard work and discipline. According to Buffett, shielding his children from the corrosive influence of wealth has meant giving them "enough money so that they would feel they could do anything, but not so much that they could do nothing."[14]

CHAPTER 3: ETHICAL LIVING

Warren Buffett's highly ethical nature is one of the hallmarks of his personage. This is especially impressive considering the history of corruption in finance and on Wall Street generally. Warren Buffett learned early on in his career that ethical behaviour is not just good in and of itself, but also that such behaviour is good for business. Establishing a reputation for honesty and candour makes others more likely to do more business with you in the future. Conversely, behaving in a conniving way might earn you a little more profit in the short run, but is sure to affect you negatively in the long run. One of Buffett's favourite principles is that "it takes 20 years to build a reputation and five minutes to ruin it. If you think about that, you'll do things differently."[15]

Buffett has also been an avid follower of the Newspaper Test, an ethical technique that this book steadfastly recommends to the reader. If you are thinking of engaging in a course of action that might be unethical, imagine if that action were written about on the front page of tomorrow's newspaper by a crass reporter. Would that bother you? If the thought even irks you a little bit, don't take that course of action. It's a principle that is as simple as it is effective.[16]

CHAPTER 4: FINANCIAL LITERACY

Given Buffett's predilection for all things financial, it should be no surprise that he has great insights on this particular topic. The first principle we espoused in Chapter 4 is spending less money than you make, and then investing those savings into assets. Saving and investing, of course, has always been an integral part of Buffett's lifestyle. Never has he ramped up his consumption to conspicuous levels, even upon reaching the status of billionaire.[17] Buffett first began saving when he was only a small child, going door to door and selling bottles of Coca-Cola for 5 cents each and buying six-packs as inventory for 25 cents, netting him 5 cents in profit per six-pack.[18] This profit was then further saved and invested into future ventures. With the magic of compound interest, these first small savings grew into the billions that Buffett has today.

The next point I made was to suggest to the reader that they avoid credit card debt at all costs. It is not unusual to see credit card interest rates starting at 18% and as high as 30% or more. It is nearly impossible to build your financial future when you are paying that much interest on your debt. "Avoid credit cards. Just forget about them", says Buffett.[19] Sage advice, indeed.

In this chapter we also discussed how banking fees and expenses can eat into your investing efforts. Even the difference of 1 percent in management fees can mean the difference of hundreds of thousands of dollars of savings by the time you retire. Investing is about owning productive assets. The more fees the intermediary (the bank or financial institution) charges you, the less return on investment you will receive from the asset itself. Paying high fees for investment management is a "fool's game" says Buffett.[20] Do everything you can to reduce your fees and expenses. Your wallet and your retirement funds will both thank you for it.

CHAPTER 5: HEALTH AND FITNESS

This is the one area of The Paradigm of Happiness where I have to admit that Buffett may not be the best role model. Instead of a diet that consists mostly of fruits and vegetables, as recommended by nutritionists, Buffett has been known to drink five servings of Coca-Cola daily, along with ice cream for breakfast and peanut brittle throughout the day. In Buffett's defense, he was raised in the 1930s, an era in which our knowledge of nutrition was not as extensive as it is today. Despite the less than ideal diet, Buffett is now well into his eighties and in seemingly good health.

However, even Buffett appears to take his health reasonably seriously. Buffett exercises with a personal trainer three times a week, and limits his calorie intake to an average intake of 2,700 calories per day.[21] In addition, Buffett gets regular physical checkups with a doctor.[22] So, even though he doesn't eat the foods recommended in this book, Buffett clearly stays within certain bounds when it comes to taking care of himself.

CHAPTER 6: PERSONAL HABITS

"Don't sleepwalk through life," says Warren Buffett.[23] Since his childhood, Buffett has used his time effectively to pursue his interests and passions in life. He has not been idle and has always tackled problems and challenges head-on. In Chapter 6, I introduced tools to help the reader stay organized and productive. Buffett himself dedicates the majority of his time to the activities that he knows will benefit his passion of building his company. Reading is his primary activity. Whether it be through reading newspapers, trade magazines, company reports, or other related materials, reading gives him the edge in the investing and business world. "I've never known anyone as focused as he is," notes Susan, Buffett's daughter. [24]

When it comes to personal habits, Buffett lives by the philosophy that "the chains of habit are too light to be felt until they are too heavy to be broken."[25] Thus, it makes sense to develop good habits early in your life. Buffett has taken care to develop as many good habits as possible, from avoiding drugs, alcohol, and cigarettes to always being reliable, honest, and punctual.

According to Buffett, success in life is largely a matter of habit, not of flashing brilliance or stratospheric IQ.[26] It's more about doing the few things in life every day that you know will make a positive difference to your future, and having the courage to say "no" to the many things that can be distracting or injurious. Maintaining rationality at all times and making decisions based on an analysis of projected costs and benefits is a hallmark of Buffett's personality.[27] Success is about not letting emotions corrode your framework of rationality. This attitude is perhaps the most important component of personal habits that all but guarantee success in life.

CHAPTER 7: GENUINE RELATIONSHIPS

One of the first principles I enunciated in Chapter 7 was that happiness is derived from experiences with friends and family. If you are going to be spending time and money, this is who you should be spending it on. This is in stark contrast to what many people do, which is to spend their money on the accumulation of material goods and possessions.

As I mentioned above, Buffett has always lived a modest life. He has focused on building his relationships with his family and children and his friends such as Charlie Munger, rather than spending his billions on luxury cars and mansions. These things don't fulfill you; your life experiences are likely to fulfill you more. Sharing life experiences with those around you is a key way to cultivating deep and meaningful relationships.

In Chapter 7, we next talked about authenticity in communication. Buffett's openness in his communication style is one of his hallmark characteristics. According to business partners, friends, and observers when Warren Buffett tells you something, you know that you can trust him.[28] This has led to him enjoying countless favourable and enduring relationships over the years. Those who know him state that the people he does business with quickly become friends, and the managers of his subsidiary companies remain loyal, often for decades.[29] Being open and honest isn't just a good trait in itself—it's great a tool for business.

Our final principle in this chapter is that of unconditional caring for others. "Every human life has equal value," says Buffett.[30] That's not just rhetoric either: Buffett puts his money where his mouth is. He has pledged to donate the vast majority of his multi-billion dollar fortune to the Bill and Melinda Gates Foundation, a foundation which will help to combat disease, poverty, and inequality all across the world.[31] Helping every human life that he can seems to be more important to him than owning any amount of luxuries in the world. This makes him tremendously admirable and lovable to those around him. In a certain sense, it seems that Buffett sees the entire human race as a type of family to be cared for.

CHAPTER 8: SOCIAL CONTRIBUTION

In this chapter, we discussed the virtues of using our time and effort for the benefit of society at large, rather than just working hard for our self-interest. There doesn't have to be a conflict between doing good for oneself and for society, and most often the modern system of free markets prevents such conflicts. However, even the market system and a rule of law isn't perfect. Rather than just following the rules of society, it is far better to embrace a commitment to constructive action guided by positive intentions. One of the key takeaways from this chapter is that *making others happy makes you happy*. When you think about that and adopt such a philosophy in earnest, your life will change tremendously for the better. As covered in this chapter, there has been much scientific study that has confirmed the therapeutic benefits of helping others.

We've already discussed how Buffett is incredibly altruistic as an individual, having pledged to donate billions. However, his charitable activities aren't the only place where this has been true. Even in his everyday work, Buffett has always made sure that his activities have been for the benefit of society at large. Even when he was just starting out managing small sums of money in his twenties, Buffett set up his compensation arrangement so that he would only earn money if his partners were earning money.[32] This is in sharp contrast to many other individual and institutional money managers. Unlike those managers, Buffett wanted to add value to the lives of his partners, not just earn a paycheque. Later on, Buffett also refused to invest in cigarette manufacturers despite the tremendous profit opportunities. He did not want to own a business that was not in keeping with his morality.[33] These actions seem to have not only made Warren Buffett happy with how he has lived his life, but also have helped him grow his company.

In this chapter, we also discussed how motives matter when it comes to doing good in society. Buffett has never gone out of his way to try and create celebrity around his charity or altruism.[34] He wants to do good for other people. He doesn't seem to care about the attention lavished on him, and has never tried to get a building named after him or a monument made in his image. In life, we reap what we sow.

CHAPTER 9: YOUR LIFE PURSUIT

Self-actualization is achieved primarily by *realizing your full potential through your life's passion*. Self-actualization is the process of becoming everything you are capable of becoming. This is what forms the cornerstone of your life pursuit. Warren Buffett knows this full well.

Buffett offers the following advice on the subject of self-actualization: "You should really take a job that, if you were independently wealthy, you would take. That's the job to take, because that's the one you'll have great fun in. You'll learn something, you'll be excited about it. You can't miss."[35]

I will repeat a key principle emphasized in Chapter 9: that is, if you do not know what you want to do in life, your *immediate* task is to find your purpose. Explore the world and find your passion. It seems that Warren Buffett never wasted time, even in his childhood, and got right to working on the things that interested him in business, investing, math and numbers, and, for a time, even weightlifting.[36] Investing ended up being his calling, and he charged ahead with full effort and intensity.

Because of his dedication to his craft, and supported by the other levels of The Paradigm of Happiness, Buffett is a happy man. He calls Berkshire Hathaway his masterpiece, and claims that he would be doing the same thing with his life regardless of whether he had just a little money or a fortune. With his accomplishments, he is one of the few people who has truly reached self-actualization in life. However, since we now know The Paradigm, we can now reach this level, too.

CHAPTER 10: CONTINUOUS GROWTH

Self-actualization and achievement are an endless journey. While there is no limit to what you can do or achieve, the *time* you have available to you in life *is* limited. Make the most of it, and never allow yourself to think that you can put things off until tomorrow. Buffett seems to know this intrinsically. Despite his advancing age, he has elected not to retire, and probably never will as long as he is able to continue with his day-to-day responsibilities.[37] Despite having come as far as he has in life, Buffett will not stop building his legacy and doing what he loves. According to news reports, he has even joked that he will run Berkshire Hathaway via ouija board after he passes away.[38]

Some people dream of retirement after working hard over a 40-year career that they regard as a real-life purgatory. Retirement is their promised land. However, spending your entire life deferring meaningful work is no way to live. When you are on a journey to self-actualization via your life pursuit, your career *is* your dream, and retirement becomes something you want to put off rather than look forward to. Your work and your enjoyment become indistinguishable and real happiness enters your life. Embrace the endless journey and the limitless possibilities of life.

We can see that Buffett displays most of the qualities of a self-actualized person via The Paradigm of Happiness. Life can be messy, but the essential building blocks of a happy life are simple and straightforward. There's no mystery surrounding the route to success in life. Happiness is about adhering to rational principles that have been derived from sound logic. Once those are in place, all else follows.

Quick Reference Guide and Book Recap

Sometimes there's too much of a good thing. For instance, some books are packed with great information, but by the time you finish them, there's too much information to process all at once. What's the result? You remember nothing. I'm not sure why this is the case, but I have a theory. I think it's because there's very little context in which to actually place most of the information. You need to have some way to anchor the information you're trying to absorb to a model that is simple and familiar. I don't want you to arrive at the end of this book feeling inspired to take action in life, only to find yourself so overwhelmed with information that you are paralyzed.

The human mind is fallible, especially in these information-overload scenarios. In addition, our memory tends to fade with time. One possible solution is to revisit this book and reread it on a regular basis. However, for the most part, this isn't really practical. We all lead busy lives, and the luxury of re-reading books isn't always on the table. So, how do we solve this?

I'm going to tackle this problem by providing you, the reader, with a summary of the whole book, along with some additional principles for living an actualized life. What I want you to do is refer to this chapter whenever your memory begins to fade. I want you to refer to this chapter whenever times are tough, or when you have lost direction in your day-to-day life. Let's get started.

THE KEY IDEA: THE PARADIGM OF HAPPINESS

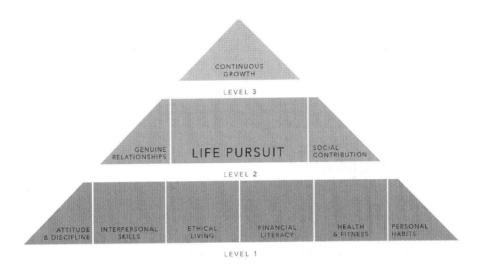

CONTINUOUS GROWTH

LEVEL 3

GENUINE RELATIONSHIPS — LIFE PURSUIT — SOCIAL CONTRIBUTION

LEVEL 2

ATTITUDE & DISCIPLINE — INTERPERSONAL SKILLS — ETHICAL LIVING — FINANCIAL LITERACY — HEALTH & FITNESS — PERSONAL HABITS

LEVEL 1

THE PARADIGM OF HAPPINESS

The Paradigm of Happiness is the central concept of this book. It's the keystone to building a satisfying and healthy life. If you remember any single concept from this book, remember this one. Refer to it often, consult it, and make an earnest effort to build your life with this concept. I guarantee it will make your life better.

CHAPTER-BY-CHAPTER RECAP OF THE KEY IDEAS

Let's also recap the most important concepts within each of the individual building blocks of The Paradigm.

CHAPTER 1: ATTITUDE AND DISCIPLINE
- Discover your Core Principle.
- The mindset for success:
  - a. Make a conscious decision to focus on constructive thoughts.
  - b. Translate constructive thoughts into constructive action.
  - c. Let constructive action lead to positive outcomes in your life.
- Repeat tasks and exercises to build confidence.
- Use the Personal Balance Sheet to take stock of your life.
- Write your Personal Constitution.

CHAPTER 2: INTERPERSONAL SKILLS
- Electronic communication and social networking cannot take the place of actually spending time with someone.
- Integrity leads to lasting relationships.
- Family is the most important of all relationships.
- Try to see things from the other person's point of view.
- Quality is more important than quantity when it comes to friends.

CHAPTER 3: ETHICAL LIVING
- Behave ethically because it's the right thing to do, and it's beneficial to ourselves.
- Practice the Golden Rule: treat others the way you would like to be treated.
- Apply the Newspaper Test: imagine the action you are about to take will be read about by everyone in the world on the front page of tomorrow's newspaper.

- Use Phronesis: a combination of instinct and accrued knowledge that gives us innate insight into the ethical makeup of a decision we are about to make.
- Beware of ethical fallacies such as Consequentialism and Universality.

CHAPTER 4: FINANCIAL LITERACY

- Budget your money. Spend less than you make to create savings.
- Invest your savings. Use your savings to buy assets.
- Take advantage of compound interest to grow your money.
- Look for the financial institution with the lowest possible fees when putting your money into investment products.
- Avoid credit card debt at all costs.

CHAPTER 5: HEALTH AND FITNESS

- Follow sensible, research-based nutrition guidelines.
- Read labels! People have a common tendency to underestimate the number of calories in their food.
- Exercise regularly to maintain a healthy lifestyle.
- Make time for meditation.
- Sleep six to eight hours a night.

CHAPTER 6: PERSONAL HABITS

- Use organizational tools such as a to-do list, calendar, Linear Progress Indicator, and Stagger Charts.
- Clean out anything you don't want out of your home, organize everything that is left, and keep it that way.
- Consider that the chains of habit are too light to be felt until they're too heavy to be broken.
- Overdress rather than underdress; take care of hygiene, clothing choices and style as they are important elements of your career and overall life.
- Behave rationally; you don't need great insights to be successful.

CHAPTER 7: GENUINE RELATIONSHIPS

- Find happiness through forming deep connections with other people.
- Accept that loss is a necessary part of having fulfilling relationships.
- Offer unconditional compassion and caring to fortify the backbone of your relationships.

CHAPTER 8: SOCIAL CONTRIBUTION

- Make positive contributions to the lives of other people: there are few things in life more gratifying than this.
- Check your motives for social contribution: engage in community and social causes because you feel strongly about them, not because you want to look good.
- Gain exposure to people from different walks of life in order to enrich your existence.

CHAPTER 9: YOUR LIFE PURSUIT

- Achieve self-actualization by realizing your full potential in your life's passion.
- Recognize that you will have found your passion in life when work and pleasure become indistinguishable.
- Do not delay finding and pursuing your passion; life passes by too quickly. Read books, talk to people, explore life until you find something you love.

CHAPTER 10: CONTINUOUS GROWTH

- Enjoy the life-long journey of self-actualization, growth, and achievement, for the journey itself is the reward.

FINAL THOUGHTS

The following are some final tips on navigating your way through life more prudently.

ALWAYS PROTECT YOURSELF

While many people are trustworthy, never let your guard down in life. Whether it be looking over your shoulder when walking home late at night, or wearing a condom during sex, protect yourself at all times.

ADAM SMITH'S INVISIBLE HAND

Building wealth requires offering goods and services to others that provide them with benefit. So, don't be ashamed of wanting to make a profit through your endeavours.[1]

SELF-MASTERY

Mastery over the self is a key ingredient to success. Through gradually creating and keeping more challenging self-promises, we grow to keep increasingly bigger commitments, which in turn allows for greater and greater success in life. Positive feedback from this process allows us to overcome procrastination—one of the ultimate killers of productivity.

MARGIN OF BENEFIT

Use this rule to make decisions in life. Always compare cost to benefit.

THINK INDEPENDENTLY AND EMPIRICALLY

Always demand evidence, and don't be afraid to question conventional wisdom. Don't be afraid to question the logic of authority.

AN INVITATION

As we wrap up this book, I also want to leave you with an invitation. As an author, I want this book to make a lasting and positive impact on your life. Know that I'm on your side. Refer to this book time and again throughout your life as you face trials and challenges. Also, feel free to send me your thoughts, comments, and criticisms. You can join our community on Facebook, Twitter, and on my website at **www.forrestwong.com/**the-paradigm/ to communicate with me or to further your learning through discussions with other people all around the world.

To repeat what I said at the outset: I am proposing a movement for all of society to adopt The Paradigm of Happiness as a way of life—to improve not only our individual lives, but the lives of society at large. Now that you have finished this book, you are automatically a part of this movement. Welcome.

I invite you not only to join this movement, but to make a difference in the lives of your friends and family by sharing this book and its philosophy with the people you care about in your life.

EPILOGUE
SAVE THE WORLD

Your prosperity and your happiness have global consequences. Indeed, the very fate of the world may depend on it. The trajectory of the lives of individuals, countries, and the entire world is determined by the *ideas and values that people live by*. As mentioned in Chapter 1, your attitude is what ultimately determines your reality.

Allow me to make my claim more concrete with a simple example. Imagine that every person in the developed world adopted a dietary plan similar to the Harvard model proposed in Chapter 5. This diet calls for a reduction in red meat consumption and an increase in one's intake of fruits and vegetables relative to the average American diet. Such changes would result in a significant reduction in the annual greenhouse gas emissions produced by humanity. This *alone* would go a long way to helping save our planet from climate change.[1,2] In addition, such dietary changes would make individuals healthier overall.[3,4,5] It would improve their happiness, and it would put less pressure on our healthcare systems—literally saving billions of dollars in the process.[6] Global productivity would also improve.[7]

The ideas we hold in our minds determine how we live our lives, and that in turn decides the trajectory of the entire human race. By doing right by yourself, you are doing right by the planet. Your happiness truly has global reach, so this "altruism" has no downside.

Let us consider another example. Five hundred years ago, China and India were the two richest and wealthiest regions in the entire world.[8] Today, these two countries are among some of the poorest nations in the world.[9] What caused this drastic reversal to happen? The clue lies in the intellectual heritage of today's wealthiest countries. Much of the balance of today's prosperity exists in countries that share similar values in regard to free markets, protection of intellectual property rights, political freedom, and equality of opportunity. This system of values — indeed, this *paradigm* — has allowed countries such as Canada to blossom and surpass countries that did not have values that were as conducive to prosperity.[10]

However, this does not mean that our system is perfect. Nor does it mean that a similar reversal in fortune cannot happen in Canada. For instance, this book provides the reader with the tools needed to make good financial decisions and warns against imprudence. Do these considerations, too, have global reach? Indeed, they do. The world learned in 2008 that the global financial system is interconnected and fragile in ways unknown to most.[11]

Consider the following. Canada is, at the moment, one of the most indebted countries in the world. Our household debt as a ratio of GDP is over 100%, and our household debt to income ratio is over 170%.[12,13] This debt can be destabilizing to the economy as an event such as rising interest rates can cause a critical threshold of defaults and cascading institutional failures to occur. It may be tempting to say that such a thing would never happen, as the Bank of Canada would not likely continue tightening monetary policy while the economy is weakening. However, this is not necessarily true in the context of, say, an inflationary scenario similar to the one seen during the 1970s.[14] This may occur without warning. As such, our high levels of personal debt may crash the entire global economy through an unforeseen domino effect and throw us into a second Great Depression.[15] It pays to be financially prudent, both for your own benefit, and for the benefit of the economy as a whole. Again, by doing right by yourself, you are doing right by society.

One final consideration is that the severity of the societal problems described above will be orders of magnitude worse in terms of their effect if they are allowed to compound on each other and occur *simultaneously*, which they very well may.

This book is about introducing a *new* Paradigm. One for individuals that can be as empowering as constitutions written for nations. One that I believe can have truly global influence because there is nothing in the world more powerful than ideas, and there is no better way to disseminate powerful ideas than through powerful words. Your happiness, your prosperity, and the way you live your life has real impact on the trajectory of humankind. It is a mistake to think that society naturally makes progress on its own. This is simply not true. A civilization only makes progress when its citizens unite behind a common set of ideas that are favourable to prosperity and empirically verifiable as being so. Without meaning to sound audacious, I believe that *The Paradigm* can provide that unity. Be happy and save the world.

APPENDIX 1
RECIPES

The following are some additional breakfast recipes you can try.

3-MINUTE BREAKFAST: SUPER CEREAL COMBO

Ingredients:
- High-fibre cereal
- Soy or almond milk
- Yogurt
- 1 apple
- 4 – 5 strawberries
- Palmful of raspberries
- Palmful of blueberries

Instructions:
- Combine high-fibre cereal and desired amount of soy milk or almond milk in a bowl.
- In a separate bowl combine slices of apple, strawberries halves, blueberries, and raspberries. Drizzle with yogurt as desired.
- Serve with two 8-ounce glasses of water.

3-MINUTE BREAKFAST: OATMEAL DELIGHT

Ingredients:
- Two packs of regular instant oatmeal
- Soy or almond milk
- 1 banana
- Handful of blueberries

Instructions:
- Combine the two packets of regular instant oatmeal into a bowl.
- Pour soy milk or almond milk into the bowl as desired.
- Heat on high in microwave for 3 minutes.
- Add banana slices and blueberries as desired; topping with a sprinkle of flaxseed or cinnamon powder adds flavour as well.
- Serve with two 8-ounce glasses of water.

FIGURE A1.1 OATMEAL WITH BLUEBERRIES, BANANA AND FLAXSEED

10-MINUTE BREAKFAST: FRIED EGG AND FRUIT

Ingredients:

- 2 slices of 100 percent whole grain bread
- 2 eggs
- Desired spread such as butter or mayonnaise
- Cheese (non-processed)
- Pepper
- Seasoning salt (optional)
- Olive oil
- 1 apple
- 1 banana
- 1 cantaloupe
- 4 − 5 strawberries

Instructions:

- Apply spread to bread.
- Apply 2 tablespoons of olive oil to a large skillet.
- Crack 2 eggs into the skillet over medium heat.
- Cook until desired level of firmness in egg yolks.
- Add seasoning salt and pepper.
- Just before eggs are cooked, place a slice of cheese over them.
- Place eggs in between the two slices of bread and cut diagonally.
- In a bowl combine apple slices, banana slices, cantaloupe chunks, and halves of strawberries.
- Serve with two 8-ounce glasses of water.

20-MINUTE BREAKFAST: OMELETTE AND FRUIT COMBO

Ingredients:

- 3 eggs
- Salt, to taste
- Ground pepper, to taste
- 1/4 of a green pepper
- 3 mushrooms (White Button or Crimini)
- 1/8 of an onion
- 1/2 cup of spinach
- Olive oil
- Butter
- Parmesan cheese
- Mixed fruits

Instructions:

- Beat three eggs in a bowl until blended. Add a pinch of salt and pepper as desired, to taste.
- Melt a teaspoon of butter in a pan or skillet on medium-high heat. (Cooking spray works as well.)
- Pour egg mixture into pan. Cook until the egg has thickened and no egg liquid is visible. Tilt the pan and push the uncooked portions with a spatula as needed.
- Place chopped pepper, mushrooms, onions, spinach, cheese, and any other fillings desired onto one half of the omelette.
- With spatula, fold the omelette in half so that the filling is covered.
- Serve immediately with mixed fruits on the side.

FIGURE A1.2: OMELETTE WITH FRUIT COMBO

Here are some additional lunch and dinner recipes you can try.

FABULOUS FRUIT SALAD

Fresh fruit combinations of almost any kind are appropriate for fruit salad, but the following is one of the author's favourites.

Ingredients:
- 1 banana
- 1 serving blueberries
- 1 serving strawberries
- 1 serving raspberries
- 1 serving cantaloupe
- Yogurt (optional)
- Honey (optional)

Instructions:
- Rinse blueberries, strawberries, and raspberries under running water.
- On a cutting board, cut cantaloupe into bite size chunks and cut banana into slices.
- Mix ingredients in bowl and serve.

Optional:
- Mix the fruit salad with a generous helping of yogurt and two teaspoons of honey for more substance.

THE QUICK LUNCH STAPLE

Sometimes, especially when we have heavy work commitments and busy schedules, we don't have time to prepare involved lunches. (See more on preparing lunches ahead of time in Chapter 6, which discusses personal habits.) So, what do we often resort to? A can of soup. However, we often don't realize that a can of soup doesn't have to stand on its own. It can serve as the base for something much tastier and more substantial. Remember, not all cans of soup are created equal. Some are loaded with salt and calories, much more than their volume and taste might suggest. I suggest opting for a broth-based soup that has fewer than 250 calories and less than 600mg of sodium per serving.

Ingredients:
- 1 can of broth-based soup (250 calories and 600mg of sodium per serving or less)
- Left over diced chicken, beans, legumes, pasta, or brown rice

Instructions:
- Open can of soup and empty into a saucepan.
- Before preparation, as per the soup's instructions, mix in your choice of diced chicken, beans, legumes, pasta, or brown rice (cooked).
- Prepare can of soup as per instructions on can.
- Serve immediately.

FIGURE A1.3: A HEARTY SOUP

TURKEY AND TOMATO TANGO

Ingredients:
- 2 slices of whole grain bread
- 1 tomato
- Sandwich spread (1 tablespoon Greek yogurt, sprinkle of parmesan, pinch of basil, pinch of pepper, a squeeze of lemon juice)
- Reduced-sodium turkey slices

Instructions:
- Mix yogurt, parmesan, basil, lemon juice, and pepper in a small bowl.
- Spread the mixture onto two slices of whole grain bread.
- Cut tomato into slices and place on top of sandwich spread.
- Top with reduced-sodium deli turkey.
- Heat 1 teaspoon of oil in a skillet over medium heat.
- Place the sandwich on the skillet with another skillet on top of the sandwich for weight and cook for two minutes.
- Flip the sandwich and cook on the other side for another two minutes.

GREEN EGGS AND SLAM

This is a very simple dinner recipe that is immensely satisfying.

Ingredients:
- 3 large eggs
- 3 cups of greens of your choice (gai-lan works well)
- 1/2 cup of grated cheese
- Seasonings of your choice (salt, pepper, paprika, etc.)
- Olive oil

Instructions:
- Steam the greens until cooked.
- Fry the eggs in a pan, leaving a small amount of runniness in the yolks.
- Place the greens on your serving plate, add seasoning and olive oil.
- Place eggs, grated cheese, and additional seasoning on top of the greens.
- Serve immediately.

PROTEIN PANCAKES FOR DINNER

Pancakes for dinner? Yup. Protein pancakes are a staple of bodybuilders, and many insist on making them using protein powder. That's a fine option, but we're going to make them using eggs.

Ingredients:
- 2 egg whites
- 1 whole egg
- 1 banana (ripe)

Instructions:
- Mix the egg contents and mashed banana into a bowl until the consistency is even.
- Over medium heat, pour about a two to three inch wide circle of batter into a greased frying pan.
- Carefully flip the pancake after about 30 seconds, or until golden brown.
- Repeat until batter is used up.
- Serve immediately.
- Blueberries, banana slices, and chopped strawberries make for a great topping on this dish.

FIGURE A1.4: STACK OF PROTEIN PANCAKES

SENSATIONAL STROGANOFF (BATCH COOKING FRIENDLY)

This comfort food is great for a hearty and satisfying lunch. In particular, it's good on cold and rainy days when warmth is at a premium. The best part of this meal is that with batch cooking you can enjoy it at a moment's notice.

Ingredients:
- 12 oz (approximately 300 grams) of packaged egg noodles
- 1 to 1-1/2 lbs (approximately 0.5 to 0.75 kg of ground beef
- 1/2 cup of sour cream (reduced fat or fat free recommended)
- 1 can of fat free condensed cream of mushroom soup
- 1 tablespoon of garlic powder
- Salt, pepper, or cumin to personal preference

Optional: chopped onions, garlic, mushrooms

Instructions - This recipe makes a business week's worth of lunches (five meals):
- Cook the egg noodles according to the package's directions.
- Over medium-high heat, sauté the ground beef till brown; this should take five to ten minutes. Include the optional chopped onions, garlic, or mushrooms as you would prefer.
- Pour out any excess liquid still present in the ground beef.
- Pour the contents of the cream of mushroom soup and the garlic powder into the skillet and stir.
- Allow the combination to simmer for ten minutes, continuing to stir occasionally.
- In a large bowl combine the cooked egg noodles with the sauce; mix in the sour cream; include salt, pepper, and cumin to personal preference.
- Pour five equal portions of the stroganoff into plastic food containers and allow time to cool.
- Store in the freezer. Heat for five minutes from a frozen state to serve.

FIGURE A1.5: SENSATIONAL STROGANOFF

THE CHICKEN DINNER TRIFECTA (BATCH COOKING FRIENDLY)

This meal provides a little taste of home and comfort food wherever and whenever you are. As with the first recipe, I've tried to aim for simplicity while maintaining a favourable nutritional profile. One of the keys to this simplicity is the choice of protein. I've elected to purchase a simple rotisserie chicken from my local grocery store at minimal cost. These are generally available at most supermarkets with in-store deli counters and aren't difficult to find. This provides a fresh source of protein at a very affordable price and without the complications of cooking or preparation.

Ingredients:
- 1 rotisserie chicken
- 1 bag of frozen and cut yams / sweet potatoes (24 ounces / 680 grams)
- Frozen mixed vegetables (A medley of vegetables including broccoli, carrots, cauliflower, etc.; any brand is fine.)

Instructions - This recipe makes a business week's worth of lunches (5 meals):
- Lay out 5 separate plastic food containers on your kitchen counter.
- Place approximately 1/5 of the bag of frozen and cut yams into each of the five containers.
- Place the desired amount of frozen veggies into each container. As vegetables are low in calories and high in nutrients, feel free to be a little generous in your portions.
- Carve the rotisserie chicken into five equal portions and place into each of the 5 plastic food containers.
- Replace the lid on each of the containers and freeze.
- Heat for five minutes from a frozen state and serve.

APPENDIX 2
EXCERCISES

The following are examples of additional exercises that can be mixed and matched with the exercises in the sample routines outlined in Chapter 5. Experiment and find which routines work best for you.

FIGURE A2.1 A-B: CROSS-ARM CRUNCH

This exercise engages the abdominals; this is a variation of the crunch, and is slightly easier to perform than the traditional crunch.

Instructions: Lie flat on your back with your hands crossed on your chest and your knees bent. Contract your abdominals as you lift your upper torso off the mat. Lower your upper torso back to the starting position to complete the movement. Notice how the lower back does not leave the mat, even at the peak of the movement. Repeat for four sets of twenty-five repetitions, or until exhaustion.

FIGURE A2.2 A-B: EXTENDED ARM SQUAT

This exercise engages the quadriceps, and is a variation of the traditional squat. The extension of the arms changes the angle of the exercise.

Instructions: Stand with your feet shoulder-width apart and your toes pointed slightly outwards. Slowly bend your knees and lower your body into a squatting position, then return to a standing position. Extend and retract your arms throughout the course of the motion. The depth of the squat determines the difficulty. You can vary the width of the stance to further change the angle of the exercise. Repeat for four sets of twenty-five repetitions, or until exhaustion.

FIGURE A2.3 A-B: PRISONER SQUAT

This exercise engages the quadriceps, and is an additional variation of the traditional squat. Having your hands at the sides of your head changes the angle of the exercise.

Instructions: Stand with your feet shoulder-width apart and your toes pointed slightly outwards. Slowly bend your knees and lower your body into a squatting position with your hands at each side of your head, then return to a standing position. The depth of the squat determines the difficulty. You can vary the width of the stance to further change the angle of the exercise. Repeat for four sets of twenty-five repetitions, or until exhaustion.

FIGURE A2.4 A-B: GOBLET SQUAT

The goblet squat is a final variation of the traditional squat. The addition of a free weight increases the difficulty of the exercise.

Instructions: Stand with your feet shoulder-width apart and your toes pointed slightly outwards. While holding a free weight in your hands like a goblet (hence the name), slowly bend your knees and lower your body into a squatting position, then return to a standing position. The depth of the squat determines the difficulty. You can vary the width of the stance to further change the angle of the exercise. Repeat for four sets of twenty-five repetitions or until exhaustion.

FIGURE A2.5 A-B: REVERSE MACHINE FLY

This exercise engages the deltoids. Notice that this is the same machine used for the pectoral fly exercise.

Instructions: Using your gym's pectoral fly machine, adjust the height of the seat so that the handles of the arms are approximately shoulder-height, and the handles themselves are in the rear position. Keeping your elbows slightly bent, pull the handles outwards in a semicircular motion. Contract your deltoid muscles for maximum effectiveness. Repeat for three to four sets of 10-15 repetitions, or until exhaustion.

FIGURE A2.6 A-B: DUMBBELL FLY

This exercise engages the pectoral muscles. Remember to maintain a *slight* bend in the elbows at all times for proper form and to avoid injury.

Instructions: Lay back on a flat bench with two free weights of appropriate weight. Start with the weights above you, as shown in the first picture. With elbows slightly bent, spread your arms out until they are parallel with the floor. Bring them back together again, while actively contracting your pectoral muscles until the weights meet in the middle again. Repeat for three to four sets of 10-15 repetitions, or until exhaustion.

FIGURE A2.7 A-B: STANDING BICEPS CURL

This exercise engages the biceps. Standing instead of sitting works the biceps at a slightly different angle.

Instructions: Stand with free weights in both hands with your palms facing forwards. With the elbows fixed in place, lift the weight so that it rises to chest level. Slowly lower it back to the starting position. Actively contract the biceps during the peak of the exercise. Repeat for three to four sets of 10-15 repetitions, or until exhaustion.

FIGURE A2.8 A-B: LUNGES

This exercise engages the quadriceps.

Instructions: Start by standing with your feet approximately shoulder width apart. Step forward with one foot while the other one stays in place. Bend both knees and lower your body while being sure to keep your back straight, your back knee off the floor, and your front knee directly over your ankle. Use the heel of your front foot to push your body weight back up and to the starting position. Alternate legs. Repeat for four sets of twenty-five repetitions, or until exhaustion.

FIGURE A2.9 A-B: REVERSE LUNGES

This exercise engages the quadriceps. This variation is particularly good for those who suffer from knee pain caused by traditional lunges.

Instructions: Start with your feet approximately shoulder-width apart. Step back with one leg while the other foot stays in place. Bend your knees and lower your body while being sure to keep your back straight, your back knee off the floor, and your front knee just above your ankle. Use the heel of your front foot to push your body weight back up and to the starting position. Alternate legs. Repeat for four sets of twenty-five repetitions, or until exhaustion.

FIGURE A2.10 A-B: INCLINE PUSH-UPS

This exercise engages the pectoral and triceps muscles. The incline increases the resistance compared to normal push-ups.

Instructions: Lie in a prone position with your weight supported by your hands and the toes of your feet on a flat bench or another stable surface. Ensure that your feet are placed close together and that your hands are placed approximately shoulder width apart. Lift your body weight via a straightening of your arms. Lower your body back down until the space between your chest and the floor is approximately the width of a fist. This exercise engages the pectoral and triceps muscle groups. You can place your hands closer or further apart to change the angle of the exercise. Repeat for four sets of twenty-five repetitions, or until exhaustion.

FIGURE A2.11 A-B: PULL-UPS

Like the lat pulldown, this exercise primarily engages the latissimus dorsi muscles.

Instructions: Using a pull-up bar, place your hands with palms forward, slightly more than shoulder-width apart, as depicted in the first picture above. Lift your body weight upwards with your chest leading the way towards the bar and your elbows moving towards your sides. Allow shoulders to arch back slightly, and continue the motion till your chin moves up past the bar. Tighten the back muscles at the peak of the movement to maximize effectiveness. Repeat for three to four sets of 10-15 repetitions, or until exhaustion.

FIGURE A2.12: SEATED GROIN STRETCH

This stretch engages the inner thighs and groin.

Instructions: Sit on the floor with the soles of your feet together and your knees pointing outward, as depicted above. Apply gentle pressure on your knees with your elbows to provide for a better stretch. Removing footwear can make the exercise more comfortable. Hold for 30 to 60 seconds.

FIGURE A2.13: PRETZEL STRETCH

This stretch engages the gluteal muscles.

Instructions: Lie flat on your back and cross one leg on top of the other, as depicted above. Your crossed leg is the "active" leg, while your other leg is "neutral." Clasp your hands around the thigh of your neutral leg and apply gentle pressure by pulling your legs towards your body. Be sure to let your head rest on the ground comfortably during the stretch. Hold for 30 to 60 seconds and alternate legs.

ACKNOWLEDGEMENTS

Writing is a team sport; I truly believe that. This book would not have existed without the support and help of many people in my life. First, a big thank you to Noel Feliciano for his tireless support and encouragement for me to both begin and finish this project. Thank you to Deirdre Maultsaid and Susan Chambers for their meticulous editing work and command of prose. To Ming Chai and Christopher Lo for demonstrating and photographing exercise techniques respectively, your skill and professionalism have been nothing short of incredible.

A special thank you goes to Sydney Barnes, whose graphic design prowess gave both the cover design and illustrations in this book their final form. In addition, Sydney's work on layout and design has given polish to an otherwise very rough stone. Dana Soviala, fashion maven and close friend, gave this book the necessary insight for the sections on personal style and fashion. To Mom and Dad, I am forever indebted to you for raising me with positive life values. I also want to thank all my friends for always being there for me.

Finally, to Miriah Reitmeier, whose love and support I could not do without.

BIBLIOGRAPHY
SUGGESTED READING

Allen, David. *Getting Things Done: The Art of Stress-Free Productivity*. London: Penguin Books, 2015.

Aristotle. *Nicomachean Ethics*. Oxford: Oxford University Press, 2009.

Aurelius, Marcus. *Meditations*. New York: Modern Library, 2003.

Bogle, John C. *The Little Book of Common Sense Investing: The Only Way to Guarantee Your Fair Share of Stock Market Returns*. Hoboken: Wiley, 2007.

Bornstein, David and Susan Davis. *Social Entrepreneurship: What Everyone Needs to Know*. Oxford: Oxford University Press, 2010.

Braun, Adam. *The Promise of a Pencil: How an Ordinary Person Can Create Extraordinary Change*. New York: Scribner, 2014.

Browne, Harry. *Fail-Safe Investing: Lifelong Financial Security in 30 Minutes*. New York: St. Martin's Griffin, 200.

Byrne, Rhonda. *The Secret*. New York: Atria Books, 2006.

Carnegie, Dale and Arthur Pell. *Public Speaking for Success*. New York: Penguin Group (USA), 2006.

Carnegie, Dale. *How to Win Friends and Influence People*. New York: Gallery Books, 1998.

Carnegie, Dale. *How to Stop Worrying and Start Living.* New York: Pocket Books, 1990.

Carnegie, Dale and Dorothy Carnegie. *The Quick and Easy Way to Effective Speaking.* New York: Pocket Books, 1990.

Centrella, Sarah. *Hustle Believe Receive: An 8-Step Plan to Changing Your Life and Living Your Dream.* New York: Skyhorse Publishing, 2016.

Chapman, Gary D. *The 5 Love Languages: The Secret to Love that Lasts.* Chicago: Northfield Publishing, 2014.

Covey, Stephen R. *The 7 Habits of Highly Effective People: Powerful Lessons in Personal Change.* New York: Simon & Schuster, 2013.

Feiler, Bruce. *The Secrets of Happy Families: Improve Your Mornings, Rethink Family Dinner, Fight Smarter, Go Out and Play, and Much More.* New York: HarperCollins, 2013.

Fox Cabane, Olivia. *The Charisma Myth: How Anyone Can Master the Art and Science of Personal Magnetism.* London: Penguin Group, 2012.

Guillebeau, Chris. *The Happiness of Pursuit: Finding the Quest That Will Bring Purpose to Your Life.* New York: Harmony, 2014.

Hill, Napoleon. *Think and Grow Rich.* Shippensburg: Sound Wisdom, 2016.

Ketchpel, Steven. *Giving Back: Discover your values and put them into action through volunteering and donating.* Berkeley: Jonquil Press, 2012.

Kirschmann, John. *Nutrition Almanac.* New York: McGraw-Hill Education, 2007.

Krech, Gregg. *A Natural Approach to Mental Wellness: Japanese Psychology and the Skills We Need for Psychological and Spiritual Health.* Monkton: ToDo Institute, 2015.

Lee, Bruce. *Bruce Lee: The Art of Expressing the Human Body*. North Clarendon: Tuttle Publishing, 1998.

Mycoskie, Blake. *Start Something That Matters*. New York: Spiegel & Grau, 2012.

Porter, Ryan. *Make Your Own Lunch: How to Live an Epically Epic Life through Work, Travel, Wonder, and (Maybe) College*. Naperville: Sourcebooks, 2014.

Richo, David. *How to Be an Adult in Relationships: The Five Keys to Mindful Loving*. Boulder: Shambhala Publications, 2002.

Robbins, Tony. *MONEY Master the Game: 7 Simple Steps to Financial Freedom*. New York: Simon & Schuster, 2014.

Robbins, Anthony. *Awaken the Giant Within*. New York: Free Press, 1991.

Robbins, Tony. *Unlimited Power*. New York: Simon and Schuster, 1986.

Schwarzenegger, Arnold. *The New Encyclopedia of Modern Bodybuilding: The Bible of Bodybuilding, Fully Updated and Revised*. New York: Simon & Schuster, 1999.

Smith, Adam. *The Theory of Moral Sentiments*. London: Penguin Classics, 2010.

Stanley, Thomas J. and William D. Danko. *The Millionaire Next Door: The Surprising Secrets of America's Wealthy*. Plymouth: Taylor Trade Publishing, 2016.

Vaz-Oxlade, Gail. *Debt-Free Forever: Take Control of Your Money and Your Life*. New York: HarperCollins, 2012.

ENDNOTES

PREFACE

1   "1997 WWDC Fireside Chat with Steve Jobs," YouTube video, 30:05, posted by "Jason Molenda," February 126, 2014, https://www.youtube.com/watch?v=6iACK-LNnzM.

INTRODUCTION

1   "Maslow's Hierarchy of Needs," last modified June 29, 2009, https://u2pload.wikimedia.org/wikipedia/commons/6/60/Maslow%27s_Hierarchy_of_Needs.svg.
2   Richard Dawkins, *The Selfish Gene: 30th Anniversary Edition* (New York: Oxford University Press, April 15, 2006).

CHAPTER 1

1   Neil R. Carlson, *Psychology: The Science of Behaviour* (Toronto: Pearson Education Canada, January 9, 2009).
2   Carlson, Psychology: *The Science of Behaviour.*
3   Stephen R. Covey, *The 7 Habits of Highly Effective People: Powerful Lessons in Personal Change* (New York: Simon & Schuster, November 19, 2013), 102 – 153.
4   Tim Dalgleish, "The Emotional Brain," *Nature Reviews Neuroscience* 5 (2004): 583 – 589, doi: 10.1038/nrn1432.
5   "Cultivating Your Mindset: The Emotion Follows The Action," Kim Martin, December 20, 2015, https://www.linkedin.com/pulse/cultivating-your-mindset-emotion-follows-action-kim.
6   "Warren Buffett speaks to UGA students," YouTube video, 7:30, posted by "Terry College of Business at the University of Georgia," April 4, 2011, https://www.youtube.com/watch?v=2a9Lx9J8uSs.
7   "Warren Buffett speaks with Florida University," YouTube video, 5:00, posted by "Leyland PAM," July 2, 2013, https://www.youtube.com/watch?v=2MHIcabnjrA.
8   "5 Lessons From Warren Buffett's Office Hours," Fast Company, May 7, 2013, https://www.fastcompany.com/3009443/bottom-line/5-lessons-from-warren-buffetts-office-hours.

9 Ron Chernow, *Titan: The Life of John D. Rockefeller, Sr.* (New York: Vintage, March 30, 2004).

10 "Rockefeller's Documentary," YouTube video, 12:30, posted by "Strategy Activists," February 26, 2012, https://www.youtube.com/watch?v=7XFKsjjPs7E.

CHAPTER 2

1 Richard Dale, *Walking with Cavemen*, video, (2003; UK; BBC), television.

2 Richard Dale, *Walking with Cavemen*.

3 Diogenes Laertius, *The Lives and Opinions of Eminent Philosophers* (Oxford: Acheron Press, November 5, 2012), Kindle edition.

4 Robin I.M. Dunbar, "Neocortex Size as a Constraint on Group Size in Primates," *Journal of Human Evolution* Volume 22, Issue 6 (1992): 469 – 493

5 Miller McPherson, et al. "Social Isolation in America: Changes in Core Discussion Networks over Two Decades," *American Sociological Review* Volume 71, Issue 3 (2006): 353 – 375

6 John Kehoe, *Mind Power Into the 21st Century: Techniques to Harness the Astounding Power of Thought* (Vancouver: Zoetic, 2011), 32.

7 Miller McPherson, et al. "Birds of a Feather: Homophily in Social Networks," *Annual Review of Sociology* Volume 27 (2001): 415 – 444

8 "Matthew 7:25," *King James Bible Online*, accessed May 22, 2017, https://www.kingjamesbibleonline.org/Matthew-7-25/.

9 Marcela Gaviria, Martin Smith, "The Madoff Affair," *Frontline* video, May 12, 2009, http://www.pbs.org/wgbh/pages/frontline/madoff/

10 "Madoff Is Sentenced to 150 Years for Ponzi Scheme," last modified July 1, 2009, http://www.nytimes.com/2009/06/30/business/30madoff.html?_r=1&hp

11 Facebook (2017). Statement of Rights and Responsibilities, Facebook.com. https://www.facebook.com/terms. Accessed July 13, 2017.

CHAPTER 3

1 "Ethics," Dictionary.com, accessed May 22, 2017. http://www.dictionary.com/browse/ethics?s=t.

2 Paul R. Ehrlich, Jill Baron, *Rocky Mountain Futures: An Ecological Perspective* (Washington: Island Press, 2002), XXVII.

3 Richard Dawkins, *The Selfish Gene: 30th Anniversary Edition* (New York: Oxford University Press, April 15, 2006).

4 "Of the Natural Condition of Mankind as Concerning Their Fidelity and Misery," Bartleby.com, accessed July 19, 2016, http://www.bartleby.com/34/5/13.html

5   "The Philosophy of Warren E. Buffett," *The New York Times*, accessed May 22, 2017, https://www.Nytimes.com/2015/05/02/business/dealbook/the-philosophy-of-warren-e-buffett.html?_r=0.

6   "Virtue Ethics," *Stanford Encyclopedia of Philosophy*, accessed May 22, 2017, https://plato.stanford.edu/entries/ethics-virtue/#PracWisd.

7   "Weakness of Will," *Stanford Encyclopedia of Philosophy*, accessed May 25, 2017, https://plato.stanford.edu/entries/weakness-will/.

8   "Why It's Hard to Admit to Being Wrong," NPR, accessed May 25, 2017, http://www.npr.org/templates/story/story.php?storyId=12125926.

9   Stice, E. et al., "An effectiveness trial of a selected dissonance-based eating disorder 32 prevention programfor female high school students: Long-term effects," *Oregon Research Institute*, Volume 79, Number 4 (2011): 500–508, doi: 10.1037/a0024351.

10 The Truth and Reconciliation Commission of Canada, *Honouring the Truth, Reconciling for the Future* (The Truth and Reconciliation Commission of Canada, 2015, pp 4-5). http://www.trc.ca/websites/trcinstitution/File/2015/Honouring_the_Truth_Reconciling_for_the_Future_July_23_2015.pdf

11 The Truth and Reconciliation Commission of Canada, *Honouring the Truth, Reconciling for the Future*.

CHAPTER 4

1   Securities and Exchange Commission, *Study Regarding Financial Literacy among Investors* (Washington: Office of Investor Education and Advocacy, August 2012), iii.

2   "Severe debt can cause depression and even suicide," CreditCards.com, accessed May 25, 2017, http://www.creditcards.com/credit-card-news/debt-depression-and-suicide-1274.php.

3   "Debt stress affects health, fuels depression," CBC News, accessed May 25, 2017, http://www.cbc.ca/news/health/debt-stress-affects-health-fuels-depression-1.3082449.

4   Christopher T.S. Ragan, *Microeconomics, Fifteenth Canadian Edition* (Toronto: Pearson, February 15th, 2016), 111 – 139.

5   Christopher T.S. Ragan, *Microeconomics, Fifteenth Canadian Edition*, 111 – 139.

6   Richard Dale, *Walking with Cavemen*.

7   Canada Mortgage and Housing Corporation, *Rental Market Report Canada Highlights* (Ottawa: CMHC, Spring 2015), 2.

8   Jeremy Cato, "How much Canadians pay on average to drive a new car," *The Globe and Mail*, last modified April 17th, 2015, http://www.theglobeandmail.com/globe-drive/news/industry-news/how-much-canadians-pay-on-average-to-drive-a-new-car/article24003473/.

9   "What is a bond? A way to get income & stability," The Vanguard Group Inc., accessed May 27, 2017, https://investor.vanguard.com/investing/investment/what-is-a-bond.

10 "Warren Buffett says index funds make the best retirement sense 'practically all the time'," CNBC.com, accessed May 27, 2017, http://www.cnbc.com/2017/05/12/warren-buffett-says-index-funds-make-the-bestretirement-sense-practically-all-the-time.html?view=story&%24DEVIC E%24=native-android-mobile.

11 "Warren Buffet: Why stocks beat gold and bonds," *Fortune,* accessed May 27, 2017, 43 http://fortune.com/2012/02/09/warren-buffett-why-stocks-beat-gold-and-bonds/.

12 "Government of Canada Bonds," TD Canada Trust, accessed May 27, 2017, http://www.tdcanadatrust.com/products-services/investing/fixed-income/government-of-canada-bonds/icrcipcb.jsp%20?iframe =true&width=100%&height=100%.

13 "How and why to build a bond ladder," last modified March 7, 2017, https://www.fidelity.com/viewpoints/bond-ladder-strategy.

14 "Best practices for portfolio rebalancing," The Vanguard Group Inc., accessed May 27, 2017, https://www.vanguard.com/pdf/icrpr.pdf.

15 "Diversify your portfolio," Fidelity Investments, accessed May 27, 2017, https://www.fidelity.com/learningcenter/investment-products/fixed-income-bonds/diversify-your-portfolio.

16 Burton G. Malkiel, *A Random Walk Down Wall Street: Eleventh Edition* (New York: W. W. Norton & Company,2015), 180 – 181.

17 Burton G. Malkiel, *A Random Walk Down Wall Street: Eleventh Edition,* 180 – 181.

18 John C. Bogle, David F. Swensen, *Common Sense on Mutual Funds: New Imperatives for the Intelligent Investor* (Hoboken: Wiley, 2009), 305.

19 John C. Bogle, *Bogle on Mutual Funds: New Perspectives for the Intelligent Investor* (Hoboken: Wiley, 2015), xiii.

20 John C. Bogle, *The Little Book of Common Sense Investing: The Only Way to Guarantee Your Fair Share of Stock Market Returns* (Hoboken: Wiley, 2007), XIII.

21 "Learn the Language of the Wealthy," Robbins Research International Inc., accessed May 27, 2017, https://www.tonyrobbins.com/wealth-lifestyle/learn-the-language-of-the-wealthy/.

22 Rob Carrick, "The 10 Commandments," *The Globe and Mail,* last updated March 14, 2009, http://www.theglobeandmail.com/report-on-business/the-10-commandments/article18149377/?page=3.

23 Burton G. Malkiel, *A Random Walk Down Wall Street: Eleventh Edition,* 410 – 411.

24 "Inflation-Control Target," Bank of Canada, http://www.bankofcanada.ca/rates/in 56 dicators/key-variables/inflation-control-target/.

25 "How Inflation Swindles the Equity Investor," *Fortune,* accessed May 27th, 2017, http://fortune.com/2011/06/12/buffett-how-inflation-swindles-the-equity-investor-fortune-classics-1977/.

26 "Germany's Hyperinflation-Phobia," *The Economist,* accessed May 27th, 2017, http://www.economist.com/blogs/freeexchange/2013/11/economic-history-1.

27 "Inflation since 1900: The price of age," *The Economist,* last modified December 21, 2000, http://www.economist.com/node/457272.

28 World Health Organization, *World Health Statistics 2016: Monitoring health for the SDGs* (Geneva: World Health Organization, 2016), 7.

29 "What is a target date fund?" BlackRock, accessed May 27th, 2017, https://www.blackrock.com/investing/retirement/what-is-a-target-date-fund.

30 "Bogle: Be Sensible about Rebalancing," *Morningstar*, last modified October 17, 2013, http://www.morningstar.com/cover/videocenter.aspx?id=615379.

31 "Principle 3: Minimize cost," The Vanguard Group Inc., accessed May 28th, 2017, https://personal.vanguard.com/us/insights/investingtruths/investing-truth-about-cost.

CHAPTER 5

1   "MyPlate," United States Department of Agriculture, last modified January 25, 2017, https://www.choosemyplate.gov/MyPlate.

2   "MyPlate," United States Department of Agriculture, last modified January 25, 2017, https://www.choosemyplate.gov/MyPlate.

3   "Start with Small Changes," United States Department of Agriculture, last modified January 3, 2017, https://www.choosemyplate.gov/start-small-changes.

4   "Got your dairy today?" United Sates Department of Agriculture, last modified October 2016, https://choosemyplate-prod.azureedge.net/sites/default/files/tentips/DGTipsheet5GotYourDairyToday.pdf.

5   "Dietary Guidelines for Americans 2015 – 2020 Eighth Edition," United States Department of Agriculture, last modified December 2015, https://health.gov/dietaryguidelines/2015/resources/2015-2020_Dietary_Guidelines.pdf.

6   "Why is physical activity important?" United States Department of Agriculture, last modified June 10, 2015, https://www.choosemyplate.gov/physical-activity-why.

7   "Healthy Eating Plate & Healthy Eating Pyramid," Harvard University T.H. Chan School of Public Health, accessed March 16, 2017, https://www.hsph.harvard.edu/nutritionsource/healthy-eating-plate/.

8   "Healthy Eating Plate & Healthy Eating Pyramid," Harvard University T.H. Chan School of Public Health, accessed March 16, 2017, https://www.hsph.harvard.edu/nutritionsource/healthy-eating-plate/.

9   "Calcium and Milk," Harvard University T.H. Chan School of Public Health, accessed March 16, 2017, https://www.hsph.harvard.edu/nutritionsource/what-should-you-eat/calcium-and-milk/.

10 "Vegetables and Fruits," Harvard University T.H. Chan School of Public Health, accessed March 16, 2017, https://www.hsph.harvard.edu/nutritionsource/what-should-you-eat/vegetables-and-fruits/.

11 "Vegetables and Fruits," Harvard University T.H. Chan School of Public Health, accessed March 16, 2017, https://www.hsph.harvard.edu/nutritionsource/what-should-you-eat/vegetables-and-fruits/.

12 "Vegetables and Fruits," Harvard University T.H. Chan School of Public Health, accessed March 16, 2017, https://www.hsph.harvard.edu/ nutritionsource/what-should-you-eat/vegetables-and-fruits/.

13 "Human Ancestors Were Nearly All Vegetarians," *Scientific American*, accessed May 28, 2017, http://blogs.scientificamerican.com/guest-blog/ human-ancestors-were-nearly-all-vegetarians/.

14 "Whole Grains," Harvard University T.H. Chan School of Public Health, accessed March 16, 2017, https://www.hsph.harvard.edu/nutritionsource/ whole-grains/.

15 "Protein," Harvard University T.H. Chan School of Public Health, accessed March 16, 2017, https://www.hsph.harvard.edu/nutritionsource/ what-should-you-eat/protein/.

16 "Eggs," Harvard University T.H. Chan School of Public Health, accessed March 16, 2017, https://www.hsph.harvard.edu/nutritionsource/eggs/.

17 "Protein," Harvard University T.H. Chan School of Public Health, accessed March 16, 2017, https://www.hsph.harvard.edu/nutritionsource/ what-should-you-eat/protein/.

18 "Fats and Cholesterol," Harvard University T.H. Chan School of Public Health, accessed March 16, 2017, https://www.hsph.harvard.edu/ nutritionsource/what-should-you-eat/fats-and-cholesterol/.

19 "Lifestyle Coach Facilitation Guide: Post-Core," Centers for Disease Control and Prevention, accessed March 16, 2017, https://www.cdc.gov/diabetes/ prevention/pdf/postcurriculum_session2.pdf.

20 "Lifestyle Coach Facilitation Guide: Post-Core," Centers for Disease Control and Prevention, accessed March 16, 2017, https://www.cdc.gov/diabetes/ prevention/pdf/postcurriculum_session2.pdf.

21 "Healthy Drinks," Harvard University T.H. Chan School of Public Health, accessed March 16, 2017, https://www.hsph.harvard.edu/nutritionsource/ healthy-drinks/.

22 M. C. E. Lomer, "Review article: the aetiology, diagnosis, mechanisms and clinical evidence for food intolerance," *Alimentary Pharmacology and Therpeutics* Volume 41, Issue 3 (2015): 262 – 275, accessed March 18, 2017, doi: 10.1111/apt.13041.

23 "Food Allergy," National Institute of Allergy and Infectious Diseases, accessed March 18, 2017, https://www.niaid.nih.gov/diseases-conditions/ food-allergy.

24 "Celiac Disease Facts and Figures," The University of Chicago Celiac Disease Center, accessed March 18, 2017, http://www.uchospitals.edu/pdf/ uch_007937.pdf.

25 "Celiac Disease Facts and Figures," The University of Chicago Celiac Disease Center, accessed March 18, 2017, http://www.uchospitals.edu/pdf/ uch_007937.pdf.

26 "Serving-Size Comparison Chart," Dairy Council of California, accessed April 1, 2017, http://www.healthyeating.org/Portals/0/ Documents/Schools/Parent%20Ed/Portion_Sizes_Serving_Chart.pdf.

27 "Estimated Energy Requirements," Health Canada, accessed April 1, 2017,

http://www.hc-sc.gc.ca/fn-an/food-guide-aliment/basics-base/1_1_1-eng.
php.

28 "Estimated Energy Requirements," Health Canada, accessed April 1, 2017,
    http://www.hc-sc.gc.ca/fn-an/food-guide-aliment/basics-base/1_1_1-eng.php.

29 "Skipping breakfast may increase coronary heart disease risk," Harvard
    University T.H. Chan School of Public Health, accessed March 18, 2017,
    https://www.hsph.harvard.edu/news/features/skipping-breakfastmay-
    increase-coronary-heart-disease-risk/.

30 "How to Drink Enough Water," The University of Chicago, accessed May
    28, 2017, http://kidneystones.uchicago.edu/how-to-drink-enough-water/.

31 David E. Nelson, et al., "Alcohol-Attributable Cancer Deaths and Years of
    Potential Life Lost in the United States," *American Journal of Public Health*
    Volume 103, Number 4 (2013): 641 – 648, accessed March 18, 2017, doi:
    10.2105/AJPH.2012.301199.

32 "How Much Sodium Should I Eat Per Day?," American Heart Association,
    accessed March 18, 2017, https://sodiumbreakup.heart.org/how_much_
    sodium_should_i_eat.

33 "Apple and peanut butter," iStock, accessed April 1, 2018, https://www.
    istockphoto.com/ca/photo/apple-and-peanut-butter-gm488662823-
    39352362.

34 "Green salad with grilled chicken slices and roasted pine nuts," iStock, accessed
    April 1, 2018, https://www.istockphoto.com/ca/photo/green-salad-with-
    grilled-chicken-slices-and-rosted-pine-nuts-gm181851581-25071930.

35 http://www.foodsafety.gov/keep/charts/storagetimes.html.

36 "How to Choose Frozen Dinners," University of South Florida, accessed
    March 18, 2017, http://health.usf.edu/NR/rdonlyres/D5168BE9-98A7-
    4809-97E8-3EAA23A7006A/42725/HowtoChooseFrozenDinners.pdf.

37 Philip J. Brooks, et al., "The Alcohol Flushing Response: An Unrecognized
    Risk Factor for Esophageal Cancer from Alcohol Consumption," *Public
    Library of Science* (2009), accessed March 18, 2017, doi: 10.1371/journal.
    pmed.1000050.

38 Arnold Schwarzenegger, *The New Encyclopedia of Modern Bodybuilding:
    The Bible of Bodybuilding, Fully Updated and Revised* (New York: Simon & Schuster,
    1999), xxii.

39 "Body image concerns more men than women, research finds," *The
    Guardian*, last modified January 6, 2012, https://www.theguardian.com/
    lifeandstyle/2012/jan/06/body-image-concerns-men-more-thanwomen.

40 Dittmar, H., et al., "Does Barbie make girls want to be thin? The effect of
    experimental exposure to images of dolls on the body image of 5- to 8-year-old
    girls.," *NCBI* Volume 42 (2006):283 – 292, doi:10.1037/0012-1649.42.2.283.

41 "Trauma and Eating Disorders," National Eating Disorders Association,
    accessed May 28, 2017, https://www.nationaleatingdisorders.org/sites/
    default/files/ResourceHandouts/TraumaandEatingDisorders.pdf.

42 "Films," Jean Kilbourne, accessed March 18, 2017, http://www.
    jeankilbourne.com/films/.

43 Luminita D. Saviuc, *15 Things You Should Give Up to Be Happy: An Inspiring Guide to Discovering Effortless Joy* (New York: Penguin Random House, 2016), 118 – 131.

44 "Fitness," Reddit, accessed May 28, 2017, https://w 106 ww.reddit.com/r/Fitness/.

45 "Sleep and Disease Risk," Division of Sleep Medicine at Harvard Medical School, accessed March 18, 2017, http://healthysleep.med.harvard.edu/healthy/matters/consequences/sleep-and-disease-risk.

46 "Sleep and Disease Risk," Division of Sleep Medicine at Harvard Medical School, accessed March 18, 2017, http://healthysleep.med.harvard.edu/healthy/matters/consequences/sleep-and-disease-risk.

47 "Sleep and Disease Risk," Division of Sleep Medicine at Harvard Medical School, accessed March 18, 2017, http://healthysleep.med.harvard.edu/healthy/matters/consequences/sleep-and-disease-risk.

48 "Napping," National Sleep Foundation, accessed March 18, 2017, https://sleepfoundation.org/sleeptopics/napping.

49 "Body Mass Index (BMI) Nomogram," Health Canada, last modified February 23, 2012, http://www.hcsc.gc.ca/fn-an/nutrition/weights-poids/guide-ld-adult/bmi_chart_java-graph_imc_java-eng.php.

50 "Body Mass Index (BMI) Nomogram," Health Canada, last modified February 23, 2012, http://www.hcsc.gc.ca/fn-an/nutrition/weights-poids/guide-ld-adult/bmi_chart_java-graph_imc_java-eng.php.

51 Julian B. Rotter, "Generalized expectancies for internal versus external control of reinforcement," *Psychological Monographs: General & Applied* 80 (1966): 1 – 28, accessed March 19, 2017, doi: 10.1037/h0092976.

52 Julian B. Rotter, "Generalized expectancies for internal versus external control of reinforcement," *Psychological Monographs: General & Applied* 80 (1966): 1 – 28, accessed March 19, 2017, doi: 10.1037/h0092976.

53 William C. Compton, Edward Hoffman, *Positive Psychology: The Science of Happiness and Flourishing* (Belmont: Wadsworth, 2012), 58 – 58.

54 "Key Facts About Mental Illness," Clubhouse International, accessed March 19, 2017, http://www.iccd.org/keyfacts.html.

55 "Children, youth, and depression," Canadian Mental Health Association, accessed March 19, 2017, http://www.cmha.ca/mental_health/children-and-depression/#.WM8LmHeZPUp.

56 "Your Mental Health," Canadian Mental Health Association, accessed March 19, 2017, http://www.cmha.ca/mental-health/your-mental-health/.

CHAPTER 6

1 "Warren Buffett speaks with Florida University," YouTube video, 8:55, posted by "LeylandPAM," July 2, 2013, https://www.youtube.com/watch?v=2MHIcabnjrA.

2 Clinton Kelly, *Freakin' Fabulous: How to Dress, Speak, Behave, Eat, Drink, Entertain, Decorate, and Generally Be Better than Everyone Else* (New York: Gallery Books, 2008), 4.

3   "A Step-By-Step Guide To Getting A Job Through LinkedIn," *Business Insider. com*, last modified March 26, 2014, http://www.businessinsider.com/getting-a-job-through-linkedin-2014-3.

CHAPTER 7

1   Leaf Van Boven, Thomas Gilovich, "To Do or to Have? That Is the Question," *Journal of Personality and Social Psychology* 85 (2003): 1193 – 1202, accessed March 19, 2017, doi: 10.1037/0022-3514.85.6.1193.
2   Mark Regnerus, Jeremy Uecker, *Premarital Sex in America: How Young Americans Meet, Mate, and Think about Marrying* (New York: Oxford University Press, 2011).
3   Barry Schwartz, *The Paradox of Choice: Why More Is Less* (New York: Harper Perennial, 2005).
4   "New Love: A Short Shelf Life," The New York Times, last modified December 1, 2012, http://www.nytimes.com/2012/12/02/opinion/sunday/new-love-a-short-shelf-life.html?pagewanted=all&_r=1.
5   Gary D. Chapman, *The 5 Love Languages: The Secret to Love that Lasts* (Chicago: Northfield Publishing, December 11, 2014).
6   Gary D. Chapman, *The 5 Love Languages: The Secret to Love that Lasts* (Chicago: Northfield Publishing, December 11, 2014), 37 – 74.
7   Richard Dawkins, *The Selfish Gene: 30th Anniversary Edition* (New York: Oxford University Press, April 15, 2006).

CHAPTER 8

1   Richard Dawkins, *Nice Guys Finish First* (London, UK: BBC, 1986), TV.
2   Richard Dawkins, *The Selfish Gene: 30th Anniversary Edition* (New York: Oxford University Press, April 15, 2006), 166 – 188.
3   Gillian Brunier, et al., "The psychological well-being of renal peer support volunteers," *Journal of Advanced Nursing* 38 (2002): 40 – 49, accessed March 19, 2017, doi: 10.1046/j.1365-2648.2002.02144.x.
4   Carolyn Schwartz and M. Sendor, "Helping others helps oneself: response shift effects in peer support," *Social Science and Medicine* 48 (1999): 1563 – 1575, accessed March 23, 2017, doi: 10.1016/S0277-9536(99)00049-0.
5   W.T. Harbaugh, et al., "Neural responses to taxation and voluntary giving reveal motives for charitable donations," *Science* 316 (2007): 1622 – 1625, accessed March 23, 2017, doi: 10.1126/science.1140738.
6   "Where Asia's richest man is putting his money now," *The Globe and Mail*, last modified September 6, 2012, https://www.theglobeandmail.com/globe-investor/investment-ideas/where-asias-richest-man-isputting-his-money-now/article4170680/?page=all.
7   Ashlee Vance, *Elon Musk: Tesla, SpaceX, and the Quest for a Fantastic Future* (New York: HarperCollins, May 19, 2015).

CHAPTER 9

1   "What Is The Difference Between A Christian College & a Non-Christian College?," Online Christian Colleges, accessed June 11, 2017, http://www. onlinechristiancolleges.com/faq/what-is-the-differencebetween-a-christian-college-a-non-christian-college/.

2   "A Question of Price Versus Cost," *Christianity Today*, accessed June 11, 2017, https://www.portlandbiblecollege.org/wp-content/uploads/2016/01/AQuestionofPriceVersusCost.pdf.

3   "Undergraduate tuition fees for full time Canadian students, by discipline, by province (Canada),"Statistics Canada, last modified August 26, 2014, http://www.statcan.gc.ca/tables-tableaux/sum-som/l01/cst01/educ50a-eng.htm.

4   "University Rankings 2016: Comprehensive," *Maclean's*, accessed March 24, 2017, http://www.macleans.ca/education/best-universities-comprehensive-2016/.

5   "America's Top Colleges," *Forbes*, accessed March 24, 2017, https://www.forbes.com/top-colleges/list/#tab:rank.

6   Adam Smith, *The Wealth of Nations* (New York: Modern Library, 1994).

7   Charles Darwin, *The Origin of Species* (New York: Simon & Schuster, 2008).

8   Sir Isaac Newton, *The Principia: Mathematical Principles of Natural Philosophy* (La Vergne: Lightning Source, 2010).

9   "Bill Gates' 40th anniversary email: Goal was 'a computer on every desk,'" CNN, accessed March 24, 2017, http://money.cnn.com/2015/04/05/technology/bill-gates-email-microsoft-40-anniversary/.

10 Arnold Schwarzenegger, *Pumping Iron* (New York, NY: White Mountain Films, 1977), Netflix.

CHAPTER 10

1   Moid Siddiqui, *Leading from the Heart: Sufi Principles at Work* (Thousand Oaks: SAGE Publications, 2014), 83 – 84.

2   James Wallace and Jim Erickson, *Hard Drive: Bill Gates and the Making of the Microsoft Empire* (Hoboken: John Wiley & Sons, 1992).

3   Robert P. Miles, *The Warren Buffett CEO: Secrets from the Berkshire Hathaway Managers* (Hoboken: John Wiley & Sons, 2003), 85 – 98.

4   Patrick J. Welch and Gerry F. Welch, *Economics: Theory & Practice*, 11th Edition (Hoboken: John Wiley & Sons, 2016), 283 – 284.

5   Patrick J. Welch and Gerry F. Welch, *Economics: Theory & Practice, 11th Edition* (Hoboken: John Wiley & Sons, 2016), 4 – 5.

6   Robert G. Hagstrom, *The Warren Buffett Way* (Hoboken: John Wiley & Sons, 2013), 100 – 110.

CHAPTER 11

1 Alice Schroeder, *The Snowball: Warren Buffett and the Business of Life* (New York: Bantam Books, 2009), 41.

2 Miller, Charles. *The World's Greatest Money Maker: Evan Davis meets Warren Buffett.* London, United Kingdom: BBC, 2009. TV.

3 Jeremy C. Miller, *Warren Buffett's Ground Rules: Words of Wisdom from the Partnership Letters of the World's Greatest Investor* (New York: HarperCollins, 2016), xi.

4 "Warren Buffett speaks to UGA students," YouTube video, 7:30, posted by "Terry College of Business at the University of Georgia," April 4, 2011, https://www.youtube.com/watch?v=2a9Lx9J8uSs.

5 "Your Altitude," Ziglar Inc., accessed March 25, 2017, https://www.ziglar.com/quotes/your-attitude-notyour-aptitude/.

6 Mary Buffett and David Clark, *The Tao of Warren Buffett: Warren Buffett's Words of Wisdom: Quotations and Interpretations to Help Guide You to Billionaire Wealth and Enlightened Business Management* (New York: Scribner, 2006), 117.

7 Alice Schroeder, *The Snowball: Warren Buffett and the Business of Life* (New York: Bantam Books, 2009), 137.

8 Miller, Charles. *The World's Greatest Money Maker: Evan Davis meets Warren Buffett.* London, United Kingdom: BBC, 2009. TV.

9 "5 Lessons From Warren Buffett's Office Hours," *Fast Company*, May 7, 2013, https://www.fastcompany.com/3009443/bottom-line/5-lessons-from-warren-buffetts-office-hours.

10 Alice Schroeder, *The Snowball: Warren Buffett and the Business of Life* (New York: Bantam Books, 2009), 27.

11 "An Owner's Manual," Berkshire Hathaway, accessed March 25, 2017, http://www.berkshirehathaway.com/ownman.pdf.

12 "An Owner's Manual," Berkshire Hathaway, accessed March 25, 2017, http://www.berkshirehathaway.com/ownman.pdf.

13 Miller, Charles. *The World's Greatest Money Maker: Evan Davis meets Warren Buffett.* London, United Kingdom: BBC, 2009. TV.

14 "Should You Leave It All to the Children?," *Fortune*, accessed March 25, 2017, http://archive.fortune.com/magazines/fortune/fortune_archive/1986/09/29/68098/index.htm.

15 "Warren Buffett's Boring, Brilliant Wisdom," *Time*, accessed March 25, 2017, http://business.time.com/2010/03/01/warren-buffetts-boring-brilliant-wisdom/.

16 Alice Schroeder, *The Snowball: Warren Buffett and the Business of Life* (New York: Bantam Books, 2009), 509 – 510.

17 "The surprisingly frugal habits of 8 extremely wealthy people," *Business Insider*, accessed March 25, 2017, http://www.businessinsider.com/the-habits-of-frugal-billionaires-2016-7/#warren-buffett-chairmanand-ceo-of-berkshire-hathaway-still-lives-in-the-same-home-he-bought-for-31500-in-1958-1.

18 Alice Schroeder, *The Snowball: Warren Buffett and the Business of Life.* (New York: Bantam Books, 2009), 55 – 56.

19 "Warren Buffett Speech - How To Stay Out Of Debt," YouTube video, 7:35, posted by "Warren Buffett," December 27, 2014, https://www.youtube.com/watch?v=VpBkicb0a0s.

20 "Buffett: These investments are a 'fool's game,'" CNBC, accessed March 25, 2017, http://www.cnbc.com/2015/03/02/buffett-these-investments-are-a-fools-game.html.

21 "Warren Buffett's secret to staying young: 'I eat like a six-year-old,' *Fortune*, accessed March 25, 2017, http://fortune.com/2015/02/25/warren-buffett-diet-coke/.

22 "Warren Buffett Discloses Prostate Cancer Diagnosis," *Forbes*, accessed March 25, 2017, https://www.forbes.com/sites/steveschaefer/2012/04/17/warren-buffett-discloses-prostate-cancer-diagnosis/#713f04715fc6.

23 "Don't Sleepwalk Through Life: Warren Buffett | CNBC," YouTube video, posted by "CNBC," February 29, 2016, https://www.youtube.com/watch?v=fk0LSsRxO7g.

24 Miller, Charles. *The World's Greatest Money Maker: Evan Davis meets Warren Buffett*. London, United Kingdom: BBC, 2009. TV.

25 "Warren Buffett speaks with Florida University," YouTube video, 8:55, posted by "LeylandPAM," July 2, 2013, https://www.youtube.com/watch?v=2MHIcabnjrA.

26 "Warren Buffett speaks with Florida University," YouTube video, 8:00, posted by "LeylandPAM," July 2, 2013, https://www.youtube.com/watch?v=2MHIcabnjrA.

27 Robert G. Hagstrom, *The Warren Buffett Way* (Hoboken: John Wiley & Sons, 2013), 43.

28 Alice Schroeder, *The Snowball: Warren Buffett and the Business of Life* (New York: Bantam Books, 2009), 355.

29 Miller, Charles. *The World's Greatest Money Maker: Evan Davis meets Warren Buffett*. London, United Kingdom: BBC, 2009. TV.

30 "How Warren Buffett's Son Would Feed the World," *The Atlantic*, accessed March 26, 2017, https://www.theatlantic.com/magazine/archive/2016/05/how-warren-buffetts-son-would-feed-the-world/476385/.

31 "Warren Buffett Gives $30 Billion to Gates Foundation," *The Wall Street Journal*, accessed March 26, 2017, https://www.wsj.com/articles/SB115126355210390044.

32 Jeremy C. Miller, *Warren Buffett's Ground Rules: Words of Wisdom from the Partnership Letters of the World's Greatest Investor* (New York: HarperCollins, 2016), 60 – 61.

33 Bryan Burrough and John Helyar, *Barbarians at the Gate: The Fall of RJR Nabisco* (New York: HarperCollins, 2009), 218.

34 Alice Schroeder, *The Snowball: Warren Buffett and the Business of Life* (New York: Bantam Books, 2009), 663.

35 "Warren Buffett speaks with Florida University," YouTube video, 23:40, posted by "LeylandPAM," July 2, 2013, https://www.youtube.com/watch?v=2MHIcabnjrA.

36   Alice Schroeder, *The Snowball: Warren Buffett and the Business of Life* (New York: Bantam Books, 2009), 109.

37   "WARREN BUFFETT: Retirement is not my idea of living," *Business Insider*, accessed March 26, 2017, http://www.businessinsider.com/why-buffett-says-he-wont-retire-2015-10.

38   Carol J. Loomis, *Tap Dancing to Work: Warren Buffett on Practically Everything, 1966-2012* (New York: Penguin Group, 2012), 148.

QUICK REFERENCE GUIDE AND BOOK RECAP

1   Adam Smith, *An Inquiry into the Nature and Causes of the Wealth of Nations* (New York: Random House, 1994), 485.

EPILOGUE

1   Gidon Eshel and Pamela A. Martin, "Diet, Energy, and Global Warming," *Department of the Geophysical Sciences, University of Chicago* (2009), accessed March 30, 2018, doi: 10.1175/EI167.1.

2   Elinor Hallström, Quentin Gee, Peter Scarborough, David A. Cleveland, "A healthier US diet could reduce greenhouse gas emissions from both the food and health care systems," *Climatic Change* Volume 142, Issue 1 − 2 (2017): 199 − 212, accessed March 30, 2018, doi: 10.1007/s10584-017-1912-5.

3   Tasnime N. Akbaraly et al., "Alternative Healthy Eating Index and mortality over 18 y of follow-up: results from the Whitehall II cohort," *The American Journal of Clinical Nutrition* Volume 94, Issue 1 (2011): 247 − 253, accessed March 30, 2018, doi: 10.3945/ajcn.111.013128.

4   Rashad J. Belin et al., "Diet quality and the risk of cardiovascular disease: the Women's Health Initiative (WHI)," *The American Journal of Clinical Nutrition* Volume 94, Issue 1 (2011): 49 − 57, accessed March 30, 2018, doi: 10.3945/ajcn.110.011221.

5   Marjorie L. McCullough et al., "Diet quality and major chronic disease risk in men and women: moving toward improved dietary guidance," *The American Journal of Clinical Nutrition* Volume 76, Issue 6 (2002): 1261 − 1271, accessed March 30, 2018, PMID: 12450892.

6   Kenneth E. Thorpe, Lindsay Allen, Peter Joski, "The Role of Chronic Disease, Obesity, and Improved Treatment and Detection in Accounting for the Rise in Healthcare Spending Between 1987 and 2011," *Applied Health Economics and Health Policy* Volume 13, Issue 4, (2015): 381 − 387, accessed March 30, 2018, doi: 10.1007/s40258-015-0164-7.

7   Ron Friedman, "What You Eat Affects Your Productivity," *Harvard Business Review*, October 17, 2014, accessed March 30, 2018, https://hbr.org/2014/10/what-you-eat-affects-your-productivity.

8   Jutta Bolt et al, "Rebasing 'Maddison': new income comparisons and the shape of long-run economic development", Maddison Project Working paper 10, Madison Project Database 2018, *Groningen Growth and Development Centre, University of Groningen*, accessed March 30, 2018, https://www.rug. nl/ggdc/historicaldevelopment/maddison/releases/maddison-project-database-2018.

9   International Monetary Fund, World Economic Outlook database, February 2014, accessed March 30, 2018, http://www.imf.org/external/pubs/ft/weo/2017/02/weodata/download.aspx.

10 Milton Friedman, *Capitalism and Freedom*, (Chicago: University of Chicago Press, 2002).

11 International Monetary Fund, "Understanding Financial Interconnectedness," October 4, 2010, accessed March 30, 2018, http://www.imf.org/external/np/pp/eng/2010/100410.pdf.

12 Mark Deen, "Canadians are the most indebted in the world, OECD says, as it warns on rising debt risk," *Financial Post*, November 23, 2017, accessed March 30, 2018, http://business.financialpost.com/personal-finance/debt/canadians-are-the-most-indebted-in-the-world-oecd-says-as-it-warns-on-rising-debt-risk.

13 Staff "Canadian household debt-to-income ratio slips: StatsCan," *Global News*, March 15, 2018, accessed March 30, 2018, https://globalnews.ca/news/4085367/canadian-household-debt-to-income-ratio/.

14 Allan H. Meltzer, "Origins of the Great Inflation," *Federal Reserve Bank of St. Louis Review*, March/April 2005, 87(2, Part 2), pp. 145-75, accessed March 30, 2018, https://files.stlouisfed.org/files/htdocs/publications/review/05/03/part2/Meltzer.pdf.

15 International Monetary Fund, "Global Financial Stability Report October 2017: Is Growth at Risk?" October 2017, accessed March 30, 2018, https://www.imf.org/en/Publications/GFSR/Issues/2017/09/27/global-financial-stability-report-october-2017.

ABOUT THE AUTHOR

Forrest Wong is an actor, writer, and investor living in Vancouver, British Columbia. He has a penchant for thinking about and approaching life's problems in unusual ways and is an avid reader of all things non-fiction.

Forrest was born into a traditional Chinese family and excelled in school, graduating with a Bachelor of Business Administration degree in 2015. He has long strived for unity and simplicity in life's endeavours, repeatedly finding that seemingly unrelated concepts have threads of underlying commonality. As an example, contrarianism is regularly cited as a quality in successful investing. One of Forrest's heroes, Warren Buffett, the famous investor from Omaha, has often famously quipped about how he is greedy when others are fearful and fearful when others are greedy. By the same token, another of Forrest's heroes, Bruce Lee, the movie star and martial artist, was frequently known as saying that he expanded when his opponents contracted and contracted when his opponents expanded.

Forrest continues to work towards contributing whatever he can to society in his own unique way.

Made in the USA
Columbia, SC
04 May 2018